Quod scriptura, non iubet vetat

The Latin translates, "What is not commanded in scripture, is forbidden:'

On the Cover: Baptists rejoice to hold in common with other evangelicals the main principles of the orthodox Christian faith. However, there are points of difference and these differences are significant. In fact, because these differences arise out of God's revealed will, they are of vital importance. Hence, the barriers of separation between Baptists and others can hardly be considered a trifling matter. To suppose that Baptists are kept apart solely by their views on Baptism or the Lord's Supper is a regrettable misunderstanding. Baptists hold views which distinguish them from Catholics, Congregationalists, Episcopalians, Lutherans, Methodists, Pentecostals, and Presbyterians, and the differences are so great as not only to justify, but to demand, the separate denominational existence of Baptists. Some people think Baptists ought not teach and emphasize their differences but as E.J. Forrester stated in 1893, "Any denomination that has views which justify its separate existence, is bound to promulgate those views. If those views are of sufficient importance to justify a separate existence, they are important enough to create a duty for their promulgation ... the very same reasons which justify the separate existence of any denomination make it the duty of that denomination to teach the distinctive doctrines upon which its separate existence rests." If Baptists have a right to a separate denominational life, it is their duty to propagate their distinctive principles, without which their separate life cannot be justified or maintained.

Many among today's professing Baptists have an agenda to revise the Baptist distinctives and redefine what it means to be a Baptist. Others don't understand why it even matters. The books being reproduced in the *Baptist Distinctives Series* are republished in order that Baptists from the past may state, explain and defend the primary Baptist distinctives as they understood them. It is hoped that this Series will provide a more thorough historical perspective on what it means to be distinctively Baptist.

The Lord Jesus Christ asked, *"And why call ye me, Lord, Lord, and do not the things which I say?"* (Luke 6:46). The immediate context surrounding this question explains what it means to be a true disciple of Christ. Addressing the same issue, Christ's question is meant to show that a confession of discipleship to the Lord Jesus Christ is inconsistent and untrue if it is not accompanied with a corresponding submission to His authoritative commands. Christ's question teaches us that a true recognition of His authority as Lord inevitably includes a submission to the authority of His Word. Hence, with this question Christ has made it forever impossible to separate His authority as King from the authority of His Word. These two principles—the authority of Christ as King and the authority of His Word—are the two most fundamental Baptist distinctives. The first gives rise to the second and out of these two all the other Baptist distinctives emanate. As F.M. Iams wrote in 1894, "Loyalty to Christ as King, manifesting itself in a constant and unswerving obedience to His will as revealed in His written Word, is the real source of all the Baptist distinctives:' In the search for the *primary* Baptist distinctive many have settled on the Lordship of Christ as the most basic distinctive. Strangely, in doing this, some have attempted to separate Christ's Lordship from the authority of Scripture, as if you could embrace Christ's authority without submitting to what He commanded. However, while Christ's Lordship and Kingly authority can be isolated and considered essentially for discussion's sake, we see from Christ's own words in Luke 6:46 that His Lordship is really inseparable from His Word and, with regard to real Christian discipleship, there can be no practical submission to the one without a practical submission to the other.

In the symbol above the Kingly Crown and the Open Bible represent the inseparable truths of Christ's Kingly and Biblical authority. The Crown and Bible graphics are supplemented by three Bible verses (Ecclesiastes 8:4, Matthew 28:18-20, and Luke 6:46) that reiterate and reinforce the inextricable connection between the authority of Christ as King and the authority of His Word. The truths symbolized by these components are further emphasized by the Latin quotation - *quod scriptura, non iubet vetat*— i.e., "What is not commanded in scripture, is forbidden:' This Latin quote has been considered historically as a summary statement of the regulative principle of Scripture. Together these various symbolic components converge to exhibit the two most foundational Baptist Distinctives out of which all the other Baptist Distinctives arise. Consequently, we have chosen this composite symbol as a logo to represent the primary truths set forth in the *Baptist Distinctives Series*.

Communion:
THE DISTINCTION BETWEEN
CHRISTIAN AND CHURCH FELLOWSHIP
AND BETWEEN
COMMUNION AND ITS SYMBOLS.

COMMUNION:

THE DISTINCTION BETWEEN

CHRISTIAN AND CHURCH FELLOWSHIP

AND BETWEEN

COMMUNION AND ITS SYMBOLS.

EMBRACING

A REVIEW OF THE ARGUMENTS

OF THE

Rev Robert Hall and Rev. Baptist W. Noel

IN FAVOR OF

MIXED COMMUNION

BY

T.F. CURTIS A.M.

PROFESSOR OF THEOLOGY, HOWARD COLLEGE, A.L.A.

With a Biographical Sketch of the Author by John Franklin Jones

PHILADELPHIA:
AMERICAN BAPTIST PUBLICATION SOCIETY
118 ARCH STREET
1850

he Baptist Standard Bearer, Inc.

NUMBER ONE IRON OAKS DRIVE • PARIS, ARKANSAS 72855

Thou hast given a *standard* to them that fear thee;
that it may be displayed because of the truth.
-- Psalm 60:4

Reprinted 2006

by

THE BAPTIST STANDARD BEARER, INC.
No. 1 Iron Oaks Drive
Paris, Arkansas 72855
(479) 963-3831

THE WALDENSIAN EMBLEM
lux lucet in tenebris
"The Light Shineth in the Darkness"

ISBN# 1579785093

PREFACE.

THE Author of the following pages had occasion, in commencing to prepare a series of Lectures on the Constitution, Government, and Discipline of our Churches, for the benefit of some young brethren studying for the Ministry, to re-examine the Mixed Communion Controversy, and especially the arguments of the celebrated Robert Hall. Some two or three years previously, while laboring as a Pastor, he had delivered a series of discourses on the subject of Communion, which had been kindly received. These, re-written and re-arranged, form in fact the basis of the first two parts of the present work. The third and fourth parts, are the application of the principles before established to the arguments of Robert Hall, and also of Baptist W. Noel.

The chief point in which this volume differs from most which have preceded it on the subject, is that instead of attempting to defend *a rule*, it aims to establish *a principle*. Most of our writers have sought chiefly to vindicate the rule that no unbaptized person is qualified for the Lord's Supper. The object of the present work is to exhibit the principle that *the*

Lord's Supper is a symbol of Church relations between those who unite in its celebration. The advantage of this course is, that whereas the rule is negative, a principle is essentially positive. One true principle will lie at the basis of many rules. A rule bounds an idea but on one side ; a principle implies its own limit on all sides. A rule restricts, a principle establishes.

It was because the writer had felt the want of some popular exposition, exhibiting in a less *negative* manner the whole subject of the present Essay, that he was induced originally to deliver, and now publishes these views. The most simple, comprehensive, and conclusive plan, even so far as the restrictive side is concerned, is to maintain that positive principle, which comprehends all the rules, and presents the subject in its wholeness to the observation of the candid inquirer. The Author is convinced that no doubt can long remain after an attentive consideration of this subject, that the Lord's Supper symbolizes visible Church relations as existing between those who unite in it. To such as admit the primitive independence of the Churches of Christ, which is a point now universally conceded by the ablest investigators of Church History in Germany, the rest will follow as a necessary consequence. Where these relations do not subsist, as they certainly do not where different denominations are concerned, the symbol of such relations must be inappropriate.

It is because, in modern times, we do not feel the warmth of that peculiar affection which existed originally among those who were members of the same Church or family of Christians, that our practice in regard to the Lord's Supper, which symbolized it, comes to be called in question.

It will be observed that this work takes for granted, that the views of our denomination on the subject of baptism are correct. To have pursued any other course, would have occupied too large a field. The writer has aimed, as much as possible, to narrow the controversy to the point at issue. Nothing, however, has been taken for granted, that was not freely conceded by the most skilful opponent of our views on this subject, Robert Hall. This volume is not sent forth into the world to provoke controversy. It is written chiefly for members of our own Churches, and for those pious persons, who, convinced of the general truth of our sentiments, as to the mode and subjects of baptism, are yet troubled with scruples in regard to the Lord's Supper.

To his brethren in the ministry, the Author offers a word of explanation as to his motives, and his hopes. The substance of this work originated, not in any special circumstances of controversy, but in the regular course of ministerial labors. It was, therefore, simply to present to a Church of our own denomination, with a congregation often increased by other evangelical Christians, and well established in Divine truth, not only clear and settled views upon a subject of controversy, but also such thoughts as a Pastor would naturally desire to present in all affection, on such a subject as that of Communion; and to promote some of the very highest and noblest of all the relations of a Christian congregation—Church fellowship, love to fellow Christians, and above all, Communion with Christ. Nor is it without the hope of entering into, and silently assisting the labors of Pastors, in this unobtrusive manner, that the Author issues this book to the world. Hence, he has not been careful to prune out some paragraphs, especially in the first Part, which might be spared from a mere theological argument.

To promote love and true Communion between all mankind and Christ; between all Christians as fellow heirs of light and glory, and members of the Universal Church; between all who sustain towards each other the solemn and endearing relation of brotherhood in the same Christian Church, is the simple object which the Author has had in view. And if this volume can in any measure set these several relations in a clearer light, and restore that fervor of primitive love, that strong (not high) Church feeling that the study of the New Testament, and the earliest records of the Christian Church shows to have existed; we are convinced that the greatest difficulty to the correct understanding of the subject will have been overcome. Our chief object will assuredly have been accomplished. T. F. C.

Howard College, *September* 27, 1849.

CONTENTS.

INTRODUCTION.

1. Distinction between the Literal, and Figurative or Symbolic use of the term Communion. 2. An error here lies at the basis of much of the reasoning on this subject. 3. Division of the subject,········13

PART I.
IN WHAT COMMUNION CONSISTS.

CHAPTER I.
MEANING OF TERMS.

1. Literal meaning of Communion and Κοινωνία. 2. Sense of Communion and Fellowship compared. 3. A closer Communion the great want of the age. 4. The Objects of Communion classified,·······19

CHAPTER II.
COMMUNION WITH CHRIST THE HEAD OF THE CHURCH.

1. How far this embraces Communion with the whole Godhead. 2. Its powerful effect upon the heart and life. 3. The great clue to the labyrinth of life. 4. The vital force and moving power of religious action. 5. Illustration,··22

CHAPTER III.
COMMUNION WITH THE CHURCH UNIVERSAL: WITH THE SAINTS IN GLORY.

1. Communion with the Church Universal—its two divisions. 2. *The Christian communes with the Saints in glory.* 3. There was much of this in primitive times. 4. How it may be enjoyed now. 5. The spirit of the age in regard to it. 6. *The Saints in glory have Communion with us.* 7. Spiritual influences. 8. Practical effects, ····27

CHAPTER IV.

COMMUNION WITH CHRISTIANS ON EARTH.

1. Distinction between Communion and its Symbols, repeated. 2. Communion with Christians on earth, of two kinds. 3. The distinction illustrated. 4. The distinction shown by the two senses of the word Church. 5. Quotation from Robert Hall. 6. The error of Mr. Hall's opinion, that a particular visible Church differs from the Invisible, only as a part from the whole. 7. The true distinction shown by Neander, ...34

CHAPTER V.

FELLOWSHIP WITH CHRISTIANS AS SUCH, AND NOT AS MEMBERS OF ANY PARTICULAR VISIBLE CHURCH.

1. The New Commandment explained. 2. This Communion may exist apart from all symbols. 3. It need not interfere with denominational preferences. 4. Baptist principles most favorable to Christian fellowship. 5. How to promote it, ...41

CHAPTER VI.

CHURCH COMMUNION, OR FELLOWSHIP.

1. Its nature. 2. Its proper subjects. 3. The two objects of it. 4. *Designed to promote the piety of the members.* 5. Unreasonable expectations in regard to it. 6. Evil effects of such expectations. 7. Modern and Primitive Churches compared. 8. We need a fellowship more sympathizing in temporal matters. 9. Church fellowship ought to include a complete vindication of character. 10. It should promote the proprieties of Christian intercourse. 11. Church fellowship as *an instrument of converting sinners.* 12. A proper *Esprit du Corps.* 13. Its power. 14. The duty of joining a Church. 15. Summary of Part I. 48

PART II.

THE SYMBOLS OF COMMUNION.

CHAPTER I.

NATURE OF SYMBOLS.

1. Definition of a symbol. 2. Simple symbols. 3. Complex symbols. 4. Those only to be used when *all* the relations are as represented. 5. Division of the subject, ...65

CONTENTS. ix

CHAPTER II.
SYMBOLS OF COMMUNION WITH CHRIST.

1. These are various, but two are chief. 2. BAPTISM, the first of these a simple symbol. 3. Ground assumed in regard to Baptism. 4. Baptism, a symbolic burial. 5. Baptism, a putting on of Christ.—Optatus. 6. The Apostle's idea. 7. Importance of practically uniting the symbol and thing signified. 8. Baptism, a pledge—contains a reciprocal assurance. 9. Importance and beauty of this symbolic garment. 10. THE LORD'S SUPPER, a symbol of frequent recurrence. 11. A fresh acknowledgment of the baptismal profession—instituted connexion between them. 12. A complex symbol. 13. A symbol of communion with Christ. 14. Meaning of $\dot{\varepsilon}\sigma\tau\acute{\iota}$. 15. A re-affirmation of the baptismal vow. 16. Contains a reciprocal assurance of our acceptance,···67

CHAPTER III.
SYMBOLS OF CHRISTIAN COMMUNION.

1. Symbols imperfect and partial. 2. They change in their symbolic character. 3. Various symbols specified. 4. The same original term used for Contributions,·······································79

CHAPTER IV.
THE SYMBOLS OF CHURCH COMMUNION.

1. Kiss of charity—feasts of charity—right hand of fellowship. 2. The Lord's Supper—in what sense the Communion. 3. A symbol of Church relations. 4. Is more than a recognition of Christian character. 5. Is a Church ordinance. 6. Not a mere symbol of Communion with the Church Universal. 7. Nor with all saints on earth. 8. But with those with whom we celebrate. 9. Illustrated by the Passover, and institution of the Supper. 10. Independence of Churches. 11. The early Christians esteemed the Lord's Supper a Church ordinance. 12. It is not to be used where there are not Church relations. 13. The Church an executive, not a legislative body. 14. Baptist Churches cannot be charged with want of charity. 15. The Lord's Supper belongs to all the members of a Church which celebrates it. 16. Injustice of debarring infants in Pedobaptist Churches,·············83

CHAPTER V.
OCCASIONAL COMMUNION.

1. Meaning of the phrase. 2. Two classes. 3. Occasional participation with members of other Churches of the same denomination. 4. With

1*

Christians of no visible Church, and of other denominations. 5. The difference is only as to *occasional* participation. 6. Shown from Methodist Book of Discipline. 7. From the Pres. Con. of Faith. 8. From the Thirty-nine Articles.—Not acted up to. 9. Any other plan of Church membership must destroy all denominations. 10. This admitted by Robert Hall. 11. Must silence Truth, if in the minority. 12. Baptist Churches originated in the desire of Pedobaptists. 13. Occasional Communion must be regulated by general principles. 14. Methodist and Presbyterian principles applied to this case,.. 95

CHAPTER VI.

OBJECTIONS CONSIDERED.

1. These Objections stated. 2. "It is only the mode of Baptism that prevents us from uniting with Pedobaptists," considered. 3. "That we do not consider the Baptism of Pedobaptists as valid," considered. 4. This true. 5. But not the only ground for our not uniting with them. 6. "That we unchurch Pedobaptists," considered. 7. The Lord's Supper not designed to express Church relations as subsisting between different Churches. 8. Custom of Baptist Associations unchurches ourselves as much as other denominations. 9. Each Church entitled to declare the terms of its own fellowship. 10. The effect of the lack of a valid Baptism in unchurching, considered. 11. Different significations of the word Church. 12. Those unbaptized cannot form *regular* Churches. 13. Our difference as to Baptism chiefly keeps us from affiliating. 14. Ought our Churches to make Baptism necessary to their membership? 15. This the Primitive plan, conceded by Robert Hall. 16. Importance of keeping the ordinances as delivered to us. 17. Ought the rule of Church Membership to be extended to *occasional* participation? 18. This conceded by Christian writers of all ages. 19. This is consistent and charitable. 20. Illustration from American citizenship,·····················112

CHAPTER VII.

REVIEW OF PARTS I. AND II.

1. Distinction between Communion and its Symbols. 2. Different kinds of Communion specified. 3. The Nature of Symbols. 4. Different Symbols of Communion. 5. Symbols of Communion with Christ. (*a*) Baptism. (*b*) Lord's Supper. 6. Symbols of Christian fellowship. 7. The Lord's Supper a Symbol of Church fellowship. 8. Further proofs of this. 9. Additional proofs—The Passover—but

one Altar to a Church. 10. May it be used for other purposes?
11. Robert Hall's "leading position" considered. 12. This confounds
the Visible and Invisible Churches. 13. " Occasional Communion."
14. The case of other denominations considered. 15. Three objections considered. 16. That we deny the validity of their baptisms.
17. That we unchurch other denominations. 18. Our own position, ...130

PART III.

THE ARGUMENTS OF ROBERT HALL CONSIDERED.

INTRODUCTORY REMARKS.

Classification of Mr. Hall's writings on the subject of Communion, ··149

CHAPTER I.

ROBERT HALL'S FIRST ARGUMENT CONSIDERED.

1. Ambiguity as to the use of the word Communion. 2. Applied to the Lord's Supper proves nothing. 3. Robert Hall's view of the signification of the Lord's Supper considered. 4. His illustration of children refusing to eat at the same table. 5. Symbolic feasts. 6. The anguish of separating from Christian friends at the Lord's Supper considered. 7. Illustration, ...152

CHAPTER II.

ROBERT HALL'S SECOND ARGUMENT CONSIDERED.

1. 'The toleration of all errors consistent with salvation,' considered. 2. No Christians practice thus. 3. The Scriptures forbid this course. 4. Consequences of Robert Hall's views. 5. Errors generally destructive, may not be so in every case. 6. Persons holding almost every species of error might become Church officers on the Mixed Communion plan. 7. The cases of John Milton and others. 8. This system would permit Roman Catholic priests to perform their ceremonies in Baptist Churches.—Arians.—Polygamists. 9. Rom. 14th and 15th, considered. 10. The command to receive, only applies when the individual is complying with the whole revealed will of God in the matter in hand. 11. The case stated in another manner by Robert Hall, considered. 12. Each Church must be allowed to declare its own terms of Communion. 13. Why Pedobaptists should not be admitted to Baptist Churches. 14. Effects of Pedobaptism as a system, ...160

CHAPTER III.

ROBERT HALL'S THIRD ARGUMENT CONSIDERED.

1. Two senses of the word Church. 2. Assertion of the Author that they 'differ only as a part from the whole,' considered. 3. The true distinction destroys his argument. 4. 'Those who commune with God fit to commune with us,' considered. 5. 'Presumptuously to aspire to greater purity than Christ,' considered. 6. The same reasoning applied to the Passover,..................................177

CHAPTER IV.

ROBERT HALL'S FOURTH ARGUMENT CONSIDERED.

1. 'The exclusion of Pedobaptists a punishment,' considered. 2. The Lord's Supper a family feast. 3. The Evangelical Alliance excommunicate, on Robert Hall's principle. 4. The charge of excommunicating considered. 5. Mr. Hall would excommunicate all Churches whose invitation to Communion he declined. 6. 'That our views make the approach of Pedobaptists to the Lord's Supper criminal,' considered. 7. The difficulty of Mr. Hall's system on this point considered,..................................183

CHAPTER V.

ROBERT HALL'S FIFTH ARGUMENT CONSIDERED.

1. 'The impossibility of reducing Strict Communion to any general principles,' considered. 2. The Lord's Table to be governed by the same rules as our Church Membership. 3. Baptism a prerequisite to Church Membership, a rule *semper, ubique, et ab omnibus*. 4. Every visible Church must have some visible profession of Christianity. 5. Visible Churches aggressive in their nature. 6. The 'general principle' of Mixed Communion, considered. 7. The distinction between tolerating imperfection and endorsing it. 8. The distinction between errors fundamental and not fundamental, considered. 9. Baptism formerly deemed necessary to salvation, admitted by Mr. Hall. 10. A further difference as to Mr. Hall's 'general principle.' 11. Some visible profession must be necessary to Church Menbership,..................................192

CHAPTER VI.

ROBERT HALL'S SIXTH ARGUMENT CONSIDERED.

1. 'The Impolicy of Strict Communion.' 2. How far policy should weigh, considered. 3. Mr. Hall's statement as to its impolicy. Effects

CONTENTS. xiii

of "party," considered. 5. The comparatively rapid 'extension of scientific truths,' considered. 6. Distinction between the extension of speculative and practical truths, considered. 7. The speculative preacher of Baptist sentiments described. 8. The Baptist reformer described. 9. The question at issue between Robert Hall and ourselves. 10. The peculiar power of social organizations. 11. Shall the power of the Churches be applied to restore the obsolete practice? 12. Singular shift of Mr. Hall. 13. Practical test of his views. 14. Comparative progress of the Baptists in England and America. 15. Effects of Baptist sentiments on other denominations in America and Europe,····201

CHAPTER VII.

REVIEW OF PART III.

1. Review of Mr. Hall's first argument. 2. Of the second. 3. Of the third. 4. Of the fourth. 5. Of the fifth. 6. Of the sixth. 7. Of Mr. Hall's "leading position." 8. Mr. Hall's leading position clearly traceable back to the fundamental error of Popery. 9. Counsels of Sir James Mackintosh to Robert Hall, ····························218

PART IV.

THE ARGUMENTS OF REV. BAPTIST W. NOEL ON FREE COMMUNION, CONSIDERED.

INTRODUCTORY.

1. Recent appearance of his book on Baptism, and its claims to general regard. 2. Shortness of the section on Communion. 3. Not many new ideas, but in general follows Mr. Hall. 4. Yet some differences in method and spirit. 5. Analysis of his remarks,···············229

CHAPTER I.

MR. NOEL'S STATEMENT OF THE QUESTION.

1. In this he agrees with Robert Hall—Regards Pedobaptists as unbaptized—pleads for their admission as such. 2. Tendencies of this course—Mr. Noel's inconsistency. 3. Concedes too much to the sincerity with which Pedobaptism is upheld. 4. Yet in effect yields the very point at issue,·····································232

CHAPTER II.

MR. NOEL'S ARGUMENTS CONSIDERED.

I. *Argument from the nature of things.* 1. Error in illustration. 2. Confounds the Visible Church with the Invisible. 3. Assumes identity of qualifications. 4. Pedobaptists are not disowned as brethren, but as unbaptized. 5. The Lord's Supper belongs to visible churches. 6. The question resolves itself into this, Is it the duty of Churches, *as such*, to uphold Christian Baptism ?

II. *Arguments from the Scriptures.* 1. The main reliance here. 2. (*a*.) John 13: 35, and 17: 20, considered. 3. Nature of Christian union. 4. On whom rests the blame of breaking the Visible Church fellowship. 5. (*b*.) Rom. 14: 1—7, and 15: 7, considered. 6. Mistakes and their consequences. 7. The proper grounds of Church toleration. 8. The proper grounds of exclusion. Gal. 5: 12, 1 Cor. 5: 11—13, Rom. 16: 17, 2 Thess. 3: 14, compared with v. 6. 9. Result—There are other terms of communion than such as are terms of salvation. 10. Practical importance of this principle. 11. A fundamental distinction explained. 12. (*c*.) Mr. Noel's concessions;—1. Of an instituted connection between Baptism and the Lord's Supper. 2. Of the close Scriptural connection between Regeneration and Baptism, ...235

CHAPTER III.

MR. NOEL'S OBJECTIONS TO STRICT COMMUNION CONSIDERED.

1. These might be passed over. 2. State of the case.

I. *Prohibitory aspect of the system.*—1. Each visible Church independent. 2. No conscientious Christian is forbidden to commune at the Lord's Table with those who hold similar views.

II. *Implied usurpation over conscience.*—1. Peculiar impropriety of this objection from Mr. Noel after his concessions. 2. Supposes two serious misconceptions. 3. Singular reasoning. 4. Results to which it tends.

III. *Apparent inconsistency.*—1. It is not *real*. 2. Evidence of this. 3. The first Christians worshiped with the Jews in the Synagogues. 4. Unique relation of Baptism and the Supper, intuitively felt. 5. The alternative forced upon us. 6. Acknowledgment of Drs. Ypeij and Dermont of Holland. 7. Remark of Andrew Fuller. 8. Illustrations.

IV. *Impolicy of exclusiveness:* especially where a doctrine is unpopular, though true.—1. The Author's theories. 2. They strike at the root of *investigation*, by denying its necessity. 3. Action is here more necessary than investigation. 4. Action produces action. 5. Such exemplary action does not diminish *spirituality*. Comparison of United States and England shows this. 6. Mr. Noel's grand concession. 7. It amounts to the surrender of his whole argument,.. 250

GENERAL CONCLUSION.

1. The bearing of these views on the Churches. 2. The power of the Churches, to spread right views of the ordinances. 3. The ordinances specially committed to the Churches. 4. The relative position of the Church and the Bible to the world. 5. Duty of the Churches in view of the corruption of the ordinances. 6. Objection—'part to be sacrificed to the good of the whole.' 7. The duty of Pedobaptist Churches—their Baptism a nullity. 8. Position of the Baptists towards them—we ask them to defer Baptism to believing. 9. The duty of such Churches. 10. The duty of such ministers. 11. Why we offer these remarks. 12. All Christians love Christ better than any symbols. 13. Fate of Sects. 14. Prevailing ideas of this age—*Voluntariness.* 15. *Self-government.* 16. Baptist sentiments embody these. 17. Changes progressive. 18. The Home of the Christian. 19. It embodies the results of all the changes of Time, ·········265

APPENDIX.

A. Experience of President Edwards, ·····························281
B. Usage of the terms "Church,"—"Kingdom of God," ··········282
C. Moral Maxim of Confucius, ·····································289
D. Rev. B. W. Noel's reasons for being baptized, ·· ··············289
E. Augustine's account of the baptism of Victorinus, ·············291
F. Pliny's account of the Lord's Supper, ························293
G. Criticism on 1 Corinthians, 10: 17, ·························294
H. Effects of Mixed Communion in England, ····················296
J. Baptist views do not tempt to Superstition, ····················299
K. An early opinion of Mr. Jefferson on our churches, ············299
L. Conservative and Reviving influence of Baptist Principles, ······300
M. Fundamental Evil of Infant Baptism, ·························302

COMMUNION.

INTRODUCTORY REMARKS.

1. Distinction between the Literal, and Figurative or Symbolic use of the term Communion. 2. An error here lies at the basis of much of the reasoning on this subject. 3. Division of the subject.

1. THE word Communion is used, amongst Christians, in different senses. Of these the reader of the following pages will need carefully to distinguish two, the Literal and the Figurative.

Literally, as we shall see more fully in the next chapter, it is a spiritual union and interchange of feeling, and is nearly synonymous with fellowship.

Figuratively, the word Communion is used, in one verse of Scripture, in relation to the Lord's Supper. There, (1 Cor. 10: 16,) by a rhetorical figure, that ordinance is termed "the communion of the body and blood of Christ." Although the figurative has now become a prevalent and technical sense of this word, the above is the only passage, we believe, in the New Testament, in which it, or the corresponding Greek term κοινωνία, which occurs at least twenty times, is thus used. It is also figuratively used in the New Testament for the "*contributions*" of Christian benevolence.

In the present Essay, we propose to consider the subject of Communion, first, according to the more strict and literal meaning of the term, and then in its figurative sense, as denoting the symbols of Communion.

The reader should guard at the outset of this discussion, against losing sight of the distinction between Communion and its Symbols. From very early ages, and in the Roman Catholic Church to this day, the symbols of religion, and the things signified by them, have ever been strangely confounded; Penance and Repentance, Baptism and Regeneration, the Lord's Supper and Communion with Christ. Indeed, this is the very worst and most essential error of Roman Catholicism. By no means confined, however, to this system, it will continually be found leading theological writers of all classes, even the most completely Protestant, into error.

So entirely distinct have the literal and symbolic uses of this word become, that as accurate a lexicographer as Crabbe, treats them in his Synonymes, without the least explanation, as two separate words, classified, as to signification, under altogether different heads.

2. On the other hand, it is singular to find a writer, generally so exact in his use of terms as Robert Hall, employing this word so ambiguously, as unfairly to prejudice the views of his opponents. He thus takes for granted that what is true of the term, used in one sense, is of necessity equally so, when used in the other,—the very thing denied. Thus, in the Terms of Communion, Part II., the title of the very first section reads, " Free Communion [with all true Christians,] *urged from the obligation of brotherly love.*" We do not question that all such ought to interchange the warmest affection, and spiritual Communion, as Christians. The only point of dispute respects that symbolic Communion, which denotes church member-

ship. The ground we assume on this point, in the following pages, though opposed to his, we think more reasonable, that we should spiritually commune with those to whom we are spiritually united, and ceremonially with those who also agree with us as to the ceremonies which Christianity enjoins.

3. The present work, therefore, will be divided into four Parts, corresponding respectively with the Literal and the Popular uses of the word, and with the application of the whole to the arguments of Robert Hall and Baptist W. Noel for Mixed Communion.

PART I. IN WHAT COMMUNION CONSISTS.

PART II. THE SYMBOLS OF COMMUNION.

PART III. THE ARGUMENTS OF ROBERT HALL CONSIDERED.

PART IV. THE ARGUMENTS OF BAPTIST W. NOEL CONSIDERED.

Upon the first part of our subject, as being not only more vital, but also more spiritual, and therefore more difficult to apprehend, we shall dwell at greater length than is perhaps strictly necessary to its elucidation. To avoid confounding the Literal and Figurative senses of the term Communion, we shall, where there can be the least danger of mistake, USE IT ONLY IN ITS LITERAL SIGNIFICATION.

PART I.

IN WHAT COMMUNION CONSISTS.

CHAPTER I.

MEANING OF TERMS.

1. Literal meaning of Communion and Κοινωνία. 2. Sense of Communion and Fellowship compared. 3. A closer Communion the great want of the age. 4. The Objects of Communion classified.

1. COMMUNION! How grateful this word to the ear of the believer in Christ, connected as it is with all his happiest associations and highest blessings. While we contemplate its nature, may we, through the Spirit, be in true Communion with the Great Head of the Church.

This term is probably from the Latin *communis*, common; as κοινωνία, the corresponding Greek term, is from κοινωνεο, *to share in common*, (and radically, therefore, from κοινος, *common*). Κοινωνία, in the New Testament, is generally translated *Fellowship*. "That which we have seen and heard declare we unto you, that ye also may have *fellowship* with us: and truly our *fellowship* is with the Father, and with His Son Jesus Christ." Perhaps this fact may be useful, in enabling us not only to extend, but also to spiritualize our idea of the word Communion, if indeed this be necessary of a term which Crabbe discriminates from Converse, by saying, that it "may take place *without any corporeal agency.*"

2. Even when we escape the common error of confounding Communion with something outward and corporeal, we still are so far affected by it as to circumscribe Communion to some particular *act* or *time*, while *Fellowship*

seems to express the more habitual state of our affections and hearts. It was doubtless on this account that our translators rendered κοινωνία, *fellowship*, rather than *communion*, in the passage quoted above. It certainly would not convey precisely the same meaning, rendered "Truly our *communion* is with the Father, and with His Son Jesus Christ." Communion is most used to denote *an act*. Fellowship, *a state*. Communion implies the more *intense*, Fellowship the more *enduring* and habitual union. Thus we speak of "Communion with God in prayer," and of "living in Fellowship with our Christian brethren." We need some term for our purposes in this Essay, that shall, like the original, embrace all that is contained in both these words.* We shall use them in the following pages almost interchangeably, or vary or unite them as the occasion requires.

3. The great truth which we wish to develope in the First Part of these meditations is this:—that *A closer Communion of Christians as such, and of members of churches in their church relations, is the great spiritual want of the present time.* In the first ages of Christianity, the sword of persecution acted like pressure on the arch of a bridge, and bound all its followers firmly and closely together. This pressure is now taken off, and the whole arc and fabric of our piety has, as it were, sprung up and sprung apart, until it seems ready to drop to pieces. There wants something to bring Christians, as such, together, in a more true and well-defined fellowship, without pretending to pledge them to an agreement as to the constitution of a church, on which so many differ.

---

* For some further remarks on the senses of Κοινωνία, see Macknight on the Epistles. 1 John, i. 3. Note 3.

This is the great want of the age. There are scattered elements of piety and of power enough to erect a glorious and imposing edifice of true religion. But they need combining and cementing by a more earnest fellowship, a warmer, higher, holier, and more perpetual communion. Accurate views of the nature and proper manifestations of Christian fellowship, as distinct from Church fellowship, it is hoped, may lead to the increase at least of the former. The want of this discrimination has certainly led to many of the most serious heart-burnings that have afflicted Christendom.

4. The different objects of religious Communion may be classified as follows:

I. Communion with the Head of the Church.

II. Communion with the Church Universal: "the whole family in heaven and in earth."

The latter division will embrace,—

(1.) Communion with the Saints in glory.

(2.) Communion with Saints on earth.

The latter of these will embrace,—

   (*a*) Communion with Christians, as such, and not as members of any particular visible Church.

   (*b*) Communion with the particular Church to which each one respectively is attached.

CHAPTER II.

COMMUNION WITH CHRIST THE HEAD OF THE CHURCH.

1. How far this embraces Communion with the whole Godhead. 2. Its powerful effect upon the heart and life. 3. The great clue to the labyrinth of life. 4. The vital force and moving power of religious action. 5. Illustration.

"Whom having not seen, ye love."—1 Pet. 2: 8. "Truly our fellowship ($\varkappa o\iota\nu\omega\nu\iota\alpha$) is with the Father, and with His Son Jesus Christ."—1 John, 1: 3.

1. IN order to conceive of the abstract and essential nature of Christian Communion most perfectly, let us begin by considering *that Communion which the believer enjoys with Christ, the Head of the Church.*

It is indeed true, that the believer enjoys Communion with the Father of Spirits, but in the present state, this is chiefly through the Mediator. The period will come, when Christ, "having delivered up the kingdom to God, even the Father," our Communion with Him shall be immediate and direct. But thus is it not with us now. It is also true that all Christians enjoy "the Communion of the Holy Ghost," but this is rather a communion which He awakens in us with the Father and with the Son, so that in our proposed contemplations we shall substantially include all our Communion with the Godhead.

2. This Communion is the most intense in its nature, and powerful in the influence it has upon the spirit. It is not confined to any means or channel. "If a man love me," says the Saviour, "he will keep my words, and my

Father will love him, and we will come unto him, and make our abode with him." It may be in Baptism, or in the Lord's Supper, under preaching or in prayer, that the Christian enjoys it. Or it may be without any outward means, other than the written word, or in solitary contemplation. One of the most marked and beautiful instances of this latter kind, is mentioned by President Edwards, in his account of his own conversion.* This Communion is, of all things, the most essential to the maintenance of the Christian life, character and happiness. What is existence itself without it, to him who has tasted of the grace of God? A howling wilderness, a sandy desert. If cool streams seem flowing before him in the distance, they are but phantoms, which only disappoint and lead astray. Without Christian principles to guide a man, without communion with Jesus to cheer him, life itself is all a hopeless mystery,—a labyrinth, in which the traveller is continually losing his way, or ever vainly coming round, again and again, without progress, to the same point. "That which hath been, shall be," seems stamped on every thing, and the highest merely intellectual processes bring him round to the sickening conclusion, that "all is vanity and vexation of spirit." Without this grace, a man stands at the close of existence, no nearer its true goal than at the beginning. Life is but a circle, and death a "leap in the dark."

3. Communion with Christ illumines this darkness, and affords a clue to this maze; giving to life a definite aim, an animating hope, and rendering it in every case successful in its issue. The story of Rosamond's Bower is familiar to all. It was said to be surrounded by a labyrinth so constructed, that amid a thousand devious paths,

* See Appendix, A.

but one conducted to the centre. None could penetrate it without the clue. That clue, formed of a single thread of silk, was so suspended that it was difficult to keep it in sight, and so slender that a touch would snap it. Yet only by following that delicate guide could one penetrate the maze successfully, or escape being utterly lost in its windings. Just such a hidden guide through life is Communion with Christ. A single golden thread running unperceived by most, along the labyrinths of life, affording to those who possess it, a clear and certain clue, and conducting safely all who follow it through the world's mazes and mysteries. It comes from heaven and therefore conducts to it. Mysterious clue! So sure when truly followed with a sincere and humble footstep, yet so delicate; so often unperceived even by the most careful; so hard to regain when missed. O Holy and Most Blessed Guide, to whom we owe it, sole Leader of the pilgrim here below! grant us thine aid; leave us not orphans; ever be thou present; let us never lose sight of thee.

4. We need ever to feel that communion with Christ is the first and chief thing in Christianity. It gives life to all the rest. Let it be there, and every Christian grace and virtue will regularly and naturally follow. It is the vital force, the great moving power of all truly religious actions.

5. It is like the main-spring of a watch, which, though boxed around, and covered up from sight, moves all the wheels by its concealed, but steady and drawing power. Without it, the mechanism might seem perfect, the wheels all adjusted, but they could never move. Thus it is with man. His intellect may be clear, his knowledge complete, his morals excellent, he may have the Bible in his hand; but without the love of God in his heart, without com-

munion with Christ, what is he? He knows not how to make the first right movement in anything religious.

Much more evidently is it thus in a Church. If it hold not the Head,—if its members have not communion, daily personal spiritual communion with Christ, what is that Church? A watch, without a main-spring. It may have hundreds of members, great intelligence, regularity, and ability; all the wheels and mechanism of Christian membership may be there; yet what is it after all, but a cold, dead, motionless uniformity, with the regularity of order, but the rigidity of death. Such a body is a mere formality. Church fellowship is a lifeless and powerless thing, unless fellowship with Christ be its basis. But let that be there as the moving principle, and it will make all the routine of Church duties, order, and discipline, work easily and frictionless. The more earnest and powerful the Communion with Christ, the more easily will all other duties be performed. If we wish to make all the machinery of a large factory perform with most perfect regularity and ease, and if there are a hundred complicated wheels and joints, all rusty and stiff, how shall we hope to effect our purpose? By turning around each little wheel by hand, retailing thus our strength by driblets? No, but by concentrating force in the engine, by kindling a flame, and piling up fuel, and generating the steam, and when the main-shaft moves with a powerful stroke it will carry everything around, large and small. From the great driving wheel to the most remote spindle, all then will work harmoniously and well. Just thus is it in the Church of Christ; one-half of the wheels turn not at all in ordinary times; and when they do, they speak with creaking, rusty eloquence, of the disorder that corrodes each part, and disturbs the motion of the whole.

What is the remedy? More Communion with Christ. That secured, all duties and discipline of the Church, with its glorious and goodly fellowship, will work smoothly and sweetly, without harshness or formality, without strife or jarring. This is the true and only remedy.

CHAPTER III.

COMMUNION WITH THE CHURCH UNIVERSAL: WITH THE SAINTS IN GLORY.

1. Communion with the Church Universal—its two divisions. 2. *The Christian communes with the Saints in glory.* 3. There was much of this in primitive times. 4. How it may be enjoyed now. 5. The spirit of the age in regard to it. 6. *The Saints in glory have Communion with us.* 7. Spiritual influences. 8. Practical effects.

1. WE turn now to consider the Communion of the child of God with the Church Universal. This may be divided into Communion with the Saints in glory, and with the Saints on earth.

In the present chapter we treat of *The Christian's fellowship with the Saints in Glory.* This communion is mutual. He communes with them; they with him.

2. *The Christian communes with the Saints in Glory.* There is not a more unscriptural dogma, than that of the Romish Church, which teaches us to pray to and for the dead. But there is not a more scriptural or delightful doctrine than that of the spiritual communion of the whole church, the living and the dead, of all ages and of all climes. "We are come," says Paul, "to the heavenly Jerusalem, and to an innumerable company of angels, to the general assembly and church of the firstborn, whose names are written in heaven, and to God, the Judge of all, and to the spirits of just men made perfect."

3. Primitive Christians lived much nearer to their brethren who had passed into the world of spirits, than

we do in modern times. Paul speaks of them continually, as all forming a part of that same great company; two divisions of the same army, one on this side of the river of death, and the other beyond it; one division having "entered into rest," the other, by small detachments, entering in; both as having the same leader, Christ, "who died, and rose, and revived, that he might be Lord both of the dead and living," so that "whether we wake or sleep, we might live together with him."

> " One family, we dwell in him;
> One church, above, beneath;
> Though now divided by the stream,
> The narrow stream of death.
>
> One army of the living God,
> To his command we bow;
> Part of the host have crossed the flood,
> And part are crossing now."

The saints of primitive times walked so closely to the gates of Paradise, and lived so completely in communion with the unseen world, that it appeared to them but a short and easy step from the Church below to that above, as if a person on a journey, should go to sleep to-night in Time, and awake to-morrow in Eternity.

Hence it was, that anciently the bodies of pious Christians were brought for a time into the churches, and so often buried in and around them; even because the early Christians loved the idea of uniting their praises and worship in company, as it were, with those who having passed through the trials of the church militant, were now enjoying the repose and blessedness of the church triumphant. Their names were read, and their lives and actions of piety mentioned at the Table, during the celebration of the

Eucharist, and solemn praise was offered that they had been enabled to maintain a holy and virtuous life to the end. Their memory was cherished, and every means taken to keep up the idea that we are now worshipping the same Being below, that they adore around the Throne above. This was done, we are expressly informed by the Author of Dionysius, "partly to excite the living to the same course, and partly to show that they were still living according to the principles of religion and not properly dead, but only translated by death to a more Divine life."*

No doubt superstition very early corrupted all this into praying for the dead; for what will not superstition corrupt? But the idea of the essential oneness of the whole Church, militant and triumphant, is true, scriptural and ennobling.

"Let saints below in concert sing
With those to glory gone;
For all the servants of our King,
In heaven and earth are one.

The Church, triumphant in thy love,
Their mighty joys we know;
They sing the Lamb in hymns above,
And we in hymns below."

4. In studying the holy deeds and writings of Prophets, Apostles, Martyrs, and Reformers of all ages, we enjoy a true spiritual fellowship with them. While we meditate upon the history of the people of God, the struggles and piety of men of former ages, we imbibe their spirit, and become wiser and holier by their examples. And in proportion as we do this, do we enjoy the true Communion with Saints. Even when, from time to time, we bend

* Bingham's Antiq. Christian Church, bk. 15, ch. iii., sec. 17.

weeping over the remains of those whose virtues we have known, and bedew their coffins with our tears, and resolve to follow their faith, to imitate their example, and to worship as they also worshipped, we enjoy this fellowship and communion. Who has not felt the influence of a pious Mother or Father, a Sister or Wife, animating their devotions, long years after their departure to the skies? Robert Hall lost his theoretical materialism in praying by the grave of his Father. How often are the saints of Christ cheered by the hope, that their eyes will one day gaze upon their departed friends, upon Apostles and Prophets, whose example they have followed, and whose deeds have encouraged them here;—Paul the logician,—Peter the zealous,—John the beloved,—Moses and Elias,—Samuel and David,—Daniel and Isaiah,—the glorious company of the Apostles,—the goodly fellowship of the Prophets, and the noble army of Martyrs! And those hopes shall not be disappointed. Our eyes shall gaze upon them. Even now are they worshipping as we worship, all forming part of that "general assembly" to which we also belong. With all, from the saint most newly arrived in the kingdom of bliss, whose life and sufferings we have witnessed, to the holy Apostle who leaned on the breast of Jesus at the Last Supper, we have fellowship, a true and living communion even now: it is our privilege as saints, our birth-right as Christians.

5. But how little of all this do we realize! How far below it do we live! The tendency of the age draws men to live only in the present, and to forget the past. This infects even the temper of our piety. There is too often a forgetfulness of the maxims and experience of those of our Christian brethren and friends who have fallen asleep before our very eyes. "The righteous perisheth, and no

man layeth it to heart." The saints of Christ die, and their memory seems lost, almost before their bodies are cold. They fall asleep in Jesus, their spirits fly to the throne of God, but what eye of faith follows them? They are put into the cold, damp earth, and then, oh! how soon are their labors and piety forgotten.

We dread this temper of the times, so cold, so careless. He only who looks *backwards*, with piety and reverence, to the past, knows how to move forward with wisdom into the future. Reader, have you had pious relatives and friends? Think of them. Where are they? On what contemplations are they now employed? How would you act if you felt their eyes at this moment resting on you?

6. It is certain that *the Saints in Glory have a true Communion with us.* We know that "the great cloud of witnesses," who all died in faith, "compass us about," to animate and strengthen us to run the race of life eternal. We know, too, that there are "ministering spirits sent forth to minister unto those who shall be heirs of salvation." These proffer us the communion of their love, sympathy, and example, in order that we may draw spiritual sustenance through our knowledge of their purified natures.

7. The soul has, doubtless, powers of attraction and repulsion for different orders of spiritual beings, by a magnetism of its own, and according to its own character. The spirit of the man of evil dispositions, repels holy influences and agents, just as one point of the loadstone repels substances magnetized for the opposite pole; but it will perhaps attract and draw unto itself other spirits more wicked than itself, and they, entering in, dwell there. Hence the demoniacal possessions of ancient times, and hence probably much of the perfect madness and folly of wickedness, so often exhibited in outbursts, by men of

depraved characters. But the soul of the pious man, quickened by the Holy Ghost, will draw towards it influences only of light and glory, and repel all others. Thus is it that those happy spirits, "who do always behold the face of the Heavenly Father," guide us through the snares, and elevate and comfort us amid the depressions of the present state. In this manner it is, that the believer in Christ is made so fully one with the spiritual and invisible Church, of all climes, and of all ages. Hence, too, the whole Church militant, united as it is with the Church triumphant, possesses the combined wisdom and experience of all the past, and moves forward, "fair as the moon, clear as the sun, and terrible as an army with banners."

8. Christians in this way stand, in each successive age, upon a more elevated platform. We may, if we will, mount upon the shoulders of those who have gone before us. We must do this, if we would effect anything. The hosts of sin are wiser and more subtle by the experience of the past. Good and evil are assuming greater force; becoming more compact, condensed, and tremendous. Between **these** two classes of influence, we have to choose. To **one** or the other of these powers, we must ally ourselves. It is impossible to be neutral.

There is in the spirit of man, an instinctive choice of good or evil, momentarily going on; a choice between the fellowship of Christ and his Saints, and the fellowship of the hosts of evil. But with one party or the other, we must side. There is a battle to be fought, and life is one vast scene of conflict. If we choose the elevated course, the heavenly fellowship, which has just been discussed, we become allied to that cause whose final triumph is certain. The Son of God goes forth to war. Victory is written on his thigh,—angels are his attendants,—spiritual powers watch and guard those who love him,—the nations fall before him,—the kingdoms of this world are rapidly becoming the kingdoms of the Lord and of his Christ. He sweeps all his enemies away before his face. The whole earth and all heaven will finally be embraced in one *vast fellowship of Holiness*, and "the knowledge of the Lord shall cover the earth, as the waters cover the depths." But who shall stand among that holy throng? Let the beloved Apostle reply—"If we walk in the light, as He is in the light, *we have fellowship one with another*, and the blood of Jesus Christ, his Son, cleanseth us from all sin."

CHAPTER IV.

COMMUNION WITH CHRISTIANS ON EARTH.

1. Distinction between Communion and its Symbols, repeated. 2. Communion with Christians on earth, of two kinds. 3. The distinction illustrated. 4. The distinction shown by the two senses of the word Church. 5. Quotation from Robert Hall. 6. The error of Mr. Hall's opinion, that a particular visible Church differs from the Invisible, only as a part from the whole. 7. The true distinction shown by Neander.

1. WE are now about to treat of our Communion with the followers of Christ on earth, however this may exist, or in whatever way it may be expressed. Whether they are members of any visible church, or not, if they are Christ's, they are Abraham's seed, heirs of the Covenant, and therefore, partakers of the Communion of Saints.

We would again remind the reader of the necessity of distinguishing the Communion of the Saints, from the tokens of Communion. The one may exist, as we have seen, with Christ, and with the saints in glory, apart from all outward tokens, and so the tokens may be present, when all true Communion with Christ, and with Christians, is absent. Indeed, the expressions of Communion must be partial and varied, compared with the fellowship or Communion signified, which is often far more extensive and perpetual. True Communion is a spiritual, and not a visible thing. It may, in part, be symbolized, as in united prayer, or the Lord's Supper; but no Christian ever yet, on the most extensive sacramental occasion, partook of the same elements with one thousandth part of those with whom he would acknowledge true Christian Communion, for this he has, with all saints in heaven, as well as on earth. Nor will the two ever be co-extensive, until he shall sit down with Abraham, Isaac and Jacob, to eat bread in the kingdom of God, at the marriage supper of the Lamb.

2. The Communion with the Saints on earth is of two kinds. I. *Christian fellowship*, II. *Church fellowship*. The former embraces that spiritual Communion which we hold with our brethren in the Lord as such, and not in consequence of any visible Church relations. The latter is that which we have specially with those to whom we sustain such relations.

3. The distinction which we would here point out, may be most readily illustrated by the difference which there is in civil life, between the affection which a man owes to his own particular family, and the regard which he bears to his friends and fellow-citizens. It is his duty to cherish toward all around him, sincere friendliness and good-will; there may even arise cases, where it will be so far necessary to sacrifice the family to the community, that he should be willing to die for the good of his country. Yet who doubts that there is a vast distinction between the affection due to a wife and family, and a proper regard to all others, neighbors, fellow-citizens, or even friends? The peculiar family affection can be, and ought to be, shared only by members of that family. For a man to love any other children as his own, would be far from a virtue.

Just so must we cherish not only a fellowship with all Christians upon earth, rendering us willing, if need be, to "lay down our lives for the brethren," but a still closer Communion and fellowship with those who, by providence and grace, are members of the same particular Church or family of visible Christians.

4. This distinction is neither arbitrary, nor artificial. It originates in the Bible, or rather in the plan of Church government instituted by the Apostles of Christ, who established, wherever they went, societies, independent of each other, and completely organized within themselves, consisting of those professed Christians who were able, conveniently and regularly, to assemble together. These Societies were termed Churches. Whoever carefully studies the New Testament will find that the word Church, when applied to a Christian assembly, is used in two distinct senses. (1.) For a particular Congregation of professed believers. (2.) For the Universal Church,—the general assembly and church of the first-born. Dr. Robinson, in his New Testament Lexicon, defining εκκλησια finds two, and but two ecclesiastical senses in which it is used, (a) a particular Church, e. g. The Church in Jerusalem, Acts 8: 1. Antioch, Acts 11: 26, &c. (b.) The Church Universal, Heb. 12: 23, &c. (See Appendix B.)

5. Robert Hall has, in like manner, remarked, that "in the New Testament we shall find the word Church, as a religious appellation, occurring in two senses only, denoting either the whole body of the faithful, or some one assembly of Christians associated for the worship of God. * * * * In this [the former] sense, Jesus Christ is affirmed to be 'Head over all things to the Church, which is his body.' When the term is employed to denote a particular assembly of Christians, it is invariably accompanied with a specification of the place where it was accustomed to convene, as for example, the

Church at Antioch, at Corinth, at Ephesus, or at Rome. It is never used in the New Testament, as in modern times, to denote the aggregate of Christian assemblies throughout a province or a kingdom; nor do we ever read of the Church of Achaia, Galatia, &c., but of the churches, in the plural number."*

Fully concurring in the above observations, we quote them here only for the purpose of showing that, according to Robert Hall himself, the New Testament treats specifically of our communion or fellowship with the particular or visible Church with which we are associated, as quite distinct from that general fellowship which we have with all other Christians, as members of the Universal or Invisible Church.

Each separate Church then, is recognized in Scripture as a divinely organized Society, having its own special prerogatives and relations independently of all other bodies; and for the employment of which, it is answerable to the Head of the Church alone. Its fellowship is peculiar; just as in every state, each member of a family has peculiar relations and obligations to the other members, in regard to which the State has no concern; he is answerable only to them, and to the God of the families of all the earth. Such is the distinction between Christian fellowship and Church fellowship.

6. It is far indeed from our intention to represent Robert Hall as carrying out this distinction as we have done. He seems, on the contrary, to us, first to admit its Scriptural basis, and then quite to fail in erecting upon the foundation thus laid, any appropriate edifice. He takes for granted, as a matter of course, rather than

---

* R. Hall, on Communion.—Part 2, sect. 3.

attempts to prove that the Universal Church, (which is an *Invisible* body,) "differs from a particular assembly of Christians (which is a visible body,) *only* as the whole differs from a part," and that a single Church, such as the Church of Ephesus or Corinth, differs from the general assembly and Church of the first-born, "*only* as a part differs from the whole."* In this case, it would be difficult to perceive why the sacred writers so carefully avoid using it, as in the former extracts he admits and contends that they do, to denote the aggregate of Christians throughout a province or a kingdom. Here, the chief fallacy lies in that able author's Treatise on Communion. We can by no means admit that a particular visible Church differs from the Church Universal invisible, "*only*" as a part differs from the whole. With equal justice might it be said, that a family differs from a nation only as a part from the whole. The membership of the two bodies is based upon different principles. As no man can read the heart of his fellow-man, so a *credible profession* of piety is all that is requisite for membership in a particular visible Church, whatever may be the state of the heart. The Invisible or Universal Church, on the other hand, as Robert Hall would allow, is entirely a spiritual body, and consists of such only, whatever their professions, as *possess* sincere piety.† Indeed, from the meaning of words, it is not difficult to show that the terms of *visible* Church membership must embrace that which he himself admits not to be requisite to membership in the Invisible Church. For although true faith in Christ, which alone is necessary to salvation, or admission to the Invisible Church, may be said perhaps to include the disposition to confess him, it

---

* Terms of Communion.—Part 2, sect. 3.
† Dr. Dagg, on Communion.—Part 2, sect. 3.

cannot always embrace any actual profession of religion; whereas, in the very nature of things, some credible profession of religion must be one of the pre-requisites to visible Church membership. To contend that the terms of admission into the two bodies are identical, must therefore be a fallacy.

7. That in the plan of government developed in the New Testament, the distinction between the term of visible and invisible membership is recognized clearly, the following extract from Neander's "Planting and Training of the Christian Church," well illustrates: "John also describes an *inward* community, the assemblage of those who stand in communion with the Redeemer, and which embraces the whole development of the divine life among mankind; and an *outward* community of believers, which it is possible for thou to join who have no part in the former. . . . . We find here, as in St. Paul's writings, the distinction of the visible and the invisible church." Bk. 6, chap. 4, pp. 320–321.

To the visible churches of Christ belong ordinances and means of grace, things temporary in their nature, and to be observed only "till He come," who is the Head of the Church. To the Universal Church, as such, which is a spiritual and therefore invisible body, ordinances are impossible, since it cannot be convened; and means of grace are unnecessary, since its members all drink from the fountain head, and enjoy the grace of the means.

There are radically, therefore, two, and but two kinds of communion, which we can hold with the followers of Christ on earth. First, *Christian Communion*, or fellowship with the followers of Christ at large, as such; and secondly, *Church Communion*, or fellowship with the particular church to which, by the grace and providence of God, we belong. The fellowship of Associations, Conventions, Synods, and Denominations, is a voluntary and advisory matter, to be regulated on general principles of expediency, not being laid down in the Word of God.

CHAPTER V.

FELLOWSHIP WITH CHRISTIANS AS SUCH, AND NOT AS MEMBERS OF ANY PARTICULAR VISIBLE CHURCH.

1. The New Commandment explained. 2. This Communion may exist apart from all symbols. 3. It need not interfere with denominational preferences. 4. Baptist principles most favorable to Christian fellowship. 5. How to promote it.

"Whoso loveth not his brother whom he hath seen, how shall he love God whom he hath not seen." 1 John, 4:20.

1. THE object of the present chapter is to show, or rather to illustrate what will hardly be denied, though it is often forgotten; that, as Christians, we must and ought to have a true fellowship with those whom we esteem Christians, as such, though they may not be members of our own, or indeed of any particular visible Church, but only of Christ's mystical body, the Church Universal; such characters as the penitent thief of primitive, or a pious Quaker of modern times.

It was in relation to this love for all who love Christ, that our blessed Saviour said, "A new commandment give I unto you, that ye love one another. As I have loved you, that ye also love one another." But wherein, it will be asked, is the *newness* of this command? Not in the injunction laid on Christians to love one another, in common with the rest of mankind. Had Christ never come, this duty would have been binding upon them. "Thou shalt love thy neighbour as thyself," is the universal command, not only of Christianity, but also of the Jewish, and even of natural religion. And while Infidels have cavilled at it, even heathen philosophers have laid it down as the foundation of all Ethics.* Wherein then, consisted the newness of the command? It was in the peculiar *manner* and *degree* of the love enjoined, "*as I have loved you* that ye also love one another." Christ here makes out that "especial dearness, that watchful disciplinary love and loving-kindness, which, over and above the affections and duties of philanthrophy and universal charity," were to form the basis of a new, a Christian fellowship. "By a charity, wide as sunshine, and comprehending the whole human race," says Coleridge, "the body of Christians was to be placed in contrast with the proverbial misanthropy and bigotry of the Jewish Church, while yet they were to be distinguished and known to all men, *by the peculiar* love and affection displayed by them towards the members of their own community. How kind these Christians are to the poor, without distinction of religion or country, but how they love each other."† This new, this higher, this holier affection that binds Christian to Christian, is of the most heavenly nature. The love of Christ to the Church Universal is the highest exhibition, the full measure of it. He loved the Church, not as, but better than himself, for "He loved the Church and *gave* himself for it." "Love one another as I have loved you," saith he: "Greater love hath no man than this, that a man lay down his life for his friend."

2. This love, this Communion, may exist truly and per-

---

* See Appendix C.
† Coleridge's Aids to Reflection, p. 325.

fectly where there is and can be no interchange of any particular tokens of fellowship. This has, in substance, been already shown, for our fellowship with the saints in light, and with Christ, the Head of the Church, is of this spiritual character. Our fellowship with the saints on earth as such, our "brethren whom we have seen," may be of the same nature in this respect, with those whom "we have not seen."

This may be the case, even although our earthly fellowship be much more close and sympathizing than that which we have with the saints in glory. The great cloud of witnesses in heaven, bending from their lofty seats, may sympathize with us, because they have passed through our state of trial, but we cannot so well sympathize with them, not having yet attained to their excellence and holiness, and they not being encompassed, as we are, with infirmities. But our brethren in the flesh, however holy, are imperfect still; they need our prayers, they are comforted and sustained by our love. They are often materially assisted by our efforts, and stimulated by our example. Hence, we can assist and sympathize, and therefore commune with them more perfectly. And yet, notwithstanding all this, Communion of spirit is easily distinguishable from any particular tokens or symbols of Communion.

There is needed in the present day, a greater feeling of oneness among Christians of every name and denomination; one existing, primarily at least, apart from signs and tokens.

3. This need not, and would not, in any degree interfere with a firm maintenance and vindication of denominational peculiarities, or church customs. Should we not rather trust a man who was warmly and actively attached

to his family and kindred, to be a fast friend in the hour of adversity, than he who had no particular zeal or love for any one, and was almost indifferent to his own wife and children? So it is a good general rule, that unless a Christian love his own church, and his own denominational peculiarities, warmly and strongly; unless, in their place, he maintains them firmly up to the measure of truth and justice, he will not prove very warmly attached to the cause of Christ, or the true fellowship of Christians as such. No genuine Christian love will be promoted by attempting to break down Church peculiarities.

But on the other hand, where party zeal is a blinding thing, infidels mock while Christians quarrel. Every noisy controversy, all the selfishness of mere sectarian zeal, all the quibbles and the quirks, the party manœuvring and scheming, the pride and tricking of sectarianism, (and there is far too much of this,) rend and mar the Communion of saints, the true and proper fellowship of those to whom Christ said, "by this shall all men know that ye are my disciples, if ye have love one toward another."

That there must be different denominations, so long as there are different opinions on essential truths, or on the divinely instituted order of the churches, is to us clear. Truth must be upheld. Each Christian must follow the truth of God for himself, so far as he see it, not loving the errors of good men, because he loves them; not following a multitude, even of the most pious, to do any thing forbidden, or to omit what is commanded him by the Word, the Spirit, or his own conscience. That there must, and ought to be an ever increasing number of particular churches, in proportion to the greater number of Christians, is quite clear, if only from local causes; and the members of each of these must uphold what they believe to be truth.

4. But we may have true Christian fellowship with many whom from other, as well as local causes, we cannot join in Church fellowship; and those churches are to be regarded as having most truth and piety that have the most extensive fellowship and real love for Christians, *as such*, apart from the name they bear. Take those denominations, beginning at the Roman Catholic, who are the most proud, the most selfish, the most contemptuous of others, and those are the sects, and those the Churches, that have the least of the life of religion. Men of the world, the mass of Christians even, do not go into niceties, but they can easily see *the spirit that is manifested*. If it is a spirit of love for those who love Christ and bear his image as such; it is a good, a Christian spirit. "By this shall all men know that ye are my disciples, if ye have love one toward another." How far, as Baptists, we may have actually attained to the practice of this grace, it is not for us to say; but that *our principles* are more favorable to its developments than those probably of any other denomination, admits, we think, of demonstration. We never baptize any persons, until we first believe them to be true Christians. Hence we are obliged, in each instance, to keep Christian and Church fellowship distinct, and to have the former kind of Communion with them prior to, and apart from receiving them to the latter. Pedobaptism tends rather to destroy this distinction of feeling. Especially is this the case, when Baptism is supposed to *confer* Christian character.

5. With all true Christians, we ought to cherish and cultivate a spiritual communion as our strongest and most powerful feeling. We should strive to promote it by all

consistent means. Properly carried out, it will not be found to interfere with our more immediate duties to the particular Church of which we are members.

Let Christians pray, and preach, for and with each other; let them "speak often one to another" of heart experiences of religion. Is a church revived? Let her not be selfish, and unwilling for other congregations to share in the good work, and catch the heavenly flame from her altar, but rather let her pray that it may be so. Let her members and ministry urge others to use the means which they have found successful. And let all the other churches around, praise God for it, as a blessing to them, and pray that it may extend to them also. Let them exercise no narrow and sectarian jealousy, as if they would prefer that people should remain unconverted, rather than be converted to any creed but their own. Is a church divided, or tried? Let others sympathize and weep, and never aim to exaggerate and foment the disorders of their brethren, or tear open their wounds.

It is the want of this kind of spiritual interchange of affections among the different congregations and denominations in our towns and villages, it is the scheming and selfishness, the grasping sectarianism, trying in every way to get the advantage, and regarding all others as in antagonism, that cuts at the root of true Christian fellowship and real communion, such as we all feel with the saints in glory, and hope to enjoy in eternity with every Christian. This is the spirit which makes infidels rejoice and angels blush.

There is, it is true, a momentary success which seems to attend all this grasping. Strenuous exertions will produce a certain effect. But the motive will soon be discovered, and the means rejected as an imposture. The mass of people never yet could be convinced that such is the Spirit of Christ. It may be set down as a certain rule, that where there is most bitterness of spirit, most manœuvring and scheming, there is least of truth and least of piety. These are the resorts and refuges of that conscious weakness that cannot bear honest investigation.

So it is also certain, that where there is most real, earnest love, most simplicity, candor, and spirituality, there is most truth, most of that Charity which is the bond of perfectness, most of that "communion of saints", which is one of the clearest evidences and noblest features of Christianity.

CHAPTER VI.

CHURCH COMMUNION, OR FELLOWSHIP.

1. Its nature. 2. Its proper subjects. 3. The two objects of it. 4. *Designed to promote the piety of the members.* 5. Unreasonable expectations in regard to it. 6. Evil effects of such expectations. 7. Modern and Primitive Churches compared. 8. We need a fellowship more sympathizing in temporal matters. 9. Church fellowship ought to include a complete vindication of character. 10. It should promote the proprieties of Christian intercourse.—11. Church fellowship as *an instrument of converting sinners.* 12. A proper *Esprit du Corps.* 13. Its power. 14. The duty of joining a Church. 15. Summary of Part I.

1. WE have seen that the word Church is used in two distinct senses; first, for the whole body of believers in Christ, the Church Universal or Invisible; and secondly, for a particular visible congregation of believers, habitually associating for worship, and uniting in the ordinances of the Christian religion. In the present chapter, we are about to speak of the Communion, *i. e.* the spiritual fellowship peculiar to the members of these latter bodies within themselves respectively, over and above that general fellowship which they have with the whole body of the faithful in Christ.

This fellowship, though having its origin in the more general affection which binds all Christians together, is far more specific, and very different in some of its manifestations; just as family affection may, in some respects, be analogous to that general love of Society, which makes social intercourse so preferable to solitude, while yet it has many relations peculiar to itself. It is not too much to say, that as the happiness of mankind is more dependent upon a properly regulated family affection, than upon any of the more general feelings which bind men together, as tribes, as nations, or as human beings,—so to Christians, in the present state of existence, the proper affection of the particular members in the churches of Christ to which they respectively belong, is productive of more important effects for the good of themselves, and for the extension of the cause of Christ, than the most correct views and feelings as to their more remote relations to " the whole family in heaven and on earth." These separate Churches of Christ's professed people, though so small and insignificant, so widely and irregularly scattered through the whole earth, do yet produce the most powerful effects upon mankind. They are the salt of the earth, and the light of the world, the leaven that is ever working and permeating and fermenting the surrounding mass, infusing into it the most heavenly activities.

2. There is, as was shown in a previous chapter, a distinction between the proper *subjects* of Christian and of Church fellowship, the former extending to all the followers of Christ in heart, whether members of any visible Church or not, the latter subsisting between those who make a credible and appropriate profession of faith in Christ, whatever may be the state of their hearts, and who are in the habit of associating for the promotion of their mutual piety, and the extension of the Redeemer's kingdom. There are also other important distinctions. Christian fellowship is more extensive; Church fellowship more definite. The one contains perhaps a more spiritual sentiment, but the other, a more stirring and practical efficiency. If indeed the latter is more artificial and earthly,

it is for that reason more visible, tangible, and better adapted to the present state of human nature,—of the Church and of the world. The purely spiritual communion of the whole true Church of Christ, may suit the peaceful and triumphant state of glory in heaven, where there is no enemy to oppose, or discipline to be carried on; but the more visible fellowship, though circumscribed by place and time, professions and ordinances, is far better adapted to the militant state of Christ's followers upon earth. When a town is besieged, or a country is in a state of insurrection, the stringency of military law affords the greatest real liberty for all, compatible with their security. Or, to recur to a former figure, as the prosperity of society in the aggregate, is best promoted by the citizens all segregating themselves into families, for the enjoyment of household comforts, the education of the young, and the accumulation of property; and as thus a nation attains to a higher degree of riches and happiness, morality and refinement, than it could under any other social system, more compact and central, whether that of ancient Sparta or of a modern Fourier,—even so the prosperity and progress of the Universal Church will be best promoted by the distinct and independent organization of visible Churches.

3. The *objects* of the peculiar fellowship of Church members, as such, are two. To promote piety among themselves, and to convert others. We offer a few remarks on each of these points.

4. *First*, as to the fellowship of a visible church, so far as it is designed to promote the piety and grace of its own members. Some have, indeed, very unreasonable expectations in regard to this fellowship, desiring it to be closer than it ever can or ought to be on earth. They

would wish, for instance, such a oneness among the members of a Church, as would break down all individuality of character. There are not probably any in our Churches now, who carry this to the extent of desiring a community of property. But some professors of religion would wish all acquaintances, and all the familiar intercourse of private friendship in common, and expect all the members of a church to be equally unreserved and unqualified in the concerns of private life. They are jealous of those more intimate with others than with them, and are disposed to regard private friendships, and particular attachments in the Church of Christ, as so many violations of a proper fellowship.

5. This is altogether unreasonable. It arises sometimes from a shallow acquaintance with the Scriptures, and then a closer study of the Bible will correct it. Let any man read the Epistles, and he will see that even the intimacy of the Apostles was not alike with all. Paul preferred Silas to Mark, and had a personal warmth of friendship for Priscilla and Aquilla, that he had not with every Christian. John was emphatically "the beloved" of Jesus, and, with Peter and James, enjoyed more of his intimacy than the rest. We would even put the young Christian on his guard against expecting, suddenly at any rate, a perfect communion with all his brethren, even in the holiest church on earth. A Christian is a man who must dare to be singular, must dare to stand alone, and walk alone with God in prayer, with conscience in self-communion. He must be careful not to make Christians, but Christ his guide. He must follow the Bible, and light, and truth, and duty, wherever they may lead him, and without regard, beyond a certain point, to the feelings, or the friendships, or the practices, even of the members of his own church.

6. There is a weakness about most Christians here, that keeps them ever in leading strings, and makes them think it hardly proper to hold an opinion, or to practice a virtue, beyond what their church requires. This it is that makes our religion so dwarfish, our devotion so weak. They follow Christians, not Christ. They go as far as the church to which they belong, make the average of its piety their standard, but go no further, and attain no higher. The stream cannot rise above its fountain, but may fall below; and such a communion as this, destroying, as it must, the individuality of Christian character, levelling downwards the noblest spirits in the Church of Christ, puts all upon a Procrustes' bed, to shape them according to the newest pattern of orthodoxy. All this, however, is not to be identified with the scriptural doctrine of Church Communion.

7. Were we to compare our present Churches with those of primitive times, we should perhaps find that our members live, upon an average, in even greater regularity of *outward* deportment, peace and harmony, than anciently. Not even in these things as they ought, not as did the Apostles, and holier members and ministers, but more than a large part of the professors of those times actually attained. We cannot forget that there were serious disorders and divisions in the first Churches, Jewish teachers, doting about strifes and fables, and endless genealogies, and meats and drinks and new moons. Things were suffered in the first Churches, that would not for a moment be tolerated now. There was the thief at Ephesus, of whom St. Paul wrote, " let him that stole, steal no more." There was the incestuous man at Corinth. There were those who, even at the Lord's Table, took "each before other his own supper, and one was hungry and another

drunken." It must at least be conceded, that great as are the faults of our present Churches, they are more regular and orderly than all this would indicate. And these cases are no doubt left on record, in order that Christians may not plead the inconsistencies and errors of Church members now, as an excuse for not uniting themselves to a society constituted on the same principles with those to which holy Apostles scrupled not to attach themselves.

But on the other hand, if we have not the errors and divisions of the early Churches, neither have we their life nor their love. If we have not their strife and their failings, neither have we their Christian faithfulness, or affectionate zeal, rebuking and reproving. They could afford to take in rough-hewn Christians, full of faults and inconsistencies, as we cannot afford, seeing that they in the zeal of their holy affection would reprove and exhort them with a vigor of discipline, in which we are altogether lacking. They melted them down, and they moulded them over; and they turned them out as quickly as they took them in, if heretical, contumacious, or schismatic. Our church life is a petrified life. It is said that in Sweden, a physician has discovered a process of applying gradually increasing degrees of cold to all kinds of animals, from lizards up to man, and thus reducing them to a perfectly torpid state, without destroying life. Some culprits of the government have been taken through these different stages, and so long as kept at the proper temperature, preserved insensible for weeks, months, and even years; after which by restoring warmth, they have been brought back to consciousness. The fellowship of Church members thus exists, all petrified and frozen up for long periods. It is not dead. It is there. It is alive; but only now and then, after months and years of torpor, is it thawed out into consciousness and activity. There is in our Churches, a mysterious energy, that only needs waking up. There is a real life, a something between which and the spiritual death of false and formal systems of religion, there is placed an immeasurable and impassable gulf. Still it is only a spark of life. It wants waking up, drawing out, and fanning to a flame.

We pause to specify some of those things which are needed to render our Church fellowship more efficient, and like that enjoined in the New Testament.

8. We need a Church fellowship that shall be *more sympathizing and compassionate, in temporal matters*, to those members who need assistance. There is, indeed, much of this compassion exhibited every where in this country, and beyond what is common in any other. But while there is much of this love to man as man, and to a neighbor as a neighbor, there is little to a member of the same Christian Church as such, beyond this general social feeling. The cup of cold water, even when given to a disciple, is not given to him *in the name of a disciple.* Numerous are the societies formed and flourishing in our cities, towns, and villages, for the especial purpose of affording mutual support, visiting the sick, burying the dead, educating the orphan, or encouraging particular reformations. If one of the members of these fraternities is sick or suffering, he is visited, nursed, and relieved, as the case may require; or if he dies, is buried by his Order. But a Church of Christ, whose comprehensive relations to her members involves far more of these duties than any other society on earth, will often neglect these to a degree which would bring disrepute on any other.

Now we believe that the heart to perform these offices exists nowhere so strongly as in Christian Churches, and it is only from the lack of system in our arrangements, that so much of all this goes undone. A Christian may be sick and require nursing and kind attention, and though belonging to a Church, he will often be neglected to a degree that he would never have been in primitive times. There were orders of men and women anciently appointed to these very duties, even to digging the graves of Christians.* A large proportion of the funds of the Church were also appropriated for these purposes. This it was that won for Christians the love of all mankind, and caused them to grow so rapidly. And not only in pecuniary matters, but in all the duties of mutual service and benevolence, was this spirit manifested. To belong to a Christian Church was to be one of a society, each of whom loved the other with a new love, and in a peculiar degree, and who strove constantly to forward each others' interests. Our union is too often a merely spiritual or rather nominal thing; a mere intellectual fiction. We meet at the Lord's Table, and there we shake hands and unite in prayer, and are warm friends inside the Church doors. But how is it in the street, in the transactions of business? There is sometimes, we fear, a sharpness in making bargains and trading, and a selfishness, not to say an over-reaching, wherever there is opportunity, that destroys the unbounded confidence which should exist in a Christian brother, as a Christian brother. There are men of the world of such integrity, that a person would prefer to trust their honor in dealing for a tract of land or for a house, rather than the virtue, love, friendship, and word, of a Christian brother united. The word of a Christian ought to be sufficient assurance that what is said is not only true and honorable, in everything, but that there is as much con-

---

* See Bingham's Christian Antiquities, Bk. 23, chap. 3, sect. 7.

sideration of a brother's interest, as truth, justice, and the proprieties of the case will admit.

9. There is also wanting, in our Church fellowship, *such a brotherly feeling as shall produce a complete vindication and maintenance of the characters of the worthy, and the rejection of the unworthy altogether from our Churches.* If a member of a Christian Church hear any thing against the character of another member, he should feel it a wound upon his own, until he is vindicated. He ought to be affected as he would if, in society, his own brother were accused of some dishonorable transaction. Would he not in such a case, go and tell him what was being whispered, and urge and assist him to clear his character? If this could be done satisfactorily, he would cling to him the closer, because attacked unjustly and slanderously. Or if that brother were guilty and incorrigible, he would retire from his defence, and cease to uphold him as worthy of confidence. So with a Christian brother whose character is assailed, it is the duty of the Church and of each member to vindicate him, if he can be rightly vindicated, not listening to a whisper or an insinuation without going and telling him of it, so as to give him opportunity for explanation. If he be innocent, let them put down all evil and malicious insinuations; if not, it is their duty to withdraw fellowship from such an one, that their own character may not be implicated in his baseness. But the suspicion and tattling, the whispering and backbiting which a man himself can never reach;—from these, the whole fellowship of the Church ought to protect its members by the broad shield of its high character, and by its warm and living union. Herein is one of its greatest benefits and delights, that it is a society of holy persons, full of love and sympathy, ready

to sustain and support each other in adversity, while they walk piously before God, and faithfully with each other.

10. There needs also *a more careful observance of the proprieties of Christian intercourse, especially in all matters of Church action ;*—a vigilant attendance on many duties, and as careful a forbearance from unauthorized intrusion. A punctual attendance on all the meetings of the church for worship and for business, is to be regarded as the solemn duty of each individual. A careful forbearance from tyranizing over a conscientious minority, by any undue extension of their power, is no less the duty of the body. A majority, by pressing a measure unnecessarily against the scruples even of a few, may be the cause of schism and of strife, and of breaches of Christian affection in others, if not directly guilty of them themselves. A Christian, with proper views of communion, will rarely propose any measure requiring a new course of action, for which he cannot hope to obtain the unanimous sanction of the Church, unless it be some constitutional matter, in which, not to act, would be clearly sinful. Until some course of procedure can be devised which will secure unanimity, it is generally best for all to agree in deferring action. It is not sufficient that a majority can be found to support a particular measure; for a packed and party majority may thus be obtained in favor of many things which, to force upon a conscientious minority, may be destructive of all communion of heart.

11. Secondly, Church Communion or fellowship, is designed, not alone for the edification of its own members. *One great object designed by Christ in instituting Christian Churches was thereby to convert the world.* These living organizations were intended to effect this even more directly, than the written word. " *Ye are my witnesses,*

saith the Lord," "*Ye* are the light of the world." The Churches are the chosen instrumentalities of accomplishing his purposes, and they are kept in a militant state, while on earth, for this end. Their organization is essentially *aggressive* in its object. As soon as they lose sight of this great truth their own vital energy dies within them.

12. A serious deficiency of our modern Church fellowship is the want of more of what may be termed the *Esprit du Corps* of the Christian army. It is not enough that there be "one body." There must be also "one spirit" to animate and control it. Any man who has been in battle well knows that everything there depends on the spirit and enthusiasm of the officers and men. It is this that gives them the desire to perform every operation in the best possible manner. It is this that makes the soldier ready to die at his post rather than give way, and fulfill honorably every duty entrusted to him as if the safety of the whole depended upon him alone. Thus too in the army of Christ, the most exact order and regularity, for the good of others, is what each soldier of the cross must maintain, while a member of the Church militant. There are many duties which he owes to the body of believers to which he belongs, not only for his own, or for its sake, but for the sake of the cause of Christ in the world. Regular attendance on the Sabbath, prayer and church meetings, contributions for the pecuniary support of public worship in due proportion to his means; resolution to stand at his post, and do his duty unmoved, even if all others turn back, are some of these. As then so many of the obligations of Church fellowship are for the good of the whole cause, rather than any particular section, no delinquency on the part of other members can be an excuse for the Christian in neglecting any part of them.

He is rather pledged to do the more, that is to see that the Church, as a Church, does her part to promote the cause of Christ in the earth; and therefore if some do but little, the rest should, as far **as possible**, seek to make good their deficiency. Certainly **the neglect** of others can never justify the Christian in doing less, for though the communion be with the Church, it is in part at least for the benefit of the world, and for the glory of the cause of Christ as a whole. A Church covenant is in some respects like the articles of partnership, by which each of the parties is bound not only to act in a particular manner toward the other, but also to a certain extent to see that all their joint agreements with third parties are fulfilled.

13. All or nearly all the power which Christians have upon society, is from their Church, as distinct from their Christian fellowship. And by Church fellowship, we mean that *family affection* for the particular Christian society, with which they are by the Providence of God associated, an affection which lies behind all professions, ceremonies and symbols, and is essentially distinct from them, though often shining through and blended with them. It is the holy fellowship of these societies as such, that keeps up the true worship of God in the earth, and bears a various but united testimony to the only way of salvation, to Christian morality and Christian doctrine. To its affectionate guardianship, have been committed the oracles and ordinances of God. The testimony also of a **number** of distinct witnesses, animated by one spirit, varying on a thousand minor points, but all agreeing on the most important, becomes infinitely more weighty than that of any one body could be, however imposing the multitude it embraced, or however splendid the monuments of its piety and learning.

14. From this it will be also sufficiently obvious, that it is the duty of every true Christian to become a regular member of a particular visible Church. It is not enough that he be a member of the Church Universal. Special is the fellowship, special are the relations, and therefore the blessings reserved for believers in Christ, assembling though it be but " two or three" in his name. There are some who cannot see this ;—" Why cannot I be a Christian as well out of any Church?" "Do walls make Christians?"* they ask. This, at least, must be an evident and sufficient answer,—that if one Christian may argue thus, so may all, and if all did, we should have no churches, no sabbath bells, no assemblies, no ministry, no ordinances, no public discourses or prayers. If there be any efficiency or animating spirit in these, either for the comfort of believers or the conversion of sinners, as they are the results of this more special communion, so it is the duty of all Christians to support the visible Churches of Christ. That many seemingly pious and excellent persons omit entirely the duty of embracing this fellowship by a public profession of religion, is alas, too well known. The injury such do, both to themselves and others, can be estimated alone by God. In some, it would seem as if they thought no Church sufficiently correct. In others, it is doubtless timidity and distrust of themselves. But in many cases, it is evidently a fear of the cross, and a desire to live as much like the world as possible, and even a distaste to this close and holy fellowship.

The sin of living out of all visible Church membership and communion is not sufficiently brought to the view of Christians. Those who do so may wish well to the cause of the Redeemer as a whole, and subscribe liberally to all

* See the Account of the Baptism of Victorinus. Appendix, E.

pious institutions, but unless they walk in avowed and earnest Church fellowship, they utterly fail in a great and important duty. For it is the open, hearty, warm co-operation of the pious, that gives a Church all its power. It has no authority but that of love. It has no prisons, nor penalties, nor other temporal powers at its command. What keeps it alive? What is the source of its strength? It is its love, its fellowship. Without this, it is but a lifeless formality, a figure of wax, a rope of sand. May the Lord "add to his Churches daily, such as shall be saved."

15. Such is Communion in its essential nature. It is a spiritual, not a ceremonial thing. It consists not in any symbols, nor can it be confined to them. It may at times use them as channels, but it is in its own nature too etherial and elastic to be fettered by them. It will exist when time and symbols are all no more. It is found where they are absent. "They are no more essential to it, than they are to salvation. It is as far above mere ceremonial Communion, as the heavens are above the earth. It is a portion of heaven to be found on earth." All symbols without this are cold as moonbeams, and animating, only as they reflect a nobler, higher light. But this is like the sun, which inspires the whole scene, and gives even to ceremonies and symbols, their warmth, their lustre, and their life.

PART II.

THE SYMBOLS OF COMMUNION.

CHAPTER I.

NATURE OF SYMBOLS.

1. Definition of a symbol. 2. Simple symbols. 3. Complex symbols.
4. Those only to be used when *all* the relations are as represented.
5. Division of the subject.

1. A SYMBOL is an emblem, or sign by which any moral truth or idea is intelligibly represented.

Whatever emblem or action is designed to indicate our fellowship with any party, is a symbol of that fellowship. All those actions, therefore, by which we express our Communion with Christ, or with Christians, are to be regarded as symbols of our Communion with them.

2. These symbols may be either *simple* or *complex*. A simple symbol represents our relations with one and but one party. Thus when in private prayer we bow the knee, it is a symbol of this class, that is, of Communion with God alone.

3. A complex symbol represents relations with more than one party. When, for instance, we request a Christian brother to lead our devotions, our uniting in that worship symbolizes our fellowship with him, as a sincere and pious man, in the petitions he offers, and our Communion with God in the devotions offered.

4. Where any symbol represents several relations, it is not sufficient that one of them exist in reality as represented by the symbol. To be appropriate, all of them must subsist in the measure indicated. For example, the Lord's Supper is, first of all, a symbol of our participation

in the benefits of the death of Christ. But inasmuch as it also indicates, as we shall show, certain relations as subsisting between the parties who celebrate together, it would not be proper for those persons to unite, between whom all the relations indicated did not exist, however appropriate the symbol might be so far as it related to the Great Head of the Church.

5. In the former part, we have seen that our Communion, as followers of the Lamb, has for its objects, 1st. Christ, the Head of the Church, and 2nd. The Church which is His body; this latter being again divisible into 1st. Communion with Christians, as such, and 2nd. with the members of some particular visible Church. Corresponding to this, the Symbols of Communion may be classified according to their objects thus,—

I. SYMBOLS OF COMMUNION WITH CHRIST.

II. SYMBOLS OF CHRISTIAN COMMUNION, OR WITH CHRISTIANS, AS SUCH.

III. SYMBOLS OF CHURCH COMMUNION.

CHAPTER II.

SYMBOLS OF COMMUNION WITH CHRIST.

1. These are various, but two are chief. 2. BAPTISM, the first of these, a simple symbol. 3. Ground assumed in regard to Baptism. 4. Baptism, a symbolic burial. 5. Baptism, a putting on of Christ.—Optatus. 6. The Apostle's idea. 7. Importance of practically uniting the symbol and thing signified. 8. Baptism, a pledge—contains a reciprocal assurance. 9. Importance and beauty of this symbolic garment. 10. THE LORD'S SUPPER, a symbol of frequent recurrence. 11. A fresh acknowledgment of the baptismal profession—instituted connexion between them. 12. A complex symbol. 13. A symbol of communion with Christ. 14. Meaning of $\dot{\varepsilon}\sigma\tau\iota$. 15. A re-affirmation of the baptismal vow. 16. Contains a reciprocal assurance of our acceptance.

1. WE have seen that whatever emblem or action is designed to signify our Communion with Christ, is a symbol of that Communion. It may be the yielding of our bodies to an emblematic burial in a watery grave, or a participation in the tokens of a Saviour's body, broken, and his blood shed for our sins. Passing by all emblems of human device, let us fix our minds on these two chief divinely instituted symbols of our Communion with Christ, *i. e.* Baptism and the Lord's Supper. For these, being appointed by Jesus, become, when rightly received, symbols of a reciprocal Communion, of ours with Christ, and of Christ's with us.

I. BAPTISM.

2. This, of the two, most nearly approaches to the nature of what we have termed a simple symbol. It sym-

bolizes our union with the Saviour, and so to speak, nothing else. Indirectly, indeed, it may seem to indicate a spiritual relationship between the Minister or Church, through whom we receive it.* In a world in which all our relations are so complicated, nearly every symbolic act must have some reference, indirectly at least, to more of them than one. But in baptism, all other relations are so secondary, that we shall here consider it simply in regard to the Communion it expresses with Christ the Head of the Church, (and through him with the Father and the Holy Spirit).

3. We have no space here, to go over the whole Baptismal controversy. We rather take for granted therefore, than attempt to prove at length, (for, apart from the words bestowed upon it in controversy, it is in truth a very plain case,) *first*, that Christian baptism as a symbol, necessarily embraces an immersion or burial of the body in water, and *secondly*, that the chief thing symbolized by it is personal union or fellowship with Christ by faith.†

4. (1.) It is unquestionably in allusion to the *symbolic* part of baptism, that Paul speaks of Christians as "Buried with Christ in baptism, wherein also they are risen with him, through the faith of the operation of God, who hath raised him from the dead." (Col. ii. 12.) Hence he also says, "Know ye not that so many of us as were baptized into Jesus Christ, were baptized into his death? Therefore we are buried with him by baptism

---

* For a more full discussion of the relations indicated between the particular Church and Minister through which it is received, and the Candidate in Christian Baptism, the author refers the reader to an article which he prepared a few years ago for the Christian Review, and which appeared in that Journal, July, 1846. Art. o.

† See Appendix D.

into death, that like as Christ was raised up from the dead by the glory of the Father, even so we also should walk in newness of life." Rom. vi. 3, 4. In reference to this also, he speaks in the next verses of our being "planted together" in the likeness of his death and resurrection.

5. (2.) It is in allusion to *the thing symbolized* by baptism, that in Gal. iii. 27, "as many as have been baptized into Christ," are said to have "*put on Christ.*" One of the early Fathers (Optatus) in commenting upon this passage, compares the Christian's baptismal profession to "a garment found swimming in the water, that is always one and never renewed," that decently fits all, "not too large for little children, nor too small for men, and without alteration fits women."

6. The idea of the Apostle seems to be, that as the spiritual fellowship with Christ, into which we enter at regeneration, hides all our sins and covers us in his righteousness as in a robe, and conforms us to his image and likeness, so baptism is the divinely appointed symbol of all this, the emblem by which our union with Him is *visibly* signified. In it we put on Christianity outwardly and before the world. We profess our fellowship with the Lord Jesus, and publicly assume his uniform and allegiance. Mere water baptism however, administered without the baptism of the Spirit, and where it is not a profession of *personal* faith, is at best a lifeless ceremony, a tame and vapid thing. But where the inward and the outward may justly be presumed to correspond, and thus be considered together, as they are by the Apostle in the passage above;—where through the transparent drapery—the outward garment of profession, shines the rich vesture of a living faith within, the whole assumes a symbolic

lustre and magnificence, sufficient fully to justify the warmest eulogium of the Christian. Not too extatic to be applied to it, is the language of the Prophet when he says, "I will greatly rejoice in the Lord, my soul shall be joyful in my God; for he hath clothed me with the garments of salvation, he hath covered me with the robe of righteousness, as a bridegroom decketh himself with ornaments, and as a bride adorneth herself with her jewels."*

7. If the confounding of this symbol, and the thing symbolized by it, led the early Fathers,† as unquestionably it often did, to attach too great an importance to the mere baptism of water; on the other hand, let us not forget that there is an opposite tendency, sometimes manifested, so completely to separate these two, that the symbol comes to be regarded quite too much apart from the truth it signifies, and as a mere meaningless form. Thus all due sense of its worth is lost, and it comes to be regarded as of no importance. But as in nature, soul and body are so mysteriously blended, by the All-wise Creator, that they cannot be separated, without so etherealizing the one that we cannot grasp it, and reducing the other to a loathsome mass of dust and decay, so in the New Testament, has the Author of Redemption inwrought the spiritual essence into, and clothed it upon with the substantial body of symbol, that while the anatomists of spiritual influences may speculatively separate them, to ascertain the respective properties of each, it must be our care in practical life, to keep them relatively as he has placed them, that both may thrive. What he has joined, let none separate. For as by the union of two in marriage, each receives a benediction, neither could obtain alone, and both have bestowed

---

* Isaiah lxi. 10. † See Appendix E.

on them a relationship, neither had before, so by the uniting of the spiritual essence of baptism with its appointed symbol, both the consciousness of spiritual communion becomes more clear and strong, as being embodied in visible form, and the visible form assumes vitality, color and warmth from the animating spirit within; so also those who rightly receive baptism, not only in it give to the world a profession of their faith, but also obtain thereby a direct *Divine assurance and pledge of Christ's present and eternal fellowship with them*, a *palpable* covenant, that assures them by a formal act, that they actually *are* "heirs of God, joint heirs with Christ."

8. Indeed even this is not a full view of the importance of Christian Baptism, as it is placed in the New Testament. For it is also to be regarded, on our part, not only as a profession of present fellowship with Christ, but as a *public pledge* before the Church of God, and men and angels, of our whole future course. The baptized is regarded by the Apostle Paul, as having by this act, placed himself under a moral and public obligation, to live a new and holy life. Speaking of baptism, Paul adds therefore, "Likewise reckon ye also yourselves to be dead indeed unto sin, but alive unto God, through Jesus Christ our Lord. Let not sin therefore reign in your mortal body, that ye should obey it in the lusts thereof." (Rom. 6: 12.)

9. A pious mind properly instructed, will never think lightly of this ordinance, or regard it as of no importance, because a symbol. How can it be a matter of indifference? In it we enter into a public, solemn, and Divinely appointed covenant with God. We openly dedicate, and consecrate ourselves to be his. Baptism is the act of consecration. Those who are living in the neglect of baptism therefore, are living in the neglect of this consecration.

They who through indifference, or because they esteem it a matter of no importance, whatever may be their inward piety, are certainly neglecting to put on Christ publicly, in the divinely appointed way. "As many of us as have been baptized into Christ, *have put on Christ.*" This divinely appointed confession of Christ, animated by a true faith, is a garment which well befits all Christians;

> "it becomes
> The crowned Monarch better than his crown."

It can make poverty honorable, decrepitude and old age cheerful, sickness and death happy. It suits all ages and gradations of intellect. What sight on earth so beautiful as to behold the young and lovely descending into the waters of baptism, yielding up their hearts and lives to the service of the Saviour, "putting on Christ." It beseems well, even the simplicity of childhood, when entered into voluntarily and intelligently. The profession of the Gospel suits the heart and life of a child. Sin, repentance, forgiveness, the three great truths symbolized, are the three earliest moral ideas it can understand.

It is a garment that will adapt itself to the Christian's growth. If he puts on Christ while a child, he finds when his mind is cultivated and matured, in the faith to which he has attached himself, that which affords him contemplation, which warms his heart, and shelters it from the bleakness and coldness of the world. And when he is old and ready to die, and all the other relations of life have changed, and all his other fellowships have sundered again and again, the fellowship symbolized in his baptism remains as firm in texture, and as sufficient every way as at first. It is a garment that never wears out; but like those shawls of Cashmere that retain their colors brilliant for successive generations, is unfading and resplendent to the very last.

This garment is the uniform, divinely appointed for Christians upon earth. It is intended to mark them as separate from the world, soldiers of the Church Militant, members of the fraternity of Christians. It contains a significance and mystery that angels desire to look into, and that shall never be fully unravelled, until Time shall be no more, and unto all the saints is granted everlastingly to be clothed in fine linen, clean and white.

Such is the first symbol of Communion with Christ; Christian Baptism.

II. THE LORD'S SUPPER.

10. We turn now to consider the second Divinely appointed symbol of our Communion with Christ. As such it differs in two respects from baptism.

First, This is a symbol of *frequent recurrence.* Baptism is appointed for each individual once, and but once. The Lord's Supper, "*often.*" "As *often* as ye eat this bread, and drink this cup, ye do show forth the Lord's death till he come."* We will not say that Baptism confers an indelible character, but it certainly *makes an indelible profession and vow.* It pledges the candidate to be Christ's for life. It is a confession that can never be retracted, a step never to be retraced. He who has once voluntarily taken it, must if he possess a correct moral sense, ever feel that he has "opened his mouth to the Lord, and cannot go back." The Lord's Supper, on the other hand, may and ought to be frequently repeated. The first Christians made it part of their regular worship. It symbolizes our

---
* 1 Cor. 11: 26.

renewing covenant with God and Christ from time to time. It assists and enables us to do so.

11. In its relation to Baptism, it is rather like the ratification of an old deed, than the execution of a new one;— the acknowledgment of a bond, repeated again and again at different times and places, all having reference to some one original and permanent document. On this account it is that there is no instance in the New Testament of any person coming unbaptized to the Lord's Table. Those who knowingly receive this ordinance without baptism, act contrary to all the precedents of Holy Scripture, and to the instituted relations of the symbols.

12. *Secondly*, the Lord's Supper differs from Baptism, in being a *complex* instead of a simple symbol. It symbolizes first and chiefly, as also does baptism, our Communion with Christ. But it also symbolizes directly, as Baptism does not, a peculiar fellowship and relation, as subsisting between those who unite together in this ordinance. Baptism is an individual, the Lord's Supper a social ordinance. Both of these views are indicated in 1 Cor. 10: 16, 17.

13. In the present chapter, we have however, only to consider the former of these relations our communion with Christ. This is indeed the first, the chief, the most important fellowship signified. "The cup of blessing which we bless, is it not the Communion of the blood of Christ? The bread which we break, is it not the Communion of the body of Christ?" The Apostle was exhorting Christians not to partake of meats offered to idols in their temples. Why, because the idol was anything or the meat offered to idols capable of communicating spiritual taint or infection? No; but because in partaking, they would seem as if seeking and symbolizing a spiritual communion with

the idols, by giving the accustomed token of so doing. This he illustrates in ver. 18. " Behold, Israel after the flesh, are not they which eat of the sacrifices, partakers of the altar?"* As if he had said, do not they who eat together of the sacrifices offered to Jehovah, betoken to the world their joint worship of the God of Israel? In ver. 16, 17, he similarly illustrates his argument by the Lord's Supper; " the cup of blessing which we bless, is it not the communion of the blood of Christ?" Is it not a token by which we show to the world, our communion with Jesus? that we are partakers of the precious fruits of his death for our sins? The bread that we break, is it not a token that we are not ashamed to be considered as having imbibed the spirit and principles of the Crucified One? Do we not thus acknowledge ourselves to be joint worshippers with those with whom we partake. If they by partaking signify this, we by partaking with them signify it also. Such is the Apostle's thought. Idol altars and temples have crumbled into ruins before the power of the Cross, and we have happily no use here for the Apostle's argument against partaking of idol's food, but only for his illustration. From this, it will be apparent that when St. Paul speaks of the cup, being *"the communion"* of the blood of Christ, and the bread, *"the communion"* of the body, he intended these words to be understood, not in the sense put on them by Roman Catholics, as if the act of partaking was a communion in the literal body and blood of Christ, but that it was a symbolic acknowledgment to the world of our communion and faith in Christ; just as the partaking of idol meats would seem an acknowledgment of communion and faith in idol worship, although he de-

---

* See Macknight's translation of   verse.

clares that "the idol is nothing in itself, *neither that which is offered in sacrifice to the idol.*" So neither is the bread anything in itself, nor the wine anything in itself; they are but tokens to the world of that Communion we profess to feel with Christ the Head, and with those with whom we celebrate in Him. Our partaking of them is a public act of worship and fellowship.

14. In precisely what sense the bread '*is*' the Communion of the body of Christ, has been a matter of fierce controversy. "This is my body," construed literally, has been made to teach the Romish doctrine of transubstantiation. Zwingle on the other hand, put beside it Ex. 12: 11. "Ye shall eat the Lamb in haste, it *is* the Lord's Passover." Here, he argued, the Septuagint εστί *is*, can mean nothing else than "*signifies.*"* Neander most truly expresses the sense of the passage, "The cup of blessing which we bless, is it not the Communion of the blood of Christ? This can only mean that it marks, it represents this Communion, it is the means of appropriating this communion."† It symbolizes the body of Christ; and further as we have seen, that the right reception of Baptism becomes to us an act by which we obtain more than a mere outward or symbolic blessing, so in the Lord's Supper what in itself might be, and to the unworthy is, a mere symbol, becomes in the right reception of it to the child of faith, a means and act of true and living Communion with the Lamb of God.

It is on our part a ratification and re-affirmation of the Baptismal profession and pledge. It is a profession of our constant communion with Christ, of our feeding by faith upon him. As every one one needs bread daily, and

---

* See D'Aubigne's History of the Reformation, vol. iii. p. 272.
† Planting and Training, Bk. 6, chap. i. p. 277

as the bread he eats, nourishes his body, becomes indeed incorporated into and part of it, as the wine he imbibes sustains him, so do we imbibe the spirit of Christ, and feed upon him, our souls being nourished and supported by his grace and his doctrine, especially that of his atoning sacrifice. It is the death of Christ for our sins, which is the great sustenance of our hopes and life as Christians. How he himself taught this, see his memorable discourse, John 6: 24—65.

15. The Lord's Supper is also a ratification of the Baptismal *pledge*, every time it is taken; a vow to lead a holy and Christian life. That is a touching passage in Pliny's letter to Trajan, written within twenty years of the death of the Apostle John, in which he tells him, that he can get no further information in regard to the nature of Christianity than that its followers are accustomed to meet on a certain day (the Sabbath), and bind themselves "by a sacrament not to commit any kind of wickedness; to be guilty neither of theft, robbery, nor adultery; never to break a promise, or to keep back a deposit when called upon."*

The Lord's Supper is a token of our renewing covenant with Christ, and the public act by which before the world and the Church, we re-affirm the consecration and dedication of ourselves to Christ, made in baptism.

16. This as a *Divinely appointed* symbol, rightly partaken of, contains a reciprocal assurance of our acceptance; —of our being the very persons who are now living in the enjoyment of the pardon purchased by the body and blood of Christ. It is as sure and individual a token, as if the symbols were sent by a holy angel directly from the throne of God, to us alone and set before our very faces. It is a

---

* See Appendix F.

token, partaken of again and again, to repeat the assurance, and render the sense of it, habitual and certain.

It is also a symbolic pledge and promise of Christ's unchanging love; that he changes not in his relations or feelings, but is the same yesterday, to-day, and forever. Its voice is still affirming in the ear of faith that touching and beautiful testimony of Jesus—"Having loved his own which were in the world, he loved them unto the end." John 13: 1.

CHAPTER III.

THE SYMBOLS OF CHRISTIAN COMMUNION.

1. Symbols imperfect and partial. 2. They change in their symbolic character. 4. Various symbols specified. 4. The same original term used for Contributions.

1. IN the present Chapter, we consider the symbols of Communion with our fellow-Christians, as distinct from those of fellowship with Christ the Head on the one hand, and from Church Fellowship or Communion on the other. It is proper to remark however,—

(1.) That all outward symbols *must necessarily be but imperfect and partial*, and must come short of fully representing that which is so spiritual in its nature as true Communion. Even words, the most perfect of all signs, fall far short of ideas in rapidity, variety and power. We shall look in vain therefore for any one perfect token of our fellowship with all Christians as such. Union in prayer, the great symbol of Christian Communion in the third and fourth centuries, is but an imperfect indication of the extent of our fellowship; for when does the Christian pray *with* all whom he loves as the children of God? How often does he even pray *for* all such? The petition cannot grasp every particular, and he who prays is under the necessity of segregating certain objects to place them distinctly before his own mind. Thus the prayer of the blessed Saviour (John 17,) was at first limited to the disciples who stood around him. "I pray not for the world, but for those whom thou hast given me out of the world."

In that case, it was afterwards more extensively added, "neither pray I for these alone; but for them also who shall believe on me through their word." From the absence of some particular symbols, the absence of all Christian Communion is not therefore to be inferred. Omissions are not contradictions. Communion may often rightly exist, without all the possible symbols being celebrated, or even being appropriate. Better is this than the symbol without the Communion.

2. (2.) *The expressions of our fellowship change much as to their symbolic character* in different ages and in different circumstances. The Jewish symbols of religious fellowship were done away by divine command, when they had lost their significance to the Jews, and from being symbols, had come to be regarded as the things signified. Under the Christian dispensation, particular actions are symbols of closer fellowship in one age than in another. The same forms may be used, but they change their signification, and with it in measure, their propriety. In former ages of the church, that is from the close of the second century downwards, until heathenism was obliterated, it was generally, but erroneously supposed by almost all, that Christian fellowship or communion consisted chiefly in *praying together*. Christians would never unite in saying "Our Father who art in heaven," would not even pray in the same house of worship, with those whom they did not consider orthodox Christians. Heathens, unbelievers, heretics, persons suspended, or excommunicated, even catechumens or candidates for baptism, and members of other sects were admitted to hear the Psalmody, and reading of the Scriptures, and the discourses, but were invariably excluded from the building before the prayers of the church were offered. Our views of prayer are much more just

ACTS OF CHRISTIAN COMMUNION. 81

than these. Our symbols of Christian Communion are far more various and discriminating.

3. Whatever action is designed to indicate to the world, or to the parties themselves, our Christian fellowship with them, is a symbol of Christian Communion. Whether it be uniting with them in Missionary, Bible, or Tract Societies, in Evangelical Unions or Alliances, in Conventions or Associations, the interchange of the religious exercises of prayer or preaching, all or any of these may be symbols so far as they go, of Christian Communion. Indeed whatever exhibits the peculiar charity due to all Christians, as such, if it be but a cup of cold water, symbolizes it. These form its active developments. "By this shall all men know that ye are my disciples, if ye have love one toward another."

4. There are two and but two senses in which the original term for Communion is metaphorically used in the New Testament for different outward acts of Christian fellowship; the first where it is put for the Lord's Supper, which is termed "*the Communion* of the body and blood of Christ." The second, where it is put for the "*contributions*" of Christian benevolence; Rom. 15: 26. The former of these we have already considered.* In regard to the latter, it is not difficult to perceive how pecuniary contributions came to be designated by the same original term that is used for fellowship and communion, since he who has true communion of spirit with another, will be willing to "*share in common*" the necessities of the sufferer, and his own means of supplying them. See Rom. 12: 13; Heb. 13: 16. Hence we read in Rom. 15: 26. "It hath pleased them of Macedonia and Achaia to make a

---

* See Appendix G.

certain *contribution* (κοινωνία) for the poor saints which are at Jerusalem. (See also 2 Cor. 9: 13.) Contributions for the support of the ministry and of missions are also designated by the same term, as being symbols and acts of communion, Gal. 6 : 6 ; Phil. 4 : 4. This use of the term is not at all confined to the New Testament.

Such contributions may be either for the cause of Christian benevolence generally, as for missions, or for our own particular Church, as in defraying the expenses of keeping up its public worship. The neglect of either of these, in just proportion to our means, is a violation of symbolic, and if voluntary and knowingly, of true Communion. In the former case, it violates Christian, in the latter, Church fellowship.

CHAPTER IV.

THE SYMBOLS OF CHURCH COMMUNION.

1. Kiss of charity—feasts of charity—right hand of fellowship. 2. The Lord's Supper—in what sense the Communion. 3. A symbol of Church relations. 4. Is more than a recognition of Christian character. 5. Is a Church ordinance. 6. Not a mere symbol of Communion with the Church Universal. 7. Nor with all saints on earth. 8. But with those with whom we celebrate. 9. Illustrated by the Passover, and institution of the Supper. 10. Independence of Churches. 11. The early Christians esteemed the Lord's Supper a Church ordinance. 12. It is not to be used where there are not Church relations. 13. The Church an executive, not a legislative body. 14. Baptist Churches cannot be charged with want of charity. 15. The Lord's Supper belongs to all the members of a Church which celebrates it. 16. Injustice of debarring infants in Pedobaptist Churches.

1. It was remarked in the last chapter that whatever action is designed to indicate our Christian Fellowship with any, is a symbol of that fellowship. So now, it may be added, that whatever action, over and above this, is designed to indicate *Church* fellowship with any person, is a symbol of *that* Communion. There were in primitive times, many symbols of Church Communion, such as "the kiss of Charity," 1 Pet. 5: 14, the "feasts of Charity," alluded to in Jude 12, and "the right hand of fellowship," see Gal. 2: 9. But we enter at once upon the consideration of the most important and Divine of them all, the Lord's Supper as the symbol, not now of our Communion with Christ, but with those with whom we celebrate.

2. There is indeed a popular mode of expression, by

which the Lord's Supper is termed "the Communion." In Scripture, it is nowhere thus designated, except it be as "the Communion *of the body and blood of Christ.*" The popular use might seem to indicate that it is, at least, the divinely appointed and chief if not the only symbol of the Communion which the believer enjoys with all Christians as such. Even Robert Hall uses it thus; whereas, it is chiefly the symbol of our Communion with Christ, and then with those with whom we celebrate it; of a Communion, not as Christians merely, but as sustaining a peculiar, that is a Church relation.

3. We consider the Lord's Supper, then, a symbol of *Church* relations. When we say this, we mean that there is a fellowship in Church relations, professed with those Christians, with whom we visibly celebrate. We do not say that this is everything indicated, for then its chief significance would be lost, in not symbolizing our Communion with the blessed Saviour himself. But we do mean that Church fellowship and relations are uniformly expressed by it with all our fellow-communicants. It implies for example the exercise of that peculiar watchful and disciplinary love, which it is the special province of visible Church members, mutually to exercise among each other, as it is the province of none beside, by which the Lord's Table is preserved from the approach of notoriously improper persons. Hence "with such a one, no not to eat," *i. e.* the Lord's Supper, is equivalent to saying that he was not to be regarded as a member of the Church.

4. If the Lord's Supper is a Church ordinance, then it symbolizes, each time it is celebrated, a very different and much more specific relationship subsisting between the parties thus celebrating together, than a communion simply as Christians. It is much more than a recognition

of their Christian character; it indicates a visible Church fellowship as existing between them. Nor will it be a just or safe inference from parties not communing together, where there is opportunity, that they do not recognize each other as fellow-Christians, but at most that they cannot unite as members of the same visible Church.

5. We desire to show that this is the true view of the Lord's Supper. " When ye come together therefore into one place," says the Apostle, " this is not to eat the Lord's Supper. For in eating, every one taketh before other, &c. . . . Wherefore, my brethren, when ye come together to eat, tarry one for another." (1 Cor. 11: 21, 33.) The Apostle here clearly alludes to it as the universally current opinion, that the Lord's Supper was a Church ordinance, so far as this, that it was completely celebrated in one place, by one Church. Nor does he oppose, but rather takes this view for granted as correct, only objecting to the peculiar abuses of which the Corinthians were guilty, as vitiating the ordinance. When he bids them "tarry one for another," he clearly intimates that the regulation of the Supper, so far as time and place are concerned, is lodged in each particular Church; that it expresses the relations of the members of that Church, to each other as such; and that as an executive body, each Church, as such, is to decide what course is suitable for it to pursue in the observance of this ordinance, as most conformed to the laws and spirit of the New Testament, responsible to the Great Head of the Church, and to Him alone for the correctness of their interpretation. The Lord's Supper is thus committed to the guardianship of the visible Churches.

6. That this ordinance is not, as it was considered in the third and fourth centuries, and has been often since, a symbol of that Communion which belongs to the universal

Church, as such, is plain, for then it would be the symbol of our Communion with all Saints, asleep as well as alive, in heaven as well as on earth. If this were the case, it would be proper to have seasons for holding communion with the dead, by the Lord's Supper; and masses *for* and *with* the dead are not so very distinct, as to make our non-adhesion to some of the worst corruptions of Popery, plain or reasonable. Puseyism, at least, would naturally spring from the error.

7. Nor is the Lord's Supper appointed as the symbol of our Communion merely with all the saints on earth, or with this or that denomination, but each time it is celebrated, it is the token of a fellowship more specific in its nature, a Communion in Church relations. The first Churches were always willing to enter into these relations with any whom they admitted to the Lord's Table. The two always corresponded exactly to each other. The first was the thing signified; the latter, the sign.

8. We have seen, in a former chapter, the distinction between Christian and Church fellowship. That the latter, though having its origin in the same more general affection, which binds all Christians together as such, is far more specific, and hence as distinct in some of its manifestations, as family affection, and ordinary fellow-citizenship or friendship. That the origin of this distinction is not of man, but of Divine Revelation, we have also seen. In the Lord's Supper we symbolize our Church fellowship, with the Christians with whom we participate.

9. To illustrate more clearly this distinction. When the Jews celebrated their Passover, it was ordained as a general rule, that *each family* should partake apart in its own house. If any other person or persons partook with them, they did so by special arrangement and invitation.

Thus was the Passover a family ordinance. All concerning it, that was not regulated by a special divine command, was left to the arrangement of each family. The non-extension of an invitation by another family to participate with them, was not in any way equivalent to a denial of the true Israelitish character of the parties not invited. It was never intended that because they were Jews, they should be entitled to eat the Passover in any family they pleased besides their own. So when our blessed Saviour instituted the Supper, as he did upon one of these Paschal occasions, it was we say as a *Church* ordinance, that he ordained it. He did not call together all his followers. Where for instance were the seventy, whom he had sent out two and two? He simply gathered together the twelve, with whom he was wont more intimately to commune; his own special disciples, (or particular Church,) and to them he brake that bread and poured out that wine that instituted this feast. But no person has ever supposed, that in choosing, as our Saviour evidently did, to institute the Supper with the twelve, but without the seventy, and without those pious women (including even his own Mother) who were in or near Jerusalem, it was at all indicated that the rest were not partakers of a true and real fellowship with the Great Head of the Church, or that he expressed any exclusion of them from his fellowship, as true members of his spiritual body.

We say therefore that the bread and wine of the Lord's Supper, were never designed to mark the limits of our true spiritual fellowship, so that those not partaking at the same Communion Table should therefore be supposed not to have true Christian Communion or fellowship with each other.

10. In the Congregational, as well as in the Baptist

denomination, each particular Church is regarded as a perfectly distinct society. This was the primitive plan. Our Churches advise with each other by Councils, Associations, and Conventions, they fraternize in all ways that may be mutually agreeable, but each Church is an independent body. Because a Christian is a member of *one* church, he is not therefore a member of all, nor yet of any other. This can only be effected regularly by a formal vote of the Churches concerned, and transfer of membership. Nor does the mere fact that he is a member of one of them, entitle him to the privileges of any other, as for instance, to partake with them of the Lord's Supper. When he does, it is by Christian courtesy, and invitation to occasional communion. The propriety of this will be discussed in the succeeding chapter. Among Baptists, no person, because he is a member of one Church, is therefore entitled as a matter of right, to partake of the Lord's Supper with any other, even of the same denomination; any more than the mere fact of being a Jew, authorized a man to enter the house of any other Jew, without invitation, and there celebrate the Passover. Each particular Church of Christ is a separate *family* in the great Israel or nation of Christ's professed followers; and we apprehend that the blessed Saviour instituted the Supper when and where he did, that he included those whom he did, and no others, to show that such was the idea by which the administration of this ordinance was to be regulated.*

11. There is sufficient proof to convince any close stu-

---

* Neander, in his "Planting and Training of the Christian Church," Book 3, ch. 5, p. 103, says, "As to the celebration of the Holy Supper, it continued to be connected with the common meal, in which all, *as members of one family*, joined, as in the primitive Jewish Church, and agreeably to its first institution."

dent of Church History of the first three centuries, that in the very earliest ages, the Lord's Supper was regarded as strictly a *Church ordinance,* as we have defined this phrase. For even in after times, when they had departed from the primitive pattern,—when the Churches of most cities had embraced each of them several congregations, there was ever one and but one altar, at which were consecrated the bread and wine for all the assemblies under the charge of one Bishop. Sometimes a Church consisted of so few, that two deacons and himself were sufficient to supply its wants, and sometimes it embraced more than forty congregations. Still, however numerous the assemblies included in a single bishopric, each Bishop's charge was regarded as one and but one Church, separate and complete, and each Church was indicated by one, and but one altar, or communion table. Here the elements were blessed, and sent from the hands of the Bishop to the several congregations. The discipline of this body was usually and properly final within itself, and its own members. It baptized and excommunicated at pleasure. For any of these branch congregations to set up an altar, was to set up a claim to Church independence.* The two were regarded as synonymous. Hence was it that even in after ages, the High Altar of the Cathedral or Bishop's Church became so important. Thus firmly did the superstition of succeeding ages, amid many corrupting and more modern elements, embalm the form of the true and primitive doctrine, long after its vitality had fled. "One altar where there is one Bishop," is the known aphorism of Ignatius. (Epis. ad Phila.) In the time of Cyprian, Bishop and altar were correlative terms, so that both Op-

---

* Thus Novatian is on this account charged with " erecting a *profane* altar." Cyp. Epis. 672.

tatus and Augustine speak of the whole diocese, over which Cyprian presided, as having but one altar, and show that the Donatists had gone out from his church, *because they had set up another altar.* Thus at Rome as late as the time of Innocent the First, (A. D. 402—417,) Valerius speaks of his sending the bread of the consecrated eucharist, to the Presbyters ministering in the parish churches on the Lord's day.* Sufficient this to show that the Lord's Supper was anciently regarded as a Church ordinance.

12. It may here perhaps be asked, whether if a body of Christians should so desire it, and should agree to celebrate the Lord's Supper together, not in any token of Church relations, but simply as a mutual recognition of Christian character, and of their fellowship as such, it would be proper for them to do so? A few years ago, the case was practically presented in this way. The Old and the New School Presbyterian General Assemblies, meeting at the same time in the same city, and having *formally dissolved their ecclesiastical relations with each other*, although neither was prepared to deny the general Christian character of the other body, it was proposed by one of them, that they should celebrate the Lord's Supper together. This was declined. Was there sufficient reason?

That bodies of Christians, where they cannot meet as members of the same Church, should desire to recognize each other's Christianity by outward tokens, is natural and proper. It might seem desirable to a number of suitable persons to form a Christian Temperance Society, the basis of which should be a recognition and fellowship with each other, not only as friends of Temperance, but also as pro-

---

* See Bingham's Christian Antiquities, Bk. 8, chap. 6, sect. 16, 17.

fessed Christians. Such a society might be formed of various churches and denominations. In such a case whatever symbol distinguished them from members of other Temperance Societies would be a recognition of their fellowship as Christians. The question might arise, whether they should for this purpose celebrate the Lord's Supper together. As a matter of expediency, we think few would hesitate in saying that almost any other plan would be better than this. Otherwise why do not our Missionary Societies (whose members are all of the same denomination) adopt this at their Anniversaries, but that it would seem to change a mere Society into a Church.

13. But the question might be discussed as one of *right* rather than of expediency, and then it must turn upon this point; whether the churches of Christ or Christians have a *legislative*, or only an *executive* authority in regard to the ordinances of Christianity. If the former, then they have unquestionably, not only a right to make what regulations they please, in regard to it, as to time and place, but to vote whether they will celebrate it to denote a Church fellowship, or Christian fellowship; in fact, whether they will celebrate it at all, or whether Baptism and the Lord's Supper shall be laid aside or radically altered as to their object or form. The Roman Catholics have so far assumed this power as to administer the bread only, and not the wine in the Lord's Supper. Protestants have uniformly denounced this as a stretch of usurpation; but their complaints cannot be considered just, if the Churches of Christ have a legislative authority as to this ordinance. In that case they might, if more convenient, agree in Ireland to celebrate it with potatoes and milk, instead of bread and wine, and so do away with both.

No considerate person will hesitate in taking the opposite view, *i. e.* that the Church is an *Executive* and not a *Legislative* body. The laws of Christ are supreme and final. A Church of Christ cannot repeal or supersede them, but only execute. It cannot alter, it can only carry out. It is not required even to sit in judgment upon other churches to decide what is the application of the law of Christ to them. It can only decide what is proper for itself to do, or the application of the law to its own circumstances. Each Church is an executive body of the New Testament for itself. It has sufficient powers conferred to execute the Will of Christ, none to alter.

14. The effects of a right understanding of this principle will be, entirely to relieve the Baptists from all possibility of being charged with bigotry, on account of their views and practice in regard to the Lord's Supper. It is frequently urged that we refuse Christian Communion with the members of different denominations, and thus commit the most flagrant of offences against the law of Charity. This is an error. We do not refuse to commune with the members of other denominations as Christians. On the contrary, we seek communion with them all, in proportion to their piety. But we do not consider them, nor symbolize our communion with them, as belonging to the same particular Church as ourselves; and as we have shown, the Lord's Supper is a Church ordinance. Wherever we find Christians, we commune with them as such. But the Lord's Supper being a Church ordinance, none but the members of a particular Church, or Christian congregation can claim to partake of it. Even members of another Church of the same denomination only do so by special invitation, and not by right, as we shall show in the next chapter.

There is nothing in our views of the Lord's Supper to

prevent our having the most perfect charity and fellowship as Christians, with those who differ from us in many respects. We can and do commune with them as such. As indeed we never baptize any person, until we believe him to be a Christian already, his baptism never can *introduce* him to our Christian fellowship. We never do regard, and never have regarded the outward act of baptism as an essential to Christian character, and it is impossible we ever should. It is then impossible with us, (as with no other denomination,) that our Christian communion should be limited to our own church; nor do we any more refuse Christian communion with other denominations, than did the Saviour with the seventy, or with his mother Mary, the blessed and highly favored among women. On the points of baptism and church arrangements, we acknowledge a difference, just as, and where, do Presbyterians, Methodists, and all other denominations; and we say as Abraham said to Lot, "Let there be no strife, I pray thee, between thee and me, for we are brethren: is not the whole land before thee? If thou wilt take the right hand, then we will go to the left, and if thou depart to the left, then we will go to the right."

15. It only remains to be added here, that if this view is correct, and the Lord's Supper is designed to mark the peculiar fellowship subsisting between the members of a particular church, then it is an ordinance belonging of right to *all* the members of a particular church, as such.

16. It is at this point, that all denominations of Christians, except the Baptists, exhibit such a singular and inconsistent restriction of their communion. Regarding, as they all do, Baptism as the door of their several churches, they on the one hand baptize children into church membership, and on the other, refuse them the

Lord's Supper, thereby excluding half or three-quarters of their own members from the symbols of Church fellowship. What makes this inconsistency more remarkable is its contrariety to all those ancient Church customs, to which our Pedobaptist brethren appeal as their chief evidence in favor of Infant Baptism. It is notorious that the proofs in Church History of Infant participation in the Lord's Supper, are as clear, as early, and as universal as those of Infant Baptism, so that they must stand or fall together. That our Pedobaptist brethren are substantially right in not considering infants proper persons to participate in the Eucharist, we do not deny. It is one of those happy inconsistencies that result from their being so far "Baptists in theory," as Dr. Bushnell declares that they are. But a most strange and serious inconsistency there certainly is, in first declaring them members by baptism, and then refusing them the tokens of membership. Baptists have no such close communion as this.

CHAPTER V.

OCCASIONAL COMMUNION.

1. Meaning of the phrase. 2. Two classes. 3. Occasional participation with members of other Churches of the same denomination. 4. With Christians of no visible Church, and of other denominations. 5. The Difference is only as to *occasional* participation. 6. Shown from Methodist Book of Discipline. 7. From the Pres. Con. of Faith. 8. From the Thirty-nine Articles.—Not acted up to. 9. Any other plan of Church membership must destroy all denominations. 10. This admitted by Robert Hall. 11. Must silence Truth, if in the minority. 12. Baptist Churches originated in the desire of Pedobaptists. 13. Occasional Communion must be regulated by general principles. 14. Methodist and Presbyterian principles applied to the case.

1. "OCCASIONAL COMMUNION" is a technical phrase for a participation in the Lord's Supper, with those Christians who are not members of our own particular church; but who may occasionally worship with us, and so partake by special invitation, or with whom we may thus worship, and so be invited to partake. As the same principles will apply to both cases, they will be treated as one.

2. These Christian brethren may be divided into two classes, namely, members of other churches, whose sentiments are in accordance with our own, and who are therefore only prevented by local causes from becoming members of the church with which they propose to partake; and secondly, those between whom and ourselves there are such differences of sentiment, as would make it inconsistent with the constitutions of our respective churches for us to

receive them, or them to receive us, as permanent members, entitled to all the privileges of that relation.

This will involve the consideration of Occasional Participation in the Lord's Supper, with

(1.) *Those of our own denomination* not members of the same Church.

(2.) *Christians*, either belonging to churches of other denominations, or to no visible church.

3. (1.) As to the first of these cases, *i. e. occasional participation with members of other churches of the same denomination.* These occasional or exceptional instances, must of course be regulated by those principles which belong to the general administration of the ordinance, that is, as we have seen, by *Church* principles. It is the custom of the Baptists to invite members of other churches of the same denomination to participate with them in the Lord's Supper. This might at first view be thought a deviation from the principle we have laid down, that the Lord's Supper is designed to express the communion subsisting between the members of a particular church, as a church. As however the individuals so invited, are such persons as we should be willing to admit to our permanent Church fellowship, if they were permanently located amongst us, and may therefore be considered for the time being as members of the Church with which they unite in worship, they may with perfect propriety be invited to partake of the Lord's Supper. There is every consistency in this, with those Church principles that should, as we have seen, guide the administration of the ordinance. Indeed it has been practised in all ages from the very first. Acts 20: 6, 7.

4. (2.) As to *occasional participation with* the second class of persons mentioned, *i. e. Christians, either belonging*

to no particular church, or to other denominations, the same principle, *i. e.* that the Lord's Supper is the symbol of Church, as distinct from Christian fellowship, at once and finally decides against it.

So far as this decision affects those persons, (a very large and increasing class in the present age) whose title to be considered Christians we cannot deny, but who yet are members of no regular Church, our Pedobaptist brethren generally will fully concur with us. Members of the Society of Friends, who from not administering baptism have commonly been regarded as belonging to this class, have not generally been thought proper persons to be admitted to the Lord's Table. Bishop White of Penn. it is said, refused the elements to a pious Quaker who desired to partake. Indeed, as we shall shortly see, all Pedobaptist writers restrain from the Communion unbaptized persons. Instances are to be found in nearly all evangelical congregations, of persons whose lives for twenty or thirty years, have led all around them to trust that they are Christians, but who, from modesty, or mistaken views of their duty, never having joined any Church, are not invited to the Table of the Lord.

It has however, strange to say, often been brought as a most serious charge against our usages and denomination, that we do not participate in the occasional celebration of the Lord's Supper with Churches of other denominations whose members we do not consider baptized, nor invite their members to partake with us. As this is urged with great earnestness as an objection against the Baptists; as with many, it is avowedly the only objection; and as young Christians are sometimes perplexed by what they hear said on the subject, we shall consider it the more carefully.

5. (1.) In the first place, it will be observed that *this objection is only urged by other denominations in regard to the* OCCASIONAL *participation in this ordinance.* As regards permanent Church fellowship, they are perfectly agreed with us. They do not doubt that Christians ought usually to partake with the Churches to which they respectively belong; and in the formation of their Churches, they are professedly at least as distinctive as we. Such are their terms of membership, that a conscientious person, holding Baptist sentiments, could not join one of their Churches. If he did, so are their Creeds, Confessions of Faith, and Church Covenants framed, and that purposely, that he would be obliged to support Infant Baptism. If he had children, he would be *pledged* to bring them forward for Baptism. This, a conscientious Baptist could not do. It is nothing to say that many, and an increasing number, do practically neglect it;—neglect it because they have no faith in it. The standards of these Churches are purposely so framed, as to make it the covenant obligation of every member to conform to this. A person of Baptist sentiments would be acting treacherously to join a Church with the intention of subverting its order and customs, by not fulfilling his solemn pledges.

6. That these statements are correct, is easily shown. Our Methodist brethren, for instance, in their 17th Article of Faith, declare that " *the baptism of young children is to be retained in the Church,*" and in Chap. 1, sect. 16, of the Discipline, it is made, " the duty of every minister of a circuit or station, to obtain the names of the children belonging to his congregation, ... and *diligently to instruct and exhort all parents to dedicate their children to the Lord in Baptism, as early as convenient.*" In answer to the question, "How improper persons shall be kept

from joining the Church?" the answer is, "Let none be received into the Church, until they are recommended by a leader, with whom they have met at least six months on trial, and have been baptized, and shall on examination by the leader in charge, before the Church, give satisfactory assurances, both of the correctness of their faith, and *their willingness to observe and keep the rules of the Church.*" Discipline, chap. 2, sect. 2.

The whole of this answer is put in italics in the Book of Discipline, to indicate its radical importance. Hence it will be observed that all persons joining the Methodist denomination must not only be baptized according to their views, but after six months in which to learn what the rules of the Church are, and among them this, as to "the baptism of children" being "retained," they must publicly give assurances of their willingness to "observe and keep" all, and of course this rule of the Church. Thus then it is evident that according to the Book of Discipline of the Methodist Church, persons conscientiously objecting to the Baptism of Infants, not believing in, or not promising to comply with this rule of that denomination, are declared "improper persons" to join their class, or ecclesiastical society.

Among Presbyterians, the Confession of Faith is the authorized exposition of the belief of *their Teachers.* The larger Catechism seems to be a standard rather of that belief and practice expected of all *their members.* (See Form of Government, Book 1, ch. 1, § 5.) The shorter Catechism, of those more important and essential points of the belief and practice of that denomination to be impressed as such on the minds of the very *children.* In the Confession of Faith (Chap. 28, sect. 4,) it is said, "not only those that do actually profess faith in and obedience to

Christ, but also the infants of one or both believing parents *are to be baptized.*" So also the larger Catechism, (Q. and A. 166,) declares that such "*are to be baptized;*" and so even the smaller Catechism reiterates these same words, " the infants of such as are members of the visible Church, *are to be baptized."* In the Form of Government, (Book 2, of Discipline, chap. 1,) it is stated that all their baptized are members of the Church, and that these, "are bound to perform all the duties of Church members." Thus it is made by their standards, incumbent on all members of their Church, even in the loosest sense of the term, to bring their children forward for baptism, and to instruct them that Infant Baptism is of Divine authority. This a conscientious Baptist can never do. Our Presbyterian brethren seem conscious that in some of their requirements, they may err; but they feel what is unquestionably true, that it is better for those who sincerely hold the same sentiments, to unite in the same Church, rather than what they consider truth, should not be distinctly avowed and advocated for fear of offending some member, or that the conscience of a Christian should be wounded by upholding what he believes to be error. Hence, in their Form of Government, (Book 1, ch. 1, § 2,) they state that "every Christian Church, or union or association of particular churches, is entitled to declare the terms of admission into its communion, and the qualifications of its ministers and members, ... that in the exercise of this right, they may notwithstanding err, in making their terms too lax or too narrow; yet even in this case, they do not infringe upon the liberty or the rights of others, but only make an improper use of their own."

The Congregational Churches of New England hold substantially the same views. A few years ago, it was solemnly proposed by the Congregationalists of Maine to make the neglect of bringing forward infants for Baptism, a subject of regular Church discipline.

8. The Episcopalians declare distinctly in the Thirty-nine Articles, (Art. 27,) that "The Baptism of young children, is in any wise to be retained in the Church, as most agreeable with the institution of Christ."

Practically, indeed, it is true there is no denomination of professed Christians in this country, except perhaps the Roman Catholics, in which this is now uniformly made a subject of actual discipline, at least to the extent of exclusion; because the number in all Churches, who reject or neglect it from a conscientious belief that it is unscriptural, is so immense, and embraces so large a portion of the most pious of each denomination, that somewhat after the manner in which Tertullian illustrated the proportion of Christians, under the Roman government, in his day, might it now be said of these, that "if they should break away and remove" to some other Church, the mere loss of so many, would "leave a frightful solitude."* But it is still true as ever, that all persons joining any one of these Pedobaptist denominations, are most solemnly pledged to bring their children forward for infant baptism, a pledge that is always urgently exacted where practicable. We do not blame those who conscientiously believe in Infant Baptism, for making it a duty of Church membership; we only wish to show that we, in making our Baptism requisite to our Church membership, do no more than they, in making theirs;—that all are agreed so far; and that at most our only difference is as to *occasional* Communion and not as to the principles of Church membership.

* See Tertullian's Apology, sect. 37.

9. (2.) We remark further, that not only practically do all Christian denominations in this country agree with us as to the principles of Church membership, but that *any other views on this subject must result in the amalgamation of all denominations into one, or the constant changing of each Christian Church to and fro, from one denomination to another*, as any shifting majority might chance to vote, at any Church meeting.

That the plan of Church Membership proposed by R. Hall, would result in the mixing up of all creeds and denominations, both he and his followers in England have freely admitted. He indeed predicted that " the mixture of Baptists and Pedobaptists in Christian societies, would probably ere long be such, that the appellation of Baptist, might be found, not so properly applicable to *Churches* as to *individuals*, while some more comprehensive term might possibly be employed to discriminate the views of collective bodies."* In perfect harmony with these views, the Church which Mr. Hall instructed, have refused to be any longer designated by the name of Baptist.

10. It will be proper, here briefly to consider the views of the celebrated Robert Hall in regard to the organization of Christian Churches. His principle was, that "the universal Church differs only from a particular assembly of Christians, *as the whole from a part*," or that "each particular Church is to the Universal Church, as a part is to the whole." Hence he would admit all whom he considered Christians, Roman Catholics, or Protestants, baptized or unbaptized, not only to the Lord's Supper, as occasional communicants, but to full membership; and this in any numbers they desired, so that they could vote and

---

* Christian in Opposition to Party Communion. Works, vol. 2, p. 228.

act in every way, for or against any views they esteemed proper, and thus force them upon the Church, and give them its sanction if they had the majority. To use his own words his "leading position" is, that "no Church has *a right* to establish terms of Communion which are not terms of salvation." (Works, vol. I. p. 359.) Indeed he would make it a matter of indifference, whether the Ministers of the Gospel were themselves baptized, or unbaptized, or what their views were upon any subject of Theology, provided they were esteemed to be Christians. Some of them have been Universalists of the older sort, and they might perhaps be Arians, or Roman Catholics. He admits that this would effect the most sweeping reform, doing away all denominational distinctions. When his views have been adopted, it has frequently occurred that owing to the much larger number of Pedobaptists than Baptists in England, a majority for the time of the members of Churches originally Baptist, being Pedobaptists, have called and settled Ministers of other denominations. " In October, 1846, the leading mixed Baptist ministers of London participated in the formation of the Church at High Wycombe. The Rev. Joseph Angus, Secretary of the English Baptist Mission Society, was designated to deliver the address on the occasion. In that address, he says " In a Baptist Church, baptism (as we understand the term) is essential to membership. In a Christian Church, the possession of true faith is alone essential." After a protracted argument to illustrate and commend this latter term of membership, he adds, " I rejoice then that this Church is not in the common sense, a Baptist Church." A tutor of one of the Baptist Colleges, (in which candidates for the ministry are educated) and editor of one of the Magazines in England, after presenting in his paper of August, 1846, an earnest plea for mixed fellowship, imagines that it would be objected that the principle of *free communion* for which he pleads "would annihilate all denominational Churches," and exultingly replies "granted. Mr. Hall showed that long ago." Many leading men openly avow their sympathy with Mr. Hall's willingness for the extermination of Baptist Churches, for the sake of Christian Union.* The principle assumed by Mr. Hall, and on which all this was based, is erroneous. Particular *visible* Churches cannot, in the nature of things, and were never meant to be like the Church Universal or *Invisible*, and differing from it only as a part from the whole. This was shown in a former part of the work, (p. 37, 38,) to which, in order to save repetition here, the reader is particularly requested to recur.

We therefore confine ourselves here, to showing in a more practical manner the error of the course proposed by Mr. Hall; and this merely so far as the subject of Baptism is concerned. Let us suppose the connection between it and visible Church membership entirely destroyed in all the Presbyterian Churches, in order to make room for Baptist members upon the terms of that social equality as Church members, which would be necessary. Then it would become the duty of the Pastors of those Churches not to insist or urge upon their members, the rite of Infant Baptism. So on the other hand, if in all Baptist Churches, those who held to Infant Baptism were received as full members of these Churches, the duty of believers to be baptized could not be insisted on. Baptism could not be preached or practised publicly as the act of the Church,

* See Appendix H.

but only in the twilight, and as the act of the individual. What must be the result? Perfect indifference to all kinds of Baptism, and perhaps its entire neglect or rejection. Better surely is it that things continue as they are. Let those who hold to Believers' Baptism join Churches which practise thus, and those who conscientiously believe in Infant Baptism, and are prepared to practise it, join Churches, composed of those whose views are similar. We may safely assert that no Presbyterian, or Methodist, or Congregational, or Episcopal Church would be willing to agree never to have Infant Baptism publicly preached and administered, or the peculiarities of their denominational views enjoined on their members. To do this, would be to surrender what they believe, and assert to be truth. Why then should we be expected to do this?

11. Besides, whatever opinion happened to have the majority in the beginning, would, by this unnatural silence, be certain to become universal. That tendency which Truth has, to prevail, when spoken and acted upon in love, would be prevented. No errors could ever be corrected by such a course. A moral torpor, stagnation, and inanity, must ensue. That system which restricts liberty, can never be eventually favorable to truth, or even to quiet, unless it be the quietude of death. It should perhaps be regarded as a proof of the sincere and earnest desire of the Baptists for peace and union, that such a system of forming Churches should have been attempted among them, and them alone. It has arisen from a most sincere love to Christians, as such. But on the other hand, we hope that this experiment may not be tried in this country. No denomination but our own has attempted it any where. Even the Unitarians have repudiated it in their papers. It would be no compliment for a conscien-

tious Pedobaptist to give up a consistent advocacy of infant baptism, because he thought that the preaching of his own views, in his own Church, in a Christian spirit, would offend us; while as members of a Church, it would be no compliment for us to assist to propagate what we did not believe. Pious and sensible Pedobaptists are not offended at a fair and candid exposition of our peculiarities, in our own pulpits. In this way the public mind is enlightened, and insensibly the truth that there is in any set of opinions, becomes prevalent, and is adopted by universal consent, the error being dropped. Many of the most important controversies have thus been settled. It is now, for instance, generally agreed among all Evangelical Churches, that an experience of renewing grace is necessary to visible Church membership; but a hundred years ago, it was in many quarters a mooted question, whether even the ministry should necessarily be composed of converted men. The true and proper way is for Christians to form themselves into Churches with those with whom they agree in practice and opinion. Let this only be done solemnly and prayerfully; then let such a Church conscientiously carry out their views, with Christian love towards all other Churches. If they are true they will prevail, if erroneous it is well that they should fall.

12. Here it deserves to be especially remarked, that both in England and in this country, some of the first regular Baptist Churches originated in the express desire of Pedobaptists, that those who held such views should not remain members with them. In London, indeed, the first regular Baptist Church originated thus. It was found that an Independent Church had grown too large for convenience, and at the same time, that many of its members were Baptist in sentiment, if not in practice;

whereupon it was proposed and carried, that those who were of such views should be baptized, and form the new body.

In this country however, it was not until after the forcible ejectment of Roger Williams from both Church and Colony, on account of his principles, that the first Baptist Church was formed. It was thus an absolute *necessity*, and from the action of Pedobaptists, that the Baptist Churches of this country and of England originated. The desire was perhaps not unnatural in them, if convinced that their views were right. On the principle therefore, which should regulate our Church Membership, we are all perfectly agreed. It affords the greatest practicable liberty for conscience, and scope for truth; and has doubtless resulted under God thus far, in placing the views of both parties more clearly and thoroughly before the world, than they could otherwise have been. We are satisfied, both with the principle and the results, for these have brought us where we are. All parties in this country appear satisfied so far as Church Membership is concerned. And yet, it is only on account of the consistent application of the same principle to *occasional* participation that our Pedobaptist brethren find fault with us.

13. (3.) We remark in the next place, that this participation, being only *occasional or exceptional*, must conform to the principles that guide us in the formation of our Churches. It cannot fail to be to us a matter of surprise and regret therefore, that we should be charged so frequently and earnestly as we are, with illiberality, for acting in the one case exactly as we do in the other. It never can or ought to be systematic, to participate with any Church, but that to which we belong. And our course in all such cases ought to be framed on the principle of

making exceptions bend to general rules, not general rules to exceptions. The whole matter is to be regarded as one of Christian courtesy, and invitation, not of right. Such exceptive cases must not be allowed perpetually to alter regulations, upon which all agree as proper for other occasions. Why should we depart from all analogy, from all antiquity, from everything we find in Scripture, and put our occasional participation of the symbols of Communion on a footing quite different from that of our Church fellowship? We take our stand upon this; that *if the Lord's Supper is a Church ordinance, if it is the appointed symbol of Church relations, it should only be celebrated together with those with whom we can consistently sustain these relations.* To do otherwise is to symbolize more than we should be willing to realize in action.

14. There is to us a most obvious inconsistency in admitting to our *occasional* communion those whom we should be unwilling to admit to our Church Fellowship; making an exception in *favor* of irregularity. It is as much as to say that those admitted are good enough for the Lord's Table, but not for our Church. This perhaps is not intended; but it may at least be well compared to one welcoming a neighbor to his piazza, while he publicly excluded him his house. Such slender and discriminating hospitality would do little to promote good social feeling. Our Methodist brethren are about to celebrate the Lord's Supper, and they invite members of the Baptist Church to commune with them, and they feel hurt because our views do not enable us to partake or reciprocate the invitation. Perhaps they think and say that we refuse to participate with them in Christian Communion. It is in vain that we explain the difference between uniting in Christian Communion, which we do as freely with them,

as with all other Christians, and in the tokens not of Christian only, but also of Church fellowship. Or if we were to go to them and express our willingness to accept their invitation to the Lord's Table, not for once only, but permanently, our willingness to join their Churches, if they could consistently receive us, just such as we are, they would be obliged, if they should act in conformity with their standards, to refuse to receive us, and say,* "In order to prevent improper persons from insinuating themselves into the Church, none are to be received until they have given satisfactory assurances, both of the correctness of their faith, and their willingness to observe and keep the rules of the Church,"—their faith being to us antagonistically Arminian, and their rule that "the baptism of young children is to be retained in the Church." If we cannot conscientiously believe the Arminian faith, or live up to Pedobaptist rules, their standard declares that we are "improper persons" to belong to their body. We can be invited to the occasional participation of the Lord's Supper, only by their adopting one set of rules for permanent, and another for the occasional celebration of this ordinance. We can see the consistency with their own principles, in having such rules as they have in regard to their Church Fellowship; but we cannot see that those who are "improper persons" for the Lord's Supper, if it is to be received in one sense, are yet proper persons to be welcomed to the very same table in another. This, it seems to us, savors of that Romish doctrine, that the efficacy of the sacraments depends upon "the intention."

There is indeed a further inconsistency in the conduct pursued by our Methodist brethren, in regard to Ordi-

* See Discipline, chap. 2, sect. 2.

nances. For while their standards invite members of other Churches to partake with them of the Lord's Supper as often as they please, which is really a Church ordinance, they refuse to admit any, not of their own Church, "except with the utmost caution" *even to be present* at their Love Feasts, and "the same person on no account above twice or thrice, except he become a member."* One would suppose that they at least could perceive no inconsistency in our views of the Lord's Supper, when their own are so nearly similar, we were about to say, so much more exclusive, in regard to the Love Feast. We do not feel their regulation as to this feast, the least infringement upon Christian charity or fellowship, *because* the Love Feast is intended only for the members of their own Churches. We only do not see why they cannot at least, allow us to take the same view of the Supper. At times indeed, and to a certain degree, they seem to feel thoroughly, that the relation expressed towards all those with whom we partake of this ordinance, even occasionally, is quite analogous to, if not identical with that of being members of the same Church. Thus it is ordered, that "*No person shall be admitted to the Lord's Supper among us, who is guilty of any practice, for which we would exclude a member of our Church.*"† This indicates precisely our view of the Lord's Supper.

Our Presbyterian and Congregational brethren are far enough from entertaining Robert Hall's views of the constitution of Christian Churches. They would not be willing to give up all denominational peculiarities, and have their members and even their ministers, Arminians or Calvinists,

---

* Book of Discipline, chap. 2, sect. 4.
† Book of Discipline, chap. 1, sect. 23.

Pedobaptists or Baptists, just as it might happen. It is only as to occasional participation that they differ from us. And yet how can they, without inconsistency? They invite us, as Baptists, to occasional Communion. If we were to reply, that it is inconsistent to ask us to occasional Communion, while they deny us their Church Fellowship, they would perhaps answer that they did not exclude us, we excluded ourselves, for that we could join the Church also, *only complying with their rules*. If, then, we should say that we were willing to join, provided we could live and practise according to our own conscientious and avowed opinions, their standards would reply that all who join their Churches, "are bound to perform all the duties of Church members," and among these, that " the infants of one or both believing parents *are to be baptized*." We might, with at least equal propriety, say that we do not decline to receive pious Pedobaptists, only let them comply with our rules, and be baptized.

In another chapter it will be seen that we do not differ as to the principle of making Baptism a prerequisite even to "occasional communion."

CHAPTER VI.

OBJECTIONS CONSIDERED.

1. These Objections stated. 2. "It is only the mode of Baptism that prevents us from uniting with Pedobaptists," considered. 3. "That we do not consider the Baptism of Pedobaptists as valid," considered. 4. This true. 5. But not the only ground for our not uniting with them. 6. "That we unchurch Pedobaptists," considered. 7. The Lord's Supper not designed to express Church relations as subsisting between different Churches. 8. Custom of Baptist Associations un churches ourselves as much as other denominations. 9. Each Church entitled to declare the terms of its own fellowship. 10. The effect of the lack of a valid Baptism in unchurching, considered. 11. Different significations of the word Church. 12. Those unbaptized cannot form *regular* Churches. 13. Our difference as to Baptism chiefly keeps us from affiliating. 14. Ought our Churches to make Baptism necessary to their membership? 15. This the Primitive plan, conceded by Robert Hall. 16. Importance of keeping the ordinances as delivered to us. 17. Ought the rule of Church Membership to be extended to *occasional* participation? 18. This conceded by Christian writers of all ages. 19. This is consistent and charitable. 20. Illustration from American Citizenship.

1. It has often been objected against our views in regard to the Lord's Supper, that after all, it is nothing but our mode of baptism that really draws the line between us and our Pedobaptist brethren; that not recognizing their baptism as valid, we *unchurch* them at least, if we do not deny their title to be considered Christians.

It will be observed that there are here in reality three objections, that may be thus stated more at length.

(1.) That it is only the mode of Baptism that prevents

Baptists and Pedobaptists from celebrating the Eucharist together.

(2.) That at least, Baptists do not recognize the baptism of Pedobaptists as valid, and on this account refuse to celebrate with them.

(3.) That by not uniting with Pedobaptists in the Lord's Supper, we *unchurch* them.

2. (1.) With regard to the first of these, that it is only the *mode* of baptism that prevents our denomination from uniting with Pedobaptists at the Lord's Table, it is quite an error to suppose that it is simply because they are not immersed, that we do not admit the validity of their Baptism, or celebrate the Lord's Supper with them. We hold indeed that the word Baptism essentially and necessarily embraces the idea of immersion; that as a Scriptural ordinance, it always was in primitive times, and ever ought to be administered in the way indicated by the term itself; and while we fully concede that our brethren in the Lord of various denominations may be as truly and spiritually "dead with Christ" to the power and dominion of sin as ourselves, yet we feel that of no person who is not immersed in the name of the Trinity, as a profession of the Christian faith, can it be said, as St. Paul said of all the members of primitive Churches, that they are "buried with him *by baptism.*" Rom. 6: 4.

But Dr. Griffin greatly erred, when in his letter on this subject, (See Appendix to Fuller on Communion, p. 244,) he asserted that "the separating point is not about the *subjects* of baptism, but *merely* the mode" . . . . . "in other words, whether baptism by sprinkling, is valid baptism." That this is not the chief difficulty is easily demonstrable; for it is well known that none of the baptisms of the Greek Church, though always performed by immersion would by us be esteemed valid, and this simply because they are administered in infancy, and not as a profession of personal faith in Christ.

3. (2.) With respect to the second objection, that we do not recognize the baptism of Pedobaptists as valid, and on this account refuse to celebrate with them; it is indeed true that we do not regard the sprinkling of an infant as valid Christian baptism. Our reasons for this are open to the world; they have been expressed again and again, in all charity and affection; they have never been answered, and we feel sure they never can be. This does not however prevent our entertaining the warmest affection for and Communion with Pedobaptists as Christians. It causes us to desire them to be truly baptized, before we can unite with them in Church relations, or the symbols of those relations; on the same principle that their attachment to infant baptism makes their standards require conformity to that practice, of all who unite permanently with them.

4. Certainly, the most important, though not the only point of our difference on the subject of baptism is, that we hold it to be intended essentially as a public confession of personal faith in Christ. Infant baptism is not, and cannot be at all the same in its purpose. It is no profession of the faith of the party baptized, and therefore as utterly void, as any bond or deed executed in the name of an unconscious infant by a third party would be in law. We hold baptism to be, not only the profession of a past change, but a voluntary pledge of future obedience; *a divinely appointed act of personal dedication and consecration* of the heart and life to the service of God. See Rom. 6: 11—13. Hence it is that the baptisms of the Greek Church are as utterly void in our esteem as those of the

Church of Rome. If our views are correct all those who have never voluntarily submitted themselves to this ordinance, have omitted the divinely appointed method of publicly consecrating themselves to the service of God.

It is quite true therefore that we do not admit the validity of the baptisms in question. The above are some of the reasons. We sincerely ask and urge all Christians to ponder well the ground we take. The further discussion of it belongs more properly to the Baptismal controversy, and must here be dropped.

5. But it may be remarked in passing, though we do not stop to urge it, that it is not quite correct to say, as often is said, that *the only* ground of our not uniting in the occasional celebration of the Lord's Supper with all Pedobaptists is their baptism; for we do not commonly celebrate with Free-will Baptists, who agree with us in regard to that ordinance, but are Arminians, nor with immersed members of other Churches, nor with the Campbellites. That which draws the line is, that the Lord's Supper is considered by us a symbol of Church fellowship; so that those with whom we could not unite in the one, we do not feel at liberty to unite with in the other.

6. (3.) As to the third objection, that by not uniting with our Pedobaptist brethren in the Lord's Supper, we *unchurch* them, it will be evident, on the least consideration, that our practice in regard to this ordinance, our "close communion," as it is often termed, does not intimate this, either directly or indirectly; since we do not profess to partake of that ordinance with all Christians, or with the members of all true Churches, any more than the Methodists in their Love Feast; or any more than the Jews in celebrating the Passover professed to be ready to

unite in observing it at the same table with all whom they considered to be true Israelites.

7. That the Lord's Supper is not designed to express Church relations as subsisting between different Churches as such, is evident; for this would imply either that many of them together form one great Church, or that all are parts of a Universal Visible Church, implying a visible central government, perhaps a universal bishop, and thus Roman Catholicism. This would certainly destroy Church independence.

8. It is on this account, that it has not been usual for the Associations and Conventions of Baptist Churches, when assembled, to celebrate the Lord's Supper together. When this is done, it is always by special invitation of the particular Church with which the body meets, to the delegates, as so many brethren of the same faith and order. We invite them only as *individual Christians*. We do not regard all the Churches represented as, for the time, thrown into one, even of our own denomination. We might therefore, with at least equal propriety, be charged with declaring our own not true Churches, because *as such* we refuse to celebrate with them, as to be charged with unchurching those of other denominations by the course we pursue.

9. In our view, each particular Church is a separate and independent body, with authority derived immediately from the Great Head of the Church, and "entitled to declare the terms of admission into its Communion, and the qualifications of its members;" (Form of Government of the Presbyterian Church, Bk. 1, ch. 1, sec. 2;) and the Lord's Supper is a token, divinely appointed, which symbolizes, among other things, the relation which each mem-

ber of that Church sustains to every other. Hence we unite in that ordinance, only with such as are, or but for local causes might be, and therefore are temporarily considered, members of the same Church. All that our course, in declining to celebrate with members of other denominations, exhibits, therefore, is that such persons do not belong to Churches of our order. In this, however, we no more unchurch all other Churches, than the Presbyterian, when he insists that in his Church, the infants of all the members " are to be baptized," or than the Methodist unchurches us, each time he celebrates the Love Feast, or refuses to give up preaching Arminianism as his creed, or instructing all the parents in his flock to bring their infants forward for Baptism.

10. What effect the lack of a valid baptism may have in unchurching those who have not made the divinely appointed profession of their faith, it belongs not to our present discussion to settle, but rather to that of Baptism. This must depend upon how far Baptism is regarded as essentially prerequisite to Church membership. Almost all Pedobaptists so regard it; and so far would seem to unchurch themselves. We do not care to discuss the abstract question here, because it belongs not to the subject in hand. We shall however express in all candor our own opinion.

11. The original word for Church is used with different significations in Scripture. In one sense, even the tumultuous assembly at Ephesus, is so designated ($\varepsilon\varkappa\varkappa\lambda\eta\sigma\iota\alpha$.) Acts 19: 32. Any Christian ' congregation,' especially if assembled for worship, would have been thus called in the time of the Saviour and his Apostles. Matt. 18: 17. All organized religious bodies, acknowledging the Headship

of Christ, and assembling for the worship of the Father through Him, we regard as Christian Churches. Certainly our opinions and rules as to occasional Communion do not in the least prevent our considering all the congregations of professed Christians as Churches, in as general or specific a sense as other things may permit. This has been again and again shown by our principal writers on Communion. We only do not consider them *regular* Churches according to the New Testament pattern, and with such alone do we partake. (See Dagg on Com. Ch. 3, sect. 1.)

12. That which alone concerns us here in regard to baptism is, that Churches of our order, are organized on the basis of all their members being baptized persons. This we consider the only *regular* plan according to the New Testament, nor do any differ from us on this point. But we in no way assert that they may not be formed irregularly, and yet be fully entitled to the appellation of true Christian Churches. It is a question we are not called upon to settle. If a company of believers without any Baptism at all, as, for instance a body of Quakers, claimed that title, we should have nothing to say against it. Many of the promises which Christ made of being with his people to the end of the world, are often realized in their assemblies.

13. But it is true that Baptism is the chief thing that prevents us from affiliating with those Pedobaptist Churches which are of similar faith, and of Congregational government. The separation did not however originate with us, but with them. Our Churches are formed on a clear and distinctive basis, as much so as those of any other denomination, Episcopal, Presbyterian, Congregational or Methodist. Dr. Bushnell concedes to us even a much more distinctive basis.

The only possible questions then remaining (if indeed the reader is not already satisfied as to them) are, first, if it is proper for our Churches to make Baptism necessary to their membership; and, secondly, if it is proper that this rule as to Church membership should be extended to the occasional participation of the Lord's Supper.

14. (1.) As to the first, that it is proper for our Churches to make baptism necessary in order to their membership, there will be no question with any body of Christians in this country. There certainly will not, with our Methodist brethren, who, in italics, declare " Let none be received into the Church until . . . . they have met at least six months on trial, *and have been baptized*," &c. (Discipline, ch. 2, sec. 2.) Nor will there be any controversy on this point between us and our Presbyterian brethren, who declare that " Baptism is a sacrament . . . . for *the solemn admission of the party baptized into the visible Church.*" (Confession of Faith, ch. 28, 1.) Much less will there be any between us and our Episcopalian brethren, who declare that baptism is " a sign of Regeneration or new birth, *whereby,* as by an instrument they that receive baptism rightly *are grafted into the Church.*" The symbols of all the Reformed Churches contain the same doctrine. The Roman Catholics hold the same. So that if we are in error here, it would be impossible to find any body of Christians in this country, professing to be a Church, that could cast at us the first stone. Indeed, except a portion of our own denomination in England, whose plan we have already considered, there is probably no such body throughout the Christian world. Our Pedobaptist brethren will surely never impute to us, illiberality for not occupying a position that they themselves are unwilling to assume, and one that has left our Baptist bre-

thren in England so far behind those of America, in point of numerical increase.*

15. That our plan of Church membership is the primitive one, even Rabert Hall concedes. "On the same principle" says he, "we account for *the members of the primitive Church consisting of only such as were baptized*, without erecting that circumstance into an invariable rule of action. . . . . . We are willing to go a step further, and to acknowledge that he who, convinced of the divine origin of Christianity by the ministry of the Apostles, had refused to be baptized, *would at that period have been justly debarred from receiving the sacramental elements*. . . . . On these grounds, it is not difficult to perceive that a primitive convert, or rather a pretended convert, who without doubting that baptism, in the way in which we practise it, *formed a part of the Apostolic Communion, had refused compliance, would have been deemed unworthy Christian Communion*, not on account of any specific connection between the two ordinances, but on account of his evincing a spirit totally repugnant to the mind of Christ. By rejecting the only authority established upon earth, for the direction of conscience and the termination of doubts and controversies, *he would undoubtedly have been repelled as a contumacious schismatic.*" (See Terms of Communion, Part 1, sect. 3.)

16. It is, and must be then, abundantly conceded, that in restricting our Church fellowship to the baptized, we are but following primitive custom. All that even Mr.

---

* At the late Baptist Anniversaries in London, (1849), it was made a matter of public congratulation among our brethren, that, while, for the last seven years, the average increase had been one member to each church, per annum, it had reached during the last year, four members to each church!

Hall contends for, is, that it does not necessarily follow as a matter of certainty, that because the first Churches and Apostles did so, we are obliged to do the same, but that it may have been one of those accidental coincidences, like the celebrating of the Eucharist with unleavened bread. Something even more than this is, it seems to us, conceded, when it is allowed that he who violated this order in primitive times, *" would have been repelled as a contumacious schismatic;"* and withou there discussing the specific and necessary connection between the two ordinances, we may remark that it requires to be very clearly shown, why, if the Apostles were on earth, they would not " repel as a contumacious schismatic," now as well as at first, him who should invert the order in which they established the Church. The burden of proof clearly lies on that side. At any rate, it is fully sufficient for our justification and encouragement to feel assured, as it is by Mr. Hall himself conceded, that our customs in relation to Church membership are those followed by the Apostles; —customs, any departure from which by them would have been esteemed contumacious schism. Thus did the Apostles, and so do we. It was an occasion of praise and congratulation by the Apostle Paul in his Epistle to the Corinthians, when the primitive order was observed. *" Now I praise you, brethren, that ye keep the ordinances, as I delivered them unto you."* This is what we aim to do; to form our Churches on the primitive plan. Whether in regard to the mode or subjects of baptism, the bread and wine of the Lord's Supper, or the order in which the two ordinances respectively stand to each other, we wish to keep them " as they were delivered unto us" originally. We keep Baptism, as it was delivered unto us, not caring to enquire or discuss for ourselves, whether sprinkling or pouring might do, but unhesitatingly submitting our bodies to be "buried with Christ by baptism." It is thus also that we, and indeed all Protestants, act in regard to the two elements of the Lord's Supper. How urgently, and how justly, have we all reproached Roman Catholics, for administering the Eucharist but in one kind, and withholding the cup from the laity. Supposing that any denomination of Christians were to propose to change the elements, with what feelings would all others look upon the substitution? Who would choose even to invert the order of the administration, by giving the wine before the bread? though no reason whatever can be assigned, why all Christians should observe the order they do, except that it was that uniformly observed by Christ and his Apostles. If thus all Protestants feel and act in regard to the Lord's Supper, why should there not be an equal sensitiveness as to any deviation from primitive practice in regard to Baptism? and why should not the order of the two institutions remain with us all, even as at first? Why should it be a matter of reproach, that we "keep the ordinances, as they were delivered unto us" by the Apostles of Christ?

17. (2.) The only remaining point then is, whether this rule, which makes Baptism a prerequisite to membership in our Churches, is properly extended to the occasional participation of the Lord's Supper.

This has already been settled, so far as the general principle is concerned in the Chapter on Occasional Communion, particularly pp. 108—111; and it has been also shown that as the Lord's Supper symbolizes Church fellowship, those only can consistently be invited to the one, who are admissible to the other. We desire therefore simply to add here some remarks upon *the special connection between the Lord's Supper and Baptism.* That in conformity with primitive practice, no person could be admitted to "occasional communion," any more than to Church fellowship, if not baptized, is allowed by Robert Hall himself in the preceding extract. That *such has been the universal practice of Christians of all ages and places,* except the Mixed Communion Baptists, it will now be our object to show.

18. In his second Apology, Justin Martyr (within fifty years of the times of the Apostles,) speaking of the Lord's Supper, says, "of which it is not lawful for any to partake, but such as believe the things taught by us to be true, and *have been baptized.*"

In the third century, it was a law of the Church, " Let no one eat of these (that is of the elements of the Lord's Supper) that is not initiated, but those only who have been baptized unto the death of the Lord."* It would be idle to multiply instances of the care with which even catechumens were excluded from the Lord's Supper. In the year 607, a bitter persecution of the Christian Saxons originated in nothing else but an adherence to this view. The Venerable Bede says (lib. 3, c. 5), " After the death of Eadbald, King of the East Saxons, his sons re-established idolatry in that kingdom, and when they saw the minister (*pontificem*) . . . . give the Eucharist to the people, inflated with a barbarous folly, they said to him ' Why do you not give to us that beautiful bread, which you used to give to our Father Saba?' To which he answered, ' If ye will be washed in that salubrious font, wherein your father was washed, ye may partake of this holy bread; but if ye despise the water of life, ye cannot receive the bread of life.' Upon which they said, ' We will not

---

* Apostolic Constitutions, Lib. 7, c. 25.

enter that font, because we know we stand not in need of it, but nevertheless we desire to be refreshed with that bread.' And when they had been frequently and diligently admonished that no one could lawfully partake of the holy oblation, without that most holy washing, being at length aroused to indignation, they exclaimed, 'If you will not oblige us in such a trifling matter, you can no longer remain in our province.' And they expelled him, and commanded him to depart from their dominion with his followers." These men were not Baptists, although in those days, no other baptism but that of immersion was practised. They were monks sent from Rome, under Augustine. Yet it was clearly the sentiment of all Christians, in those days, that it was better to be expelled, better to leave the country even to Paganism, better that the sword of persecution should decimate the Church, than this rule be violated. Our object here, is not to vindicate all the views upheld by these men, but only to show that if any change were to be introduced into our plan in regard to the Lord's Supper, it could only be done at the expense of a great innovation, and of going contrary, not only to the usages of our own denomination, but of all antiquity, and of those sentiments for which Christians of every name have thought it worthy, rather to suffer martyrdom than abandon.

No denomination of Christians has ever discarded this belief. Individuals among the Baptists, who have followed Robert Hall, have done so; but numberless extracts from the chief writers of all the Churches of the Reformation, might be adduced to show that our practice on this point is held by them all.

Dr. Wall, in his History of Infant Baptism, says, " No Church ever gave the Communion to any persons before they were baptized. Among all the absurdities that ever were held, none ever maintained *that*, that any person should partake of the Communion before he was baptized."*

Dr. Doddridge, in referring to this subject in his Lectures, says, "It is certain, as far as our knowledge of primitive antiquity reaches, no unbaptized person received the Lord's Supper. How excellent soever any man's character is, he must be baptized, before he can be looked upon as completely a member of the Church of Christ."

Dr. Hopkins, the celebrated New England divine, says, "No one is to be considered and treated as a member of the Church of Christ, unless he be baptized with water; as this is the only door by which persons can be introduced into the visible kingdom of Christ, according to his appointment."

Dr. Dwight, the celebrated Theological writer, says that "it is an indispensable qualification for this ordinance that a candidate for communion be a member of the visible Church of Christ in full standing. By this, I intend that he should be a person of piety, that he should have made a public profession of religion, and *that he should have been baptized.*"†

Dr. Griffin remarks, in his Letter on this subject in 1829, "I agree with the advocates of close communion in two points: 1. That baptism is the initiating ordinance which introduces us into the visible Church; of course, where there is no baptism, there are no visible Churches. 2. That we ought not to commune with those who are not baptized, and of course are not Church members,

---

* Part 2, ch. 9.

† Sermons on Theology, 160. For several of the above quotations, I am indebted to former writers, particularly "Howell, on Communion."

even if we regard them as Christians. Should a pious Quaker so far depart from his principles, as to wish to commune with me at the Lord's Table, while he yet refused to be baptized, I could not receive him; because there is such a relationship established between the two ordinances, that *I have no right to separate them;* in other words, I have no right to send the sacred elements out of the Church." Such are the opinions and concessions of our Pedobaptist brethren.

19. The ground which we take in regard to the Lord's Supper, practically harmonizes with that of Christians of all ages and climes. It is simple, charitable, and consistent with itself. We have a full and perfect fellowship or communion as Christians, with all the followers of Christ so far as we know them. With those who agree with us ceremonially, we ceremonially commune. Where we agree as to ordinances, we celebrate ordinances together. Where otherwise, we do not. We differ from many as to what Baptism is, and we feel sure that we are right. We ask, in all love and charity, our brethren of different denominations to examine the point of difference for themselves, prayerfully, and with a fixed determination to follow wherever Christ leads. But all denominations most fully coincide with us, that those only who agree as to ordinances, *i. e.* who regard as valid, each other's baptism, should partake together of the other ordinance, the Lord's Supper.

But with all Christians, as such, we commune most heartily and truly. We commune in prayer, which was the great ancient test; in preaching, in singing, in experience, in many Christian efforts: in everything except that in which they do not agree with us, Church ordinances. Can anything be more just, truthful, and proper?

20. Suppose, in order to render this matter perfectly clear, that a foreigner should have taken up his abode in this country for many years; and from an ardent attachment to its liberties and citizens, and an honest preference of our institutions, have made it his home. For some reason, perhaps only through ignorance of the law, let us suppose that he has never gone through the ceremony of naturalization: neglected even to give the regular notice of his intention to do so. If he were to present himself at the proper place at some election, would it be right that he should be allowed to vote? None will contend that he should. He might be an excellent man, far more worthy and better qualified than thousands entitled to the privilege; still all would perceive that in removing the obstacle that hinders him from voting, we should break down the whole naturalization law,—a barrier which prevents the inhabitants of the whole world from overturning the liberties we enjoy. So it would be impossible for us to participate in the Lord's Supper with those not baptized, even occasionally, without overturning the whole New Testament law of Baptism. Robert Hall, as we have seen, fully admits that it would destroy Baptist Churches, as such.

If now, notwithstanding all that has been said, any person should be disposed to assert that we refuse Communion with those on earth, with whom we expect to commune in heaven, we reply that it is a complete error, based upon confounding the literal and figurative use of terms. We do not. We are willing to commune with all those on earth, with whom we expect to commune in heaven, and precisely in the same way, *i. e.* spiritually. We do not expect there to participate in the outward symbols of bread and wine. These were appointed to show forth the Lord's death only "until he come." All that can be said in regard to our practice is, that we decline to celebrate the symbols of a particular Church Communion with those, between whom and ourselves there is no such relation existing, as the symbols would indicate! But the injustice of this accusation can perhaps thus be most readily illustrated. It is well known that in America, a foreigner enjoys privileges, which in most countries are denied to any but citizens. He can travel unmolested, and without passport; avow any religion, engage in any business, practise any profession. He is equally protected by law; and except voting for the officers of the government, and one or two restrictions of that kind, enjoys all the advantages of a citizen, though he may never have been naturalized. He is received with friendship, according to his worth, as a man, and as a citizen of the world. Suppose however that this individual, after having lived thus for many years, respected, beloved, and happy, on being informed that it was necessary that he should go through the forms of naturalization before he could be permitted to vote, should assert that in this country all foreigners who had through ignorance or other causes neglected these regulations were denied their just privileges, were outlawed, and cast out of the pale of society,—would it not be a libel on the free institutions of the country? Might not any one reply to him, If you prefer to neglect the ceremony of naturalization, you will also see the necessity of omitting the ceremony of voting? In all other respects, you enjoy equal privileges, protection, and esteem with other members of society according to your merits, and are held in more true regard if deserving it, perhaps, than many who may be naturalized or native citizens.

This is a precise illustration of the manner in which, as Baptists, we regard the members of other Christian denominations. We enjoy with them the warmest and truest communion as Christians, in prayer, in the interchange of pulpits, as "fellow-citizens of the household of faith," in fact, in everything except those points on which we differ, *Church ordinances.* If they say that Baptism is a mere ceremony, and as such the neglect of it ought not to debar them from partaking with us in the Lord's Supper; then we reply, that the same view that would reduce Baptism to a mere ceremony, must reduce the Lord's Supper to the same level. Those who voluntarily neglect the one as a matter of no importance, will not be surprised that we should treat them as those who put an equally low estimate on the other.

CHAPTER VII.

REVIEW OF PARTS I. AND II.

1. Distinction between Communion and its Symbols. 2. Different kinds of Communion specified. 3. The Nature of Symbols. 4. Different Symbols of Communion. 5. Symbols of Communion with Christ. (*a*) Baptism. (*b*) Lord's Supper. 6. Symbols of Christian fellowship. 7. The Lord's Supper a Symbol of Church fellowship. 8. Further proofs of this. 9. Additional proofs—The Passover—but one Altar to a Church. 10. May it be used for other purposes? 11. Robert Hall's "leading position" considered. 12. This confounds the Visible and Invisible Churches. 13. " Occasional Communion." 14. The case of other denominations considered. 15. Three objections considered. 16. That we deny the validity of their baptisms. 17. That we unchurch other denominations. 18. Our own position.

1. WE have in the previous parts of this work, laid down in detail, and with some copiousness, the principles which should regulate our Communion as Christians, and as members of the visible Churches of Christ, our symbolic as well as our spiritual relations. We propose to occupy the concluding chapter of this portion of our work, with a condensed view of the whole ground over which we have gone, so far as it bears on our peculiar opinions and practice in regard to the Lord's Supper. Thus it is hoped that the reader will be enabled to perceive more clearly and comprehensively the position we occupy, and to determine, in the third part of this work, whether the principles of Robert Hall on this subject, or our own, are the more consistent with reason, charity, and Scripture.

We have seen the importance of the distinction between

Communion and its symbols. The one is purely spiritual, the other, visible. They are therefore easily distinguishable; moreover, the absence of a particular symbol is no proof of a refusal to commune with any Christian. This we never refuse knowingly, but, on the contrary, have a sincere and cordial fellowship, as Christians, with all whom we consider such. A closer fellowship with Christians as Christians, is one of the great religious wants of the present age—a fellowship, not interfering in any way with their Church relations, but loving, encouraging, and doing good to all.

2. We have seen that Communion is of different *kinds and degrees*, according to its objects. There is for example, a true spiritual Communion with Christ, the Head of the Church, which is the animating principle of all the rest; and there is also a true Communion, though not of the same character, with the Universal Church, "the whole family in heaven and earth." Even in regard to this illustrious body, our fellowship is not equally close with all the portions and members of it. With saints in heaven, it is more exalted, but cannot be so sympathizing on our part, as with the saints on earth. And even in regard to these latter, there is particularly to be noticed, the distinction between our fellowship with Christians as such and apart from their being members of our own, or even of any visible Church; and our Communion with those with whom we are united in these latter relations. This distinctness of Church fellowship, from that which we hold with all Christians, is analogous to the difference between the regard of every man for his own family, and that which he has for his country, his neighbors, and his friends. The latter may be said to have its foundation in that common love for society, which makes man a social

being. Without it, he might dwell like the spider, which sits, the solitary tenant of a web, constructed for nothing but to catch prey. We know, however, that the affection a man has, and the relations he sustains to his own family, are quite distinct from any that he bears to others. So the obligations and fellowship belonging to membership in a Christian Church, as such, is, in several important respects, quite distinct from that due to a Christian as a Christian. To lose sight of this distinction, must produce the same mischievous effects upon the cause of Christ, that losing sight of the peculiar sanctity and distinctness of family affection would have upon society. As the latter would be far from promoting social happiness, so the former would not sensibly increase, even for a time, the more general affection of Christians as a whole, while in cutting at the root of the more special fellowship of the members of each particular Church, it would destroy the germ of both the one and the other. As the welfare and happiness of society depend more upon the proper maintenance of the family tie, than any of the more general attachments which bind men together, whether as communities, as tribes, or as nations; and as the former are the basis and nursery of all true social regard; so the fostering of a proper Communion with the particular Church, with which by grace a Christian is united, is his first great duty and privilege. It is the germ of all the more extensive affections of the Christian to his fellow-believers in Christ; and is more important than them all.

3. As there are different kinds, so there are different symbols of Communion. Whatever action or emblem is intended to denote any kind of Communion, is its symbol. Some of these symbols are simple in their nature, indicating but one kind of fellowship; others, complex, indi-

cating more than one. Complex symbols are appropriate, only when all the relations they express, exist as indicated. Thus, for instance, the Lord's Supper is the symbol of our Communion with Christ. It also indicates certain relations, as existing between those with whom we participate in it, and ourselves. The Lord's Supper, therefore, can be properly celebrated, only when the relations both between the Saviour and us, and also between our fellow-communicants and ourselves, are such as indicated by the symbol.

4. The symbols of Communion may be arranged under three heads. (1.) With Christ. (2.) With Christians as such. (3.) With the particular Church to which we belong. These three classes of symbols will correspond with the different kinds of Communion pointed out before.

5. (1.) As to the first of these, the symbols of our Communion with Christ, there are two, special and divinely appointed, (a) Baptism, (b) The Lord's Supper. Of these, baptism, which is divinely termed *"putting on Christ,"* naturally comes first. It is to be received once, and but once. It is that symbolic garment of confession, by which the believer in Christ not only professes the grace which has been bestowed upon him, but also dedicates himself for the future to be the Lord's, and rightly receiving it, obtains in return a public assurance of acceptance with Christ. It is not a mere ceremony therefore, but a divinely appointed public consecration of the Christian to the service of Christ, which causes those who rightly receive it, to stand in a new relation to the world, to Christians, and to Christ, and of which, all those who omit it are living in the neglect.

The Lord's Supper, which is the other special and divinely appointed symbol of our Communion with Christ, is to be repeated "often." Every time this is done, it re-affirms the same profession as to the past, and consecration of himself for the future, which the Christian made in his Baptism. It is like a new public acknowledgment or delivery of an old bond or deed. There is an instituted connection between them. They are as uniformly mentioned in this order of sequence, as regularly as are the bread and the wine of the Lord's Supper. An alteration here would be like inverting the order of the elements in the Eucharist. To admit to the Supper without Baptism is a wrong similar to that for which we all reproach the Roman Catholics, administering one of the elements without the other.*

6. As to the second class of symbols, *i. e.* that of the fellowship of Christians, as such, and apart from their belonging to any visible Church on earth, we have seen that these are many and various. Uniting in prayer, in worship, in efforts to spread the cause of Christ, or in the *contributions* of Christian charity. With regard to the Lord's Supper, it is intended, first of all, to symbolize our Communion with the Saviour, and participation in the fruits of his death, and in the holiness which he bestows. But next to that, it expresses, in regard to those with whom we partake of it, more than a mere Christian, a Church fellowship. Indeed the latter is implied, chiefly as the more general is necessarily indicated in the more specific communion.

7. That the Lord's Supper is not a mere symbol of our Communion with the Church Universal, is plain. For as that body embraces the saints in glory, it would then be

---

* On the instituted connection between Baptism and the Lord's Supper, see Fuller's Works, vol. 2, p. 671-2. Gould, Kendall & Lincoln, Boston, 1836; or vol. 3, p. 510, Am. Bap. Publication Society, Philadelphia.

appropriate, and even a duty to have seasons of holding this kind of symbolic communion with those of our Christian friends who have passed into the world of spirits. This was an error, which, originating quite early in the history of Christianity, from confounding visible Churches with the Invisible Church, led naturally, if not inevitably, to the Romish corruption of masses for the dead.

Nor is it a mere symbol of our Communion with all saints on earth, as such. If it were, we should have no right to refuse the Communion to any man, claiming to be a Christian, unless we could prove on him some error of doctrine or practice, that would make it impossible he should be what he professed. He might hold and teach sentiments, the general tendency of which was subversive of the whole system of Christianity; Roman Catholicism, Arianism, or Universalism; but unless we were prepared to assert, in each case, that these errors were so held by that individual, as to be absolutely incompatible with his salvation, we should be obliged to welcome him to this feast. He might not only defend principles that were erroneous, but act up to them in a manner which would be most perverting to the order of the Church, and destructive to the spiritual life and welfare of thousands of souls; but unless we were prepared to assert that the individual could not be a sincere man, and even a Christian, we must receive him to celebrate the Eucharist with us.* The Apostle, on the contrary, exhorts us to "withdraw from every brother that walketh disorderly." Indeed, in this case, it would be the duty of Christians, wherever they met *as Christians*, to unite in the celebra-

* See Thoughts on Open Communion—Letter to Rev. W. Ward, Sept. 21, 1800. Fuller's Works, vol. 2, p. 667, (vol. 3, p. 503. ed. Am. Baptist Publication Society) where this point is ably stated.

tion of this ordinance; not merely when they assembled in their Churches, but in Missionary, Bible and Tract Societies, Evangelical Alliances, and assemblies of every description. Wherever prayer would be appropriate, so would be the Lord's Supper. Whoever considers the reason which has led all such societies instinctively to avoid even the mention of uniting in the Eucharist, at their anniversary meetings, will perceive that it originates in a feeling, that by so doing they would be assuming the peculiar prerogative of *a Church*, instead of acting as a simple voluntary society of Christians.

8. That the Lord's Supper is a symbol of Church relations, subsisting between those who unite together in the participation of it, which is all that is necessary to our present purpose to prove, can be shown in many ways. For it presupposes that watchfulness and discipline of holy affection, by which improper persons are kept back from the number of the communicants. This, all will admit; nor can any deny, that to the Churches of Christ, as such, and to them alone, has the power of discipline been confided. Admission to the Lord's Table, therefore, implies admission to it by a particular Church, and this in fact, settles the question that the Lord's Supper is a Church ordinance. For certainly no Church in primitive times would have admitted any to its Communion Table, whom it would have been unwilling to receive as a member of its own body. Each Church was originally independent, with full powers within itself, to receive and to exclude from its communion table.

9. The Lord's Supper being then a Church ordinance, indicates Church relations as subsisting between the parties who unite together in its celebration. Not to extend an invitation to the Lord's Supper, merely shows the ab-

THE SUPPER A CHURCH ORDINANCE. 137

sence of Church, not of Christian relations. A Jew, merely because he was a Jew, had no right to go into any house he pleased to celebrate the Passover with any other family than his own, except by mutual consent and invitation; nor was any man obliged to invite every Jew, or any person out of his own family, to partake with him. Not to invite any one out of the family to the Passover, therefore, was no indication that he was not regarded as a true and pious Israelite; because that was a *family*, as this is a *Church* ordinance. The Lord's Supper was instituted by our Saviour at one of these Paschal feasts with the twelve, his more especial *family* of disciples, and no other around him. Each Christian Church is a family of such disciples now; and the Lord's Supper was so instituted as to express, not merely the Christian, but the Church fellowship, we say, of those who united in it at the same table. If, not to extend this invitation to others, is, as Robert Hall contends, equivalent to excommunicating them, and a proof of the want of Christian affection and fellowship for them; then were the seventy excommunicated, and even those pious women, (including his mother Mary,) who had come up with him to the feast, and were

"Last at the cross, and earliest at the grave."

The records of Church history plainly show, that originally the Lord's Supper was everywhere regarded as a Church ordinance. For even after centuries of gradual corruption had altered the forms of Church government in many other respects, and many separate congregations were united under the care of one Bishop, and were considered as only one Church, there was ever one and but one altar to each bishopric, at which alone the elements of the Eucharist were consecrated. To set up another altar or Communion Table, was considered a violation of unity, or a declaration of Church independence. Each bishopric had the absolute power of receiving to, and excommunicating from the Lord's Table. The whole of this shows how, contrary to all the centralizing tendencies of the age, and amid many corruptions on all sides, this truth remained, embalmed and preserved, that the Lord's Supper was a Church ordinance.

10. Seeing then no doubt can exist, that the Lord's Supper was originally thus constituted, the only question that can remain, is, if there be in the Churches or in Christians any power to employ the ordinance for other purposes beside those originally intended; such for instance, as expressing a simply Christian fellowship, and omitting the more special one, which belonged to it originally. This however can only be done by the parties presuming to alter what God has appointed, and assuming a legislative authority equal to that of the Divine Head of the Christian Church, superior to that claimed even by Rome herself.

But if it be conceded, as it must, that the Lord's Supper is ever the symbol of particular visible Church relations, then it is impossible that Baptists should be rightly charged with bigotry, or want of charity. There is no unjust closeness of Communion in not inviting those who, as not having in our view a valid baptism, could not according to our principles be received into the membership of any of our Churches, and whose own standards would forbid them to enter into Church relations with us. Much more justly might the charge be brought against those who refuse to admit more than half their own members to the Lord's Supper; who, contrary to all the antiquity to which they appeal, first receive infants into their membership by baptism, and then withhold that token which belongs to them as members. Baptists have no such close communion as this.

11. A formidable objection has however been brought, not indeed against Baptists alone, but against all Christian denominations, in respect to their views of Church membership. The objection is, that no visible Church of Christ has a right to make any other terms of admission to its full membership, than such as are requisite to belong to the Universal or Invisible Church. This is what Robert Hall calls his "leading position," *i. e.*, " that *no Church has a right to establish terms of Communion which are not terms of salvation;* and that properly, a particular Church differs from the Universal Church, *only* as a part differs from the whole."

If this were true, it would effectually destroy the Baptists as a denomination, This Robert Hall expressly concedes. "Were that practice universally to prevail," says he, " the mixture of Baptists and Pedobaptists in Christian societies would probably ere long be such, that the appellation Baptist might be found not so properly applicable to Churches, as to individuals." It would be not less destructive of all other denominations than of our own. It is as much opposed to the Methodist Book of Discipline, the Presbyterian Confession of Faith, and the Thirty-nine Articles, as it is to our own views of Church membership. The experience of the whole Christian world of all ages is against it.

12. This "leading position," however, is founded on the palpable error of confounding the nature of Visible Churches with that of the Invisible Church. It is demonstrable that these two *must* be different. For it is admitted

by all who hold these views, that true faith in Christ alone is necessary to a state of salvation, or membership in the Invisible Church. This may and does include a willingness of heart to confess Christ, but it cannot necessarily include the *act* of confessing him in any way before men. But *some kind* of credible and visible confession of Christ, or profession of piety to man, must be a prerequisite to *visible* Church membership. Consequently, that must be essential to the latter, which is not to the former. So far therefore from this position being true, that no Church has a right to establish terms of Communion which are not terms of salvation, the truth must be exactly the reverse. No visible Church can possibly establish itself, even for a day, without terms of membership that include things not essential to salvation. Instead of this being the case, that a particular Church differs from the invisible "*only*" as a part differs from the whole, nothing is more certain, than that they must and do, and were designed to differ essentially in other respects besides.

Each visible Church must adopt such terms of membership, as seem to it most in accordance with the principles and precepts of the New Testament, and the practice of the first Christians.* That our plan of Church membership, admitting only those whom we consider baptized, was the primitive plan, is conceded by Robert Hall himself: who admits that any one offering himself without baptism, would have been "repelled as a contumacious schismatic."† All other denominations hold this as much as we. This is shown by the writings of their standard authors.

13. The only point, therefore, in which we can ever be

* Presbyterian Form of Government, Book 1, chap. 1.
† Terms of Communion, Part 1, sect. 3.

supposed to differ from other denominations, is upon the subject of OCCASIONAL communion; or the admission of those who are either members of no Church, or of other Churches, to the participation with us, in the sacramental elements, when present in our assemblies. This we grant cheerfully, so far as the members of other Churches, *similarly constituted with our own*, are concerned; because the Lord's Supper is a Church ordinance, and we are willing to consider those, who, but for local circumstances might be members of our particular Churches, for the time being as actually such. Thus far, all are agreed. With regard to persons, however sincere their piety, who are members of no Church, we, in common with all other denominations, have no hesitation in declaring that they should not be admitted to the occasional participation of the Lord's Supper. With us, this also is founded on the principle, that this is a Church ordinance.

14. But now in regard to members of the Churches of other denominations. Many do invite those to occasional participation, who are not members of Churches of a similar constitution to their own; and who could not unite with them in a regular and permanent Church fellowship; their views of its order, doctrines, and government being so different. In this way, Methodists, Presbyterians, and even Episcopalians will thus occasionally partake together. It is true that no denomination would be willing to carry this so far, as to admit any persons they consider unbaptized, even to occasional Communion.

But if the Lord's Supper is a Church ordinance, and indicates a Church fellowship among all those who partake together, it is a violation of truth in symbols to invite to occasional Communion, those whom our constitutional principles would forbid to be members of our

Churches. Indeed there is a palpable inconsistency in adopting one set of principles for admission to Church fellowship, and another to occasional Communion; one for admission to the Lord's Supper considered in the former point of view, another for it, considered in the latter. Such discriminations cannot produce real unity and fellowship; a sophism lies at the bottom of them.

As it is taken for granted in this discussion, that Christian baptism essentially involves an immersion of the body in water, as a profession of personal faith in Christ, so it follows that this whole discussion must be founded on the acknowledgment that our Pedobaptist friends are *without valid baptism.* Nor can it make any abatement from this conclusion, or any alteration in regard to our receiving them at the Lord's Table, that they do not perceive this. For Baptists to admit the validity of baptism to depend, in whole or in part, not upon the New Testament, but upon what each one chooses for himself to *consider* baptism, would destroy our principles at once.

15. It has sometimes been objected, however, that it is only *the mode* of baptism that prevents us from uniting with others at the Lord's Table. This is an error. It is not only, nor even chiefly the mode. For the baptisms of the Greek Church, which are performed in the same manner, are not regarded by us as valid, because not professions of personal faith; nor could we invite the members of that body to partake with us.

16. It is urged however, that at least the difference between us and pious Pedobaptists is merely ceremonial, and that it is merely because we do not esteem their baptism valid, that we do not unite with them at the Lord's Table. It is unquestionably true that we do not admit the validity of their baptism, and that this is the chief

point of difference between our Churches and some others, as for instance those of the Congregationalists, with whom, as to doctrine and form of government, we agree. But it must not be forgotten that the Lord's Supper is as much a mere ceremony as baptism. It is just as little a matter, to debar from the former, as to refuse the latter. The two must go together. Consistency requires Ceremonial Communion with those only with whom we ceremonially agree; Spiritual Communion with those with whom we are spiritually united. Nor must it be forgotten that originally these Churches with whom we most nearly coincide, *thrust us out*, and made us a separate denomination. If there were any schism therefore in the separation, it is theirs, not ours.

But while between our Churches and some others, baptism is nearly the only point of difference; there are principles as *distinctive*, connected with our views of this one ordinance of baptism, as those which form the basis of any other denomination. Dr. Bushnell, in his works on Christian Nurture, if he has shown nothing else, has shown this.

But while there is so little difference between us and the Congregationalists, it is not so with the most. Differences in doctrine, and in the whole system of Church government; differences in the terms of admission to the full privileges of Church membership; besides those as to the mode and subjects of baptism, separate us from most others. Nor is it accurate to say that it is either baptism alone, or any single thing that is the cause of our practice in regard to the Lord's Supper, save this only; that we regard it as a Church ordinance, the symbol of Church relations, and consequently to be united in by those only who agree as to Church relations. Otherwise, we should not only be required to invite all whom we were not prepared to declare beyond the pale of Church fellowship, to partake with us, but we must participate with all bodies claiming to be Christian Churches, on their invitation, whatever may be the state of their doctrine or discipline, unless we intended to denounce them as having so apostatized, as not to deserve that appellation.

17. It has frequently been urged that by our course, we at least *unchurch* all other denominations. But this again is a complete error. It certainly does not follow from our practice in regard to the Lord's Supper. For we do not pretend to commune with all whom we esteem Christians, nor with all that we consider Christian Churches; only with such as are *similarly constituted* with our own. While we know that baptism was originally, and now is, essential to the *regular* constitution of a Christian Church, and therefore we **have no right** to dispense with it from our own, yet as the term Church ($\varepsilon\kappa\kappa\lambda\eta\sigma\iota\alpha$) is often used, even in Scripture, for *assemblies* irregularly formed, so any organized body of professing Christians, assembling from time to time for worship, may be justly considered a Christian Church, though, if it be without valid baptism, an irregular Church.

18. Our Churches are formed upon the primitive model. In our mode of celebrating both Baptism and the Lord's Supper, we feel sure that we conform to primitive usage. In the relative order, and relation in which they stand to each other, we do the same, even by the concession of our opponents. Thus did the Apostles, and thus do we. We find fault with none. We excommunicate none. We are saved from all this by our views of Church independence, and by not professing visible Church relations where they do not exist. We respect the rights of others too much

OUR AIMS JUST AND CHARITABLE. 145

to interfere with their ecclesiastical arrangements. But our regard for truth and harmony forbids us to carry union in profession further than any would be willing to carry it in practice. We aim simply to keep the ordinances as they were delivered unto us, without unchurching any, or denying their Christianity. Nor would we see ceremonial and spiritual Communions so confounded, that by not inviting persons to partake with us at the Lord's Table, we should be supposed to express any want of fellowship with them as Christians. We only feel that where any symbol is complex, and indicates several different relations, all of them must exist in truth as indicated by the symbol to render its use appropriate.

PART III.

THE ARGUMENTS OF ROBERT HALL CONSIDERED.

INTRODUCTORY REMARKS.

CLASSIFICATION OF ROBERT HALL'S WRITINGS ON THE SUBJECT OF COMMUNION.

ALTHOUGH in the former part of this treatise, we have stated the principle on which Mixed Communion was so ably advocated by the late Robert Hall, the arguments by which he has attempted to sustain that principle, deserve a separate and special notice. His writings on this subject, were comprised in three tracts : 1. "Terms of Communion:" afterwards abridged and called "Reasons for Christian in opposition to Party Communion," by the Author. 2. "The Essential Difference between Christian Baptism, and the Baptism of John." 3. "A Reply to the Rev. Joseph Kinghorn, being a further vindication of the plan of Free Communion." It is chiefly in the first of these works, that the arguments in favor of the author's views are contained; the other two being rejoinders to the replies of his opponents. It will only be necessary to take so much notice of these latter, as that when an objection similar to any which Mr. Hall has noticed in his rejoinder is brought against the reasoning contained in the Terms of Communion, his further explanation, or vindication, shall be presented to the reader, and fairly considered. This will in each case be done. As that remarkable man has confessedly advanced all that is to be said on that side of the question, it will be a thorough and final proof of the truth of our positions, if they are capable of resisting the attacks of this ablest advocate of Mixed Communion; while it will also enable those desirous of comparing opinions on this subject, to have the arguments of both parties placed side by side, and the whole subject thus brought in review before them.

The work, entitled "Terms of Communion," consists of two parts,—Part I. "The Arguments for Strict Communion considered."—Part II. "The Positive Grounds on which we justify the practice of Mixed Communion."

The First Part, divided into four sections, considers 1st. "The Argument from the Order of Time in which Baptism and the Lord's Supper are supposed to have been instituted;" 2d. "The Argument for Strict Communion, from the Order of Words in the Apostolic Commission;" 3d. "The Argument from Apostolic Precedent, and from the different Significations of the two Institutions;" 4th. "Our supposed Opposition to the Universal Suffrages of the Church."

As it will be at once evident that, in the first Part, no attempt is made to establish any positive argument, in favor of Mixed Communion, but only to remove difficulties, and reply to objections; and as none of the arguments there considered, lead to the discussion of what we consider *the radical fallacy* of Mr. Hall's views, *i. e.*, confounding Communion with the symbols of Communion, and Church fellowship with Christian fellowship; as they do not lead him to touch the principle that lies at the bottom of all we advance, *i. e.*, that the Lord's Supper symbolizes relations subsisting only between the members of a particular Church, it will not be necessary to consider here the "plea in abatement," offered under each of the four heads above specified. What is said by our Author in regard to "the Universal Suffrages" of Christians, has been noticed incidentally in our Second Part, where that subject was considered.

In Part II., Mr. Hall advances to what he terms " *The Positive Grounds on which we justify the Practice of Mixed Communion.*" Here he presents us with six distinct arguments, in as many sections. They are as follows:

1. Free Communion urged from the Obligation of Brotherly Love.

2. The Practice of Open Communion argued from the express Injunction of Scripture, respecting the Conduct to be maintained by sincere Christians, who differ in their Religious Sentiments.

3. Pedobaptists, a part of the true Church, and their Exclusion on that account unlawful.

4. The Exclusion of Pedobaptists from the Lord's Table, considered as a Punishment.

5. On the Impossibility of reducing the Practice of Strict Communion to any general principle.

6. The Impolicy of the Practice of Strict Communion.

We will consider the force of each one of these Arguments, in the same order in which our Author has advanced them.

CHAPTER I.

ROBERT HALL'S FIRST ARGUMENT CONSIDERED.

1. Ambiguity as to the use of the word Communion. 2. Applied to the Lord's Supper proves nothing. 3. Robert Hall's view of the signification of the Lord's Supper considered. 4. His illustration of children refusing to eat at the same table. 5. Symbolic feasts. 6. The anguish of separating from Christian friends at the Lord's Supper considered. 7. Illustration.

1. THE first consideration of our Author is thus entitled: *"Free Communion urged from the Obligation of Brotherly Love."*

There is not only in this title, but running through the whole argument of this section, and indeed of the whole work, an ambiguity, arising from the different senses in which the word Communion is employed. To this we have before alluded. Sometimes Mr. Hall uses this term as equivalent to *Christian* fellowship, sometimes for *Church* fellowship, habitually sustained, and sometimes for that symbol of Church fellowship "the Lord's Supper." However our Author might consider each of these as uniformly proper, where any of them was, yet in arguing on this very question, he had no right so to use them, as to take for granted the very point in dispute.

Using the term in the first of the above senses, we should fully agree with him, that it was our duty to cherish a warm *Christian* Communion with all whom we esteem Christians, Roman Catholic or Protestant, Baptist or Pedobaptist. Thus far the passages he has quoted on the duty of loving one another bear him out, and no further.

A PETITIO PRINCIPII.

But if by "Communion," he intends *Church* fellowship, (See Part I., ch. 4,) and from the obligation of brotherly love, would urge that it is our duty to maintain habitually this particular fellowship for *all* whom we esteem Christians, then must all the *family* feeling of Church membership be broken down. (See p. 35.) For any general exhortations of Scripture however, to Christian and brotherly love, to be brought in proof of this, it must be taken for granted that the terms of visible membership in a particular Church, ought exactly to correspond to those of membership in the invisible Church Universal. This Mr. Hall does take for granted throughout his whole work. But this is just the point in dispute. In Part I., ch. 4, we have shown the distinction between these two, and there, more particularly alluded to this singular *petitio principii*.

2. In the latter part of this section, at least, it is clear that our Author distinctly intends by "Communion," nothing more nor less than the *Lord's Supper*. It is here that he concentrates his argument. "In order to place this part of our subject in its strongest light, it is necessary to recur to what we have suggested before, respecting the twofold import of the Eucharist, that it is first a **feast** upon a sacrifice, in which we are actual partakers, by faith, of the body and blood of the Redeemer offered upon the cross. Considered in this view, it is a federal rite, in which we receive the pledge of reconciliation, while we avouch the Lord to be our God, and surround his table as a part of his family. In its secondary import, *it is intended as a solemn recognition of each other as members of Christ*, and consequently, in the language of St. Paul, 'as one body and one bread.'* Now we either acknowledge

---

* For another view of the passage above quoted, see Appendix G.

Pedobaptists *to be Christians*, or we do not. If not, let us speak out without reserve, and justify their exclusion at once, upon a broad and consistent basis. But if we reject a sentiment so illiberal, why refuse to unite with them in an appointment which, as far as its social import is concerned, *has no other object than to express that fraternal attachment, which we actually feel.*"*

When any symbolic act necessarily embraces a reference to two or more distinct relations, as we have seen in a former Part, all the relations must exist as indicated, to render the sign proper. Thus, for instance, it is true that the Lord's Supper is first of all a symbol of our participation in the benefits of the death of Christ. But this will not, upon our Author's ground, justify a Christian in celebrating this feast, in connection with those who make no profession of faith in Christ; because, according to him, the Lord's Supper symbolizes not only *our* union with Christ, but is also "a solemn recognition of *each other* as members of Christ." Thus far, our Author will admit.

3. It is in regard to his "secondary import" of the Lord's Supper, that we desire to remark; for here in truth the whole controversy turns. If indeed it is, as between the parties celebrating it, "a solemn recognition of each other as members of Christ," *and nothing more;* if "so far as its social import is concerned, *it has no other object* than to express *that* fraternal affection" which subsists between all true Christians, then there can be no doubt, that all who recognize each other as members of Christ, ought to be willing to celebrate the Lord's Supper together.

But in all this assumption, the author is begging the very point at issue. We contend that the Lord's Supper

---

* Works, vol. 1, p. 324.

A MISCONCEPTION OF RELATIONS. 155

has other objects, than to express that fraternal attachment which we feel to all Christians as members of Christ. In Part II., ch. 4, we have shown that the Lord's Supper is not merely a solemn recognition of each other as members of Christ, but *as those between whom and ourselves, particular Church relations exist.* The dilemma, which is put before us, therefore, with such an air of triumph, is founded upon an utter misconception, as we believe, of some of the relations indicated by the Lord's Supper. "We either acknowledge Pedobaptists *to be Christians,* or we do not," says our author. "If not, let us speak out without reserve." We really do not see why we should be called upon to pronounce upon this question here, or what it has to do with the point in dispute. Pedobaptists certainly do not acknowledge *Church* relations with us, nor do we with them. Indeed, one would think that these relations, to subsist profitably at all, should be mutual. But as we have no wish to avoid "speaking out without reserve," we frankly take the other horn of the dilemma, and acknowledge them, many of them at least, to be Christians, perhaps better than ourselves. But what then? "Then why refuse to unite with them" in the Lord's Supper? Simply because we believe that the Lord's Supper, if united in, would symbolize much more, than that we consider them Christians. It would symbolize that they were willing to unite in Church relations with us, and we with them; neither of which is true. It would say to the world that our views of Church order and discipline, and ordinances, and government, were mutually so much alike, that we could consistently consider ourselves members of the same Church. This is a principle upon which neither our Pedobaptist brethren, nor we, would like to act, and which therefore we ought not to express; and we have before seen that where a symbolic act embraces reference to two or more distinct relations, all of them must subsist in truth as symbolized, to justify the use of the sign.

4. As an illustration is often remembered, when an argument is forgotten; and as we wish to present all that our author would advance on his side of the question, we would add the following passage. "Were the children of the same parent, in consequence of the different construction they had put on a disputed clause in their father's will, to refuse to eat at the same table, or to drink out of the same cup, it would be ridiculous for them to pretend that their attachment to each other remained undiminished; nor is it less so for Christians to assert that their withdrawing from communion with their brethren, is no interruption to their mutual harmony and affection."*

The illustration of children of the same parent refusing to eat at the same table, would be applicable, *if the Lord's Supper were to be regarded as an ordinary and not a symbolic meal.* But that this is not the case is shown by the fact, that the very parties who decline to unite in it, will join as freely as brothers in any other meal, and in any other token of Christian regard. If then the Lord's Supper is a symbolic meal, the only question is, of what is it the symbol? If of Christian fellowship *and nothing more*, then all who esteem each other as Christians should be willing to celebrate together; and were they to refuse, the consequences pointed out by Mr. Hall would ensue, and even more. But if the Lord's Supper is also a symbol of *Church relations*, then those who cannot and do not sustain these relations to each other, cannot consistently unite in the symbol.

* Works, vol. 1, p. 323.

5. It is quite common in Europe, and in this country, for political dinners to be given, in order to assemble and unite the chief members of a particular party, and promote its objects. To unite in one of those feasts, would publicly symbolize that those who partook, were all agreed as to the political party or object, to promote which the feast was given. So on the other hand, to decline an invitation of this kind, would not be a refusal to meet the same persons as gentlemen or friends; it would not indicate any want of confidence in them all as true and patriotic citizens, supporters of the same national liberties, all sworn friends of a common constitution, but simply a nonconcurrence in *all* the measures which it was the object of that particular association to promote. Brothers often refuse to partake of these *symbolic* feasts together, without the least diminution of fraternal regard.

6. The author of the "Terms of Communion" eloquently pictures "the uneasiness and anguish felt on sacramental occasions, by good men, seeing their most intimate friends, and persons of exalted piety, compelled to withdraw from the Lord's Table." That cases do occur, in which such feelings arise, we doubt not. But this is either from forgetting the symbolic character of the institution altogether, or at least from forgetting it to be the symbol of Church relations, or of anything more than our fellow-citizenship with the saints in light. Upon any other supposition, the pain could only be occasioned by being reminded that such excellent Christians had not yet been buried with Christ in baptism. But that not keeping distinctly in mind the reference of any symbolic feast, may occasion the uneasiness and even anguish, which a slight attention to that circumstance would remove, is not doubtful. The following anecdote will in part illustrate what we wish to convey.

7. Many years ago, a venerable friend travelled about two hundred miles to attend the funeral of an aged widow and relative, for whom he had entertained the highest regard. But the day before the departure of this lady, which was sudden, her only daughter had been married. The body committed to the grave, the mourners, who were from various parts of the country, returned to the house, according to the custom of the times, to dine together, before reading the will and dispersing, perhaps to assemble no more on earth. But the friends of the deceased were friends also of the newly married pair; and several, forgetting the sad occasion that had brought them together, took the opportunity to congratulate the young people on their recent marriage. Before the cloth was removed, instead of the solemnity of a funeral, the gaiety of a marriage feast was exhibited by many of the company, and one of the guests rising, formally proposed to the whole company as an opening toast, "The health of the bride and bridegroom." Wounded at what would so evidently change the nature of the assembly, the old man rose, and addressing the newly-married ones, said, "My children, I cannot drink this health on this occasion. I love you both, and freely give you my blessing; but I came here *to-day* not to attend the marriage feast of young friends, but the funeral feast of an old friend." That pledge, given at that time, would have been the symbol, not merely of friendship for the young couple, *but that the occasion of assembling was a marriage, and not a funeral feast.* The parties had no right to feel hurt with their friend, as though he "would not drink of the same cup with them," or not symbolize by any consistent means, his wishes for their happiness. Not to partake was no token of this. To partake, would in his view have been disrespect to

the particular occasion that had brought them together. Those who proposed the toast, by failing to perceive *all* that would have been expressed by that symbol, *i. e.* that this was a wedding and not a funeral feast, were the true causes of whatever pain was occasioned.

To apply the anecdote to the case in hand. The pain and the uneasiness occasioned, by feeling debarred from uniting with other Christians in the bread and wine of the Supper, arise from not fully comprehending its symbolic import;—that it is a token, not merely of *Christian*, but also of *Church* fellowship. And moreover, declining "to eat at the same table, or to drink of the same cup," if it be not a common meal, but symbolic of any relation between the parties not actually subsisting, ought not to give pain, even though some of the relations indicated may actually exist. Or, if grief should be felt, it is not those who take proper views of the relations which the Lord's Supper indicates, who are the occasions of this grief, but those who do not see what is requisite before they can be appropriate.

CHAPTER II.

ROBERT HALL'S SECOND ARGUMENT CONSIDERED.

1. The toleration of all errors consistent with Salvation, considered. 3. No Christians practice thus. 3. The Scriptures forbid this course. 4. Consequences of Robert Hall's views. 5. Errors generally destructive, may not be so in every case. 6. Persons holding almost every species of error might become Church Officers on the Mixed Communion plan. 7. The cases of John Milton and others. 8. This system would permit Roman Catholic priests to perform their ceremonies in Baptist Churches.—Arians.—Polygamists. 9. Rom. 14th and 15th, considered. 10. The command to receive, only applies when the individual is complying with the whole revealed will of God, in the matter in hand. 11. The case stated in another manner by Robert Hall, considered. 12. Each Church must be allowed to declare its own terms of Communion. 13. Why Pedobaptists should not be admitted to Baptist Churches. 14. Effects of Pedobaptism as a system.

1. "*The practice of open Communion argued from the express injunction of Scripture, respecting the conduct to be maintained by sincere Christians, who differ in their religious sentiments.*"

"WE are expressly commanded," says Robert Hall, at the opening of his remarks under the above caption, " to tolerate in the Church, those diversities of opinion which are not inconsistent with salvation. We learn from the New Testament, that a diversity of views subsisted in the times of the Apostles, between the Jewish and Gentile converts especially."

That it is the duty of Christians to tolerate some diversity of opinion in their churches, none will question. But our author asserts, and intends to assert, in the above quotation, that we are commanded to tolerate in the *same* Church, *all* those diversities of opinion which are not inconsistent with salvation. Not only do we dissent from this singular assumption, but there is perhaps no denomination of Christians who would practically agree with him. Such a plan of Church membership would lead us to tolerate Roman Catholics and Protestants, members of the Greek Church, and members of all the nominal Christian sects that have produced one good man;—would lead us to tolerate them all as of equal standing and authority in our own churches with ourselves, whether as lay members or ministers, and however erroneous their sentiments and mischievous their course of action; unless we were prepared *in each case* to declare their particular opinions or lives to be "*inconsistent with salvation.*" But of this more hereafter.

2. Where is the denomination that does not require of its members many things not necessary to salvation? The Pedobaptist symbols require infant baptism; why should we be stigmatized for requiring true baptism?

3. Robert Hall would probably reply that this may be sufficient as an *argumentum ad hominem*, when replying to Pedobaptists, but does not meet what he asserts to be the New Testament rule; by which he thinks "we are expressly commanded" to tolerate in the same Church all those diversities of opinion, not inconsistent with salvation. On the contrary, we assert that so far from any such command being producible from Scripture, we are even commanded not to tolerate, nor give place by subjection for an hour, to many errors both of faith and practice in the Churches, which may yet be quite consistent with the

possible salvation of the individual holding them. From "every *brother* that walketh disorderly," we are commanded to "withdraw" ourselves. The mode in which this command is worded is exceedingly strong. "Now we command you, brethren, *in the name of the Lord Jesus Christ*, that ye withdraw yourselves from every brother that walketh disorderly:" 2 Thess. 3: 6. "A man that is an heretic," (αἱρετικός,) literally, one who creates dissensions or introduces errors, '*a factious person*' (see Robinson's Lexicon,) "is to be rejected after the first and second admonition:" Titus 3: 10. "He that will not work, neither may he eat." Indeed, this principle is taught in many passages, that the extent of the error of the individual, or the extent to which it may be supposed to endanger his salvation, is not alone that by which the Church is to be governed in retaining or rejecting an individual, but the effect also of his error upon the discipline of the Church, and upon the world, is also to be considered. One tainted sheep may infect a flock. One disorderly soldier tolerated, will break up the discipline of a regiment. Enough this to show the error of Robert Hall's principles, for which alone it is here introduced.

4. That none but those who make a credible profession of personal piety can properly be received into regular Christian Churches is unquestionable. But that each visible Church of Christ is to tolerate in its own members every conceivable diversity in practice from what the Divine law prescribed; that those who hold and practice thus in regard to any errors, not absolutely inconsistent with their own final salvation, however destructive to thousands, shall be allowed to agitate and proselyte, and vote in the Church with equal authority as the regular and orderly members; must lead to consequences so sub-

versive of all the ends for which Churches are valuable, that we might be quite sure à priori, that such could not have been the New Testament plan of Church membership. Yet such is the toleration for which Robert Hall pleads. That Church membership would be of little worth, which permitted all errors possible to good men to receive its sanction; and those who held them to vote in their favor, and to teach and propagate them with as much zeal as others uphold truth.

And yet, that no doubt may remain as to the meaning intended, our author yet more explicitly states his views thus: "Having paved the way to the conclusion to which we would conduct the reader, we have only to remark, that in order to determine how far these apostolic injunctions oblige us to tolerate the supposed error of our Pedobaptist brethren, we have merely to consider whether it *necessarily does exclude them from being of the number of those whom Christ has received to the glory of the Father;* whether it be possible to hold it with Christian sincerity; and finally, whether its abettors will stand or fall in the eternal judgment."*

It may here be observed, on this and the preceding extract, that the author applies his remarks equally to full and permanent Church membership, as to occasional participation at the Lord's Table. All that he advances in favor of the latter, he considers as making equally for the former. There is with him no shrinking from consequences. He who is to be admitted to the Lord's Table at all, is to be admitted to all the rights and privileges of full Church membership. His vote is to have just as much influence in calling a Pastor, in deciding what doc-

* Works, vol. 1, p. 326–7.

trines shall be maintained, what allowed and what instituted. He is to be equally eligible to all the offices of the Church, and may be elected Deacon, or chosen Pastor.

5. Unquestionably, many errors, of a tendency fatal to the Church, as a body, and utterly subversive of all that is vital in Christianity, may not be pronounced necessarily so to every individual holding them; and they have actually been held by good and pious men. This is particularly the case with many errors of the Church of Rome. But unless we are ready to pronounce that an error "*necessarily* excludes the person holding it from being of the number of those whom Christ has received to the glory of the Father," or that it is "impossible to hold it with Christian sincerity," or that "its abettors will certainly fall in the eternal judgment,"—unless, I say, we are prepared to assume the prerogative of Deity, and determine that the error in question *necessarily* involves one at least of the above consequences, if not all, we are then "expressly commanded" in Scripture, our author would assert, to tolerate in the Church, of which we are members, these "diversities of opinion;" that is to say, we are to admit the holders of them to perfect social equality in voting, speaking and preaching. We repeat it, the error in question may be of the most deadly general tendency, it may be the ruin of thousands of souls; but unless we are prepared to decide that it *necessarily excludes the individual* promulgating it, from the number of those whom Christ has received, we must regard it (the error) as one of those diversities of opinion, which are to be tolerated in the Church, as not inconsistent with salvation. That all these consequences legitimately and necessarily result from our author's views, no one can deny. So far as their application to Pedobaptism is concerned, he admits them; and so

far, in Great Britain, our Mixed Communion Churches practice fully up to all that has been stated. Robert Hall himself predicted, that should these views prevail, "the Baptists and Pedobaptists, in Christian societies, would probably ere long be such, that the appellation of Baptist might be found not so properly applicable to Churches as to *individuals.*"—("Reasons," &c., Hall's Works, vol. II., p. 228-9.)

6. This is, indeed, evident. Pedobaptist Churches, especially Congregational, might be as well expected to adopt Robert Hall's plan of Church membership, as our own. If they did, the Pedobaptist pastor, deacons and members, would be members of Churches of precisely the same class as those of Mixed Communion Baptists. Baptists would have equal rights, equal authority to teach; and whichever party had the majority of members in any particular Church, or in the body of the Churches, at any time, would have a right to consider their sentiments as the prevailing ones of the Church or denomination; other views would exist only by "toleration," if there was any difference.

These results have been actually realized to a certain extent. The preaching of Baptism, or even speaking on the subject in private, has been forbidden. Pedobaptist deacons and pastors have been elected to Baptist Churches; and, we believe, instances have occurred of infants being sprinkled for the accommodation of the Pedobaptist portion of the communicants in the same Church, where believers were immersed to suit the other portion. Whatever may be thought of this, so far as Pedobaptists are concerned, Robert Hall professes himself ready to act upon the same principles in regard to *all other errors and errorists;* nay, even that the Scriptures *"expressly com-*

mand" the adoption of this principle in every case. He complains elsewhere that our course is reducible to no general principle. But the general principle on which he bases his Terms of Membership, is pregnant with such consequences, that we should be pardonable if we were even to prefer none to such.

7. According to his theory, no one of our Churches could be distinctively Calvinistic, unless we were prepared to say that Arminianism *necessarily excludes* men from being of the number Christ has received. John Milton argued in favor of Divorce. None would be prepared to say that this error *necessarily excluded* him from being received of Christ, or that it was not held with all *sincerity;* consequently, this must be placed on the list of tolerated errors. He, also, was an Arian. The doctrine of the Trinity, therefore, is no longer to be deemed a fundamental doctrine. Dr. Bushnell is understood to deny the proper vicariousness of the Atonement. Yet, unless we are prepared to pronounce that he is necessarily excluded from being of the number of those whom Christ has received, (which those who have the best means of knowing his personal character shrink from doing,) the rejection of vicarious Atonement is to be placed on the list of those "differences of opinion" that are to be equally tolerated with correct views upon Baptism.

It is proper here again distinctly to recall to the attention of the reader, that according to the plan of Church Membership, which we are here told the Scriptures "expressly command," if *any error* may possibly be held by some individuals without "necessarily excluding *them*" from salvation; whatever may be its general tendency, the holders of it are none of them on that account to be refused full social equality in the Church, unless we are prepared to pronounce them individually, not true Christians. They are to have as much liberty to consider and declare that their error is sanctioned by the voice of the Church, as we have concerning the opposing truth. It is to be preached against no more than Baptism, and the Minister holding it is to be allowed the same liberty we claim in our own Church. So far as Pedobaptism is concerned, Mr. Hall actually adopted these sentiments. Augustine, one of the most pious of all the Christian Fathers, (as his "Confessions" will show,) held to praying for the dead, and baptismal regeneration; Fenelon was a Roman Catholic; Neander and Arnold hardly believe in infallible inspiration; John Foster shrunk from the doctrine of endless punishment. And must we, then, be driven to the dilemma of either declaring such men as these "necessarily excluded," by the errors we have named, from salvation; or else of being "*expressly commanded*" by Scripture to receive them as members and ministers of our own Churches, not repelling them in any numbers on this account, if we do not see some special reason to feel assured of their not being in a gracious state?

We must thus, in fact, permit the Roman Catholic on the one hand, and the deniers of inspiration on the other, to mix so freely and equally in our Churches, that we shall not be known as favoring any views in preference to these, until the name of *Baptist* " might be found not so properly applicable to Churches as to individuals;" and ministers of every shade of opinion, from Roman Catholicism to Arianism, claim a perfect equality of sanction with our own, as a thing expressly commanded in Scripture from every one of our Churches. Thus must we surrender the ancient and apostolic motto, on which our Churches are at present based; and instead of " one Lord, one faith, and one baptism," inscribe "many Lords, many opinions, and many baptisms." Our Mixed Communion brethren do not shrink from all these consequences, so far as Pedobaptism is concerned; and they declare that the same general principle will apply to all other cases.

8. But even this is not the whole. We are, according to the Mixed Communion theory, to tolerate not only *speculative* differences of opinion, but *actual differences of practice*, until we reach that point at which we are prepared to decide that they *necessarily exclude* those who practice them from the favor of God. Thus we are not only to tolerate a speculative belief in Infant Baptism, but to allow the Pedobaptist to *practice what he believes*. This is, we admit, necessary to consistency. But observe to what it must lead. We are to tolerate John Milton's "difference of opinion" about divorce, because we are not prepared to say that it necessarily excluded him from a state of grace. It is not to be preached against in the Church, so as to give offence or hurt the conscience of any weak brother holding such views. But suppose he had practised what he believed, must we tolerate divorce at option? We must permit pious Roman Catholics to pray to the Virgin Mary, to adore the Host, and kneel in confession to a priest, and at the same time be full undisciplined members, perhaps ministers of our Churches! It is a difference of opinion not "necessarily excluding" from salvation.

It is not many years since a Minister of the Gospel, by all esteemed most pious, wrote a work to prove that every seducer should be compelled to marry his victim, even were he a married man; thus advocating compulsory polygamy, in certain cases. Suppose that opinion to be conscientiously acted upon by some penitent adulterer, must we tolerate practices in the Church, that the good of society requires to be punished by the law of the land?

9. Enough has been said to show that no such plan of Church Membership could be "expressly commanded," or ought to be supposed to be, from any process of inferential argument, from isolated passages.

The passages, however, quoted by Robert Hall, in support of these views, are Rom. 14: 1—5. "Him that is weak in the faith, receive ye, but not to doubtful disputations," &c.; and Rom. 15: 1, 6, 7. "We, then, that are strong, ought to bear the infirmities of the weak, and not to please ourselves," &c. On these Robert Hall argues thus: "A moment's attention to the connection will convince the reader that the term weak in both these passages denotes persons whose conceptions are erroneous. . . . It behooves us to examine the *principle* on which the Apostle enjoins toleration, and if this is applicable in its full extent to the case of our Pedobaptist brethren, no room is left for doubt. The *principle* plainly is, that the error in question was not of such magnitude, as to preclude him who maintained it from the favor of God. 'Let not him who eateth, despise him who eateth not; and let not him who eateth not, judge him who eateth; *for God hath received him.*' . . . . . If such is the reason assigned for mutual toleration, and it is acknowledged to be a sufficient one, which none can deny without impeaching the inspiration of the writer, it is as conclusive respecting the obligation of *tolerating every error which is consistent with a state of salvation*, as if that error had been mentioned by name. . . . . Hence, we have only one alternative, either to deny that those who differ from us on the subject of Baptism are accepted of God, or to receive them into fellowship on exactly the *same ground*, and on the *same principle* that Paul enjoined the toleration of sincere Christians."*

10. It is sufficient to remark on these passages, that they only prove what all admit, that some differences of opinion and practice, are to be tolerated in the Church, when we have reason to believe the weak brother, a person accepted of God. What the nature of the difference is, in regard to which the command to receive the brother applies, we are particularly informed; *i. e., as to matters in regard to which, there is no inspired direction, one way more than another.* In such cases, *the individual was complying with the whole will of God, as revealed by inspiration,* whichever way he might act.

The Apostle, it will be observed, then places the reception of these weak brethren, distinctly on these two grounds. 1st. That whichever way they might act, they violated no command of inspiration, but were complying with the whole revealed will of God, in regard to the matter in dispute. This is most expressly stated in the 14th verse: "I know, and am persuaded of the Lord Jesus, that there is nothing unclean of itself;" but it is also implied, and *taken for granted*, in the 2d, 5th, and 6th verses; "one believeth that he may eat all things, another who is weak, eateth herbs," (but both equally fulfill every Divine command on this subject). 2d. This being the case, and, God the Father and the Lord Jesus Christ having received them, not only in these respects, but also generally as the children of grace, it was fitting that they should be tolerated by the Church at Rome. *"Wherefore"* (on account of the principles of toleration in the Church of the different customs of those persons, not violating

---

* Works, vol. 1, p. 325-6.

any inspired command,) "receive ye one another, as Christ also received us, to the glory of God."

But to argue from the command in relation to those, ho, as to the matters in question, had fulfilled the whole revealed will of God, to tolerate their harmless whims, because "God has received them," that, therefore, we are bound to tolerate all opinions of persons living in acknowledged errors, and without having fulfilled the whole revealed will of God, in regard to the matters in question, but whom God has received as Christians; that we are bound to receive them, not as Christians only, which we do, but in other respects also, will perhaps remind the admirers of Coleridge of what he aptly terms "the ever-widening spiral *ergo*, from the narrow aperture of a single text," "the inverted pyramid, of which the apex is the base." (Aids to Reflection, on Baptism.)

11. And yet, with a firm conviction of its being unanswerable, our author triumphantly recurs to it again and again, in language like this. "From these premises, we argue thus. Since St. Paul assigned as a reason for the mutual forbearance of Christians, that they were equally accepted of Christ, it was, undoubtedly, a *sufficient* one, and admitting it to be such, it must extend to all who are in the same predicament, (who are in the same state of acceptance)."*

We desire to make but two remarks on the above. 1st. Instead of saying, "since St. Paul assigned as a reason for the mutual forbearance of Christians," he should have said, "*of those Christians who, in regard to the matters in question, have complied with all the requirements of inspiration.*" 2d. That correction being made, we may

* Reply to Kinghorn, part 3, ch. 7. Works, p. 457.

grant that his conclusion in regard to mutual forbearance will apply to all who are "in *the same predicament*," that is, not merely all who are "in a state of acceptance," but "*the same* state of acceptance," *i. e., those in whom the two conditions meet,* of complying with all the Divine commands in regard to Church Membership, and being received of God. Can it be claimed for Pedobaptists, however, (to say nothing at all of those who are permitted to hold errors of any and every description, except such as "necessarily exclude from salvation,") can it be claimed for them we ask, *under these passages,* that we are expressly commanded to receive them, not as Christians only, but to all the rights and privileges of our own particular Churches?

Suppose, in order to put a case as exactly fitted to bring out the force of the text quoted by Robert Hall as possible, and at the same time, as closely to illustrate the question on hand, as we know how,—suppose that two conditions are necessary to visible Church Membership, in any denomination, one is, that the individual be professedly in acceptance with God; and the other, that he comply with the requirements of the Inspired Volume, in regard to the ordinance of Baptism : might not a Pastor, speaking of such as had complied with these latter requirements, say, "*Wherefore*, since these brethren have complied with the command, receive them, for Christ has received them?" and would it be fair to infer from such an address, that the Pastor had taught that persons who had acted *contrary* to the Divine requirements, in regard to Baptism, were to be received into visible Church Membership, if only Christians?

12. And here we might rest, contented with having destroyed the plan of Church Membership advocated by

Robert Hall. But for ourselves, we have no hesitation in saying, that we think these passages about tolerating Jewish scruples, held modestly and without disputation, when put in connection with those which speak of withdrawing from the disorderly, and rejecting the factious, show that a discretionary power is, to a certain extent, left with each particular Church, in different states of the world, and in different ages; to declare not only what is a credible profession of piety, and what are the *divinely appointed* requisites of visible Church Membership, but (so that they do not dispense with what is thus made requisite,) also to determine for itself, to a certain extent, how high a standard of Church Membership it is best *for the promotion of Divine truth in the world* that they should adopt. A Church is a voluntary association. Each Church has a right to propound a summary of its views, and every candidate for admission can state that he receives or rejects it. This is the origin of all Confessions of Faith, and so far they need not be objected to. The whole history of revealed religion in the world, shows that many things, rightly tolerated in one age and situation of the Church and of the world, would be injurious if tolerated in another. In bodies like the Churches of Christ, formed not only for the good of the individual, but of the whole, and not only for the edification of the Church itself, but to carry on the aggressive warfare of Christian holiness upon the world, they must often require of the individual, a very much stricter compliance with the rules of discipline, than might be essential to his individual *salvation;* or the whole array of Christian discipline would soon be overturned.

13. If now it should be asked, whether, upon these principles, our churches might not well use their discretionary

power, in favor of admitting to their membership unbaptized persons, we reply, No. And for these reasons, because it would be contrary to acknowledged Apostolic usage, and contrary to the sentiments of all Christians, in all places and at all times; because practically it must destroy all liberty of speech and action upon the subject of Baptism, for fear of giving offence; stifling all that inquiry and discussion, through which truth, though at first in the minority, soon gains adherents; because, with the present vast numerical majority of Pedobaptists, it must mix up and destroy Baptist Churches as such, and so obliterate Baptist sentiments; because the plan we adopt allows more liberty and freedom of discussion; because it is adopted by all denominations in this country, and by all churches in relation to *other* differences of opinion, as in regard to Arminianism, Calvinism, and even the sale and use of ardent spirits; and because the plan of Church Membership, proposed by Robert Hall in the place of our own, cannot be carried out to its legitimate results, without the most pernicious annihilation of all the distinctive features of Christian truth.

14. Besides all this; while far be it from us to suppose a belief in Infant Baptism necessarily incompatible with the most sincere and exalted piety, yet as the peculiar harmlessness of Pedobaptism is the great plea, urged in favour of Mixed Communion; it is proper to observe, that Infant Baptism, as a system, has been fraught with the most destructive effects to Christian piety, and a regenerate Church Membership, for the last fifteen hundred years, of any system equally prevalent. To perceive this fully, we must look at it, not where, from its close contact with Baptist systems, it has lost most of its distinctive features; but we must observe it, where it is followed to its legiti-

mate results. We must behold it in Papal countries, for example, and see how it has at once swept the world into the Church, obliterating entirely the distinction between the converted and the unrenewed. Has it not led to the belief, in the Roman Catholic, the Greek, and in many Protestant Churches, that the application of a little water to an unconscious babe, can make it "a member of Christ, a child of God, and an inheritor of the kingdom of heaven?" Has it not, by a natural consequence, in regard to those dying in infancy, led to the belief, wide-spread, but most intolerable, (and as Coleridge declares, one that alone came near making him reject Infant Baptism altogether,) *i. e.*, that "the want of it may occasion their eternal loss?" Has it not, so far as acted upon, destroyed the possibility of keeping up Church discipline, and by mixing up the worldly with the pious in the Church, brought all the evils of an unconverted Ministry upon whole nations; so that when Wesley arose, he could find but about three, whom he thought converted Ministers, even in the Established Church of England? From this source sprang in New England that superficial morality, in place of evangelical repentance and obedience, which not unnaturally resulted in wide-spread Unitarianism.* So too, on the other hand, Infant Baptism has formed the chief hiding place and proof of that doctrine of Tradition, which is now exerting such a fearful influence in the

---

* The Author has alluded to the condition of the Established Church of England, in the time of Wesley. The Church of Scotland was but little better when first visited by Whitefield.

It is also worthy of special remark, that Geneva, the birthplace of modern Presbyterianism, and Boston, the cradle of modern Congregationalism, have both been saved from utterly sinking into the vortex of Socinianism, by the blessing of God on the labors of zealous Baptists. See Appendix L.   J. N. B.

Episcopal and Roman Catholic Churches. It is impossible here to trace out half the pernicious effects, both in doctrine and in practice, which have resulted from Pedobaptism, *as a system*. Doubtless, all of them have not been felt in any one case. And many of the most evangelical spirits have been reared in Pedobaptist Churches. We cannot forget that an Edwards, and a Payson, not to mention a long catalogue of others, held to Infant Baptism; but a distinguished Pedobaptist, Dr. Bushnell, in his Defence of Infant Baptism, has shown that these men were all "Baptists in Theory," in proportion as they held to the very sentiments for which we revere them; indeed, to that they owed it, and the Churches to which they belonged, that in them Infant Baptism has produced so little of the very consequences we deplore.

CHAPTER III.

ROBERT HALL'S THIRD ARGUMENT CONSIDERED.

1. Two senses of the word Church. 2. Assertion of the Author that they differ only as a part from the whole, considered. 3. The true distinction destroys his argument. 4. 'Those who commune with God fit to commune with us,' considered. 5. 'Presumptuously to aspire to greater purity than Christ,' considered. 6. The same reasoning applied to the Passover.

1. THE title of this argument is, *"Pedobaptists a part of the true Church; their exclusion on that account unlawful."* Under this head, our author commences by remarking, that "If we examine the New Testament, we shall find, that the term Church, as a religious appellation, occurs in two senses only: it either denotes the whole body of the faithful, (as where Christ is declared to be Head over all things to the Church, which is his body), or some one assembly of Christians, associated for the worship of God," (as the Church at Corinth, at Ephesus, or at Rome). "It is never used as in modern times, to denote the aggregate of Christian assemblies throughout a province or a kingdom, nor do we ever read of the Church of Achaia, Galatia, &c., but of the *Churches.*"

2. So far (as we observed, p. 36,) we fully agree with our Author, as to the technical uses of the word Church in the New Testament. There are but these two distinct senses, in which it is employed as a religious appellation

The point at which we differ from Robert Hall, as shown more fully (Part I., ch. 4.) than it will be necessary here to repeat, is, where the Author takes for granted, that "it is manifest from Scripture, that these two significations of the word differ from each other, only as a part from the whole." If he means to assert, that this is manifest, because the same term (εκκλησία) is used in both cases, it would be equally proper, to argue for this reason also, that the tumultuous *assembly* of the worshipers of Diana, at Ephesus, in regard to whom the same original term (εκκλησία) is also used, (Acts 19. 32), differed from the Universal Church, the whole body of Christ, " only as a part differs from the whole." So far from it being a manifest truth, therefore, that it is *only* a difference of numbers, that constitute the distinction between a particular Visible Church and the Universal Church, which is invisible; there are at least two obvious points of distinction as to qualification, *necessarily* arising from the fact, that the one is a visible, and the other an invisible body; *i. e.* 1. That he who possesses true piety without any profession, becomes at once a member of the invisible Church, while he only who makes some credible and appropriate profession, (without here determining what it is) is eligible to visible Church fellowship. 2. That *a credible profession of faith in Christ*, in some particular way or ways, is all that can be required for admission to the one, while no conceivable profession without the reality admits to the other. After the remarks made on the subject in Part I., it is unnecessary longer to dwell here, on a distinction so evident.

3. It remains but to be observed, that it is only from overlooking this distinction, that the argument which we are now considering, can be supposed to have the least weight. Let it be granted that Pedobaptists are a part

of the true Church. Our Author must mean by this, that they are a part of the true invisible or Universal Church, which is the body of Christ. And what follows from this? That, *"their exclusion on that account is unlawful."* Their exclusion from what? From the invisible Church? No. None but "He who has the key of David, who openeth and no man shutteth, and shutteth and no man openeth," can admit into, or exclude from that great spiritual body. Their exclusion from what, then? From the symbols of membership in the invisible Church? No; for we have before seen, that the Lord's Supper is the symbol of something quite distinct from invisible fellowship or communion, *i. e. visible* fellowship in particular Church relations. Besides; in what sense do we exclude them from the Eucharist? In no other sense than as every Jew might be said to exclude every other Jew from the Passover, whom he did not invite to participate in it, with his own family.

But passing this by, for the moment, we ask, where is the force of the argument? Pedobaptists, it is urged, are a part of the true *invisible* Church of Christ. Let it be granted; and what would follow? Therefore, we are bound to invite them, as such, to participate with us in all the symbols of *visible* Church relationship, while they are not members of our visible Churches!

We grant most fully that many Pedobaptists are members of the Spiritual Church Universal. We do not exclude them from that. We extend to them all the tokens and symbols of Spiritual Communion. We unite with them in prayer, the great symbol of antiquity; and (as was shown, Part II., ch. 3,) in all religious services, that do not imply visible Church relations. Then their Confessions of Faith forbid them to have fellowship with us, (see Part II., ch. 3,) as ours with them.

4. Whoever bears in mind this distinction, will experience no difficulty from the following passage, in which our author, with his characteristic urgency, argues in this chapter. After stating that there are certain propositions which produce, on the unprejudiced, instantaneous conviction, he gives the following as one of these obvious truths. Those whom the Divine Founder of the Church " actuates by his Spirit, and admits to Communion with himself, are sufficiently qualified for Communion with mortals. What can be alleged," asks our author, " in opposition to a truth so indubitable and so obvious?" It is not necessary for us to determine, as we have no disposition to dispute the truth of the proposition. Nor could Mr. Hall have been led into the mistake of supposing that we did dispute it, unless he had not only lost sight of the difference between fellowship in the invisible and in a visible Church, but also confounded the *literal* and the *symbolic* uses of the term Communion. We do admit to our Communion, that is to our spiritual fellowship, fully and heartily, those whom we have reason to believe the Great Head of the Church admits to his; and what is more, *we hold with them the same kind of Communion which we suppose him to do*. With those He admits to a purely spiritual Fellowship with Himself, we have and symbolize a purely spiritual Communion. With those whom we consider to observe correctly his will in the ceremonial or the visible part of Church relations and worship, we symbolize our fellowship by a ceremonial or visible union in the Lord's Supper.

5. In regard to what is urged in the same connection,

"that it is presumptuous to aspire to a greater purity or strictness, in selecting the materials for a Church, than are observed by its Divine Founder," we need only remark, that Visible Churches are equally founded by him with the Invisible Church, and their respective terms of membership. That these terms in the former case should embrace what we know is not always embraced in the latter, a public profession of his name, is so obviously necessary to the idea of *visibility*, that the absurdity would be in supposing the terms of admission to the two identical in these respects.

Nor does it follow that, according to our plan, "greater purity and strictness" are made requisite for the membership of Visible Churches, than of the Universal Church. The fact is exactly the reverse; for, while a credible *profession* is all that is required in the one case, a right state of *heart* is alone accepted in the latter. It is only that the terms are necessarily distinct, as the object of the two organizations is different. Does it follow, because none but those who are citizens by birth or naturalization are permitted to vote for the President of the United States, that we suppose every one excluded by that provision of the Constitution, every person not naturalized, all those who in Europe are permitted to vote for their respective governments, are not equally good citizens of the world, and have not equal knowledge of the principles of political science, with each and any one who is permitted, by that clause, to vote in this country? Could it be justly said, "we presumptuously aspired to a greater purity and strictness in selecting the materials" of a republic, than was necessary for the rest of the world, and that, by passing naturalization laws, we had indicated that opinion?

6. But the most obvious method of exhibiting the fal-

lacy of this species of reasoning, is to show, in such a case as the following, the false consequences to which it would lead. It is admitted by all, that under the Jewish dispensation, such was the connection instituted between circumcision and the Passover, that none could, without violating the Divine command, partake of the latter symbol of belonging to the Jewish Church, without being first circumcised. But, is it necessary to contend that circumcision was always essential to salvation; or that there were no individuals in the world, accepted of God, and in Communion with Him, by means of "that faith which Abraham had, being yet uncircumcised," (Rom. 4 : 12.) who had not submitted to this ceremony; and, consequently, could not partake with the Jew of that Paschal Lamb, which was the great antitype of the all-atoning Lamb of God?

Unless Mr. Hall would be prepared to deny this, his remarks would accuse the divinely inspired lawgiver of the Mosaic dispensation, of "presumptuously aspiring to a greater purity and strictness, in selecting the materials" of the Jewish Church, "than had been observed by its Divine Founder in adjusting those of His own." Surely, this is a sufficient refutation of such an argument.

CHAPTER IV.

ROBERT HALL'S FOURTH ARGUMENT CONSIDERED.

1. 'The exclusion of Pedobaptists a punishment,' considered. 2. The Lord's Supper a family feast. 3. The Evangelical Alliance excommunicate, on Robert Hall's principle 4. The charge of excommunicating considered. 5. Mr Hall would excommunicate all Churches whose invitation to Communion he declined. 6. 'That our views make the approach of Pedobaptists to the Lord's Supper criminal,' considered. 7. The difficulty of Mr. Hall's system on this point considered.

1. *"The exclusion of Pedobaptists from the Lord's Table, considered as a punishment."*

SUCH is the title of this argument in favor of Mixed Communion, and it is supported by the following opening assertion. "The refusal of the Eucharist to a professor of Christianity, can be justified only on the ground of his supposed criminality, of his embracing heretical sentiments, or living a vicious life." If by refusing the Eucharist to a professor of Christianity, is meant simply our not inviting him to partake with us in that ordinance, (which is all that we do,) we might reply by simply asking how much truth there would be in the assertion, if it had been applied to the Passover instead? Or would our Author have ventured to say, that, for a Jew not to invite any other member of the Jewish nation to celebrate the Passover with him, could be justified only on the ground of the supposed criminality of the party, that he must be esteemed such a heretic, or a man of so vicious a life, as to have forfeited all title to be considered a member of the Israelitish nation, or entitled to any of its privileges? If a Jew had been thus charged, might he not appropriately reply, that his not inviting his fellow-Israelite, did not in the least exclude him from the Passover, or pronounce him to be no child of Abraham; that it was not necessarily any punishment, and not so intended, but that as strictly only members of the same family, or, at most, neighbors, by special invitation and agreement, were commanded to celebrate that institution together, so not to extend the invitation, indicated simply that he was not regarded as one of the parties included in the terms of that regulation?

2. We regard the Lord's Supper in the light of a *family* feast, *i. e.*, a Church ordinance, to be celebrated together by members of the same Visible Church, or at most, in company with persons whom they could consistently receive as such by special invitation. There is no more idea of *punishment*, in not inviting others or partaking with them in the case of the Lord's Supper, than of the Passover.

3. It is well known, that of late years a society has been formed of various denominations, both in England and America, termed the Evangelical Alliance, formed of the members of various denominations. We believe, it has never yet at any of its meetings celebrated the Lord's Supper. This has probably arisen, more than anything else, from the feeling, that it would seem to unite them more in Church relations than all parties could agree to, however willing to unite with each other as Christians. But we see not why an advocate for Mixed Communion, would not be bound in all consistency, to rise in such

bodies and proclaim, that unless they were prepared to assert, that some at least of the parties uniting held to errors of such a nature, as would "necessarily exclude them from being of the number that Christ has received to the glory of the Father," it would be contrary to "the express command of Scripture," for the Alliance to omit to celebrate the Eucharist together; that "such a refusal could only be justified on the ground of the supposed criminality of a portion, at least, of the Alliance, that is of their embracing heretical sentiments, or living a vicious life." That the exclusion of the Lord's Supper from such a body of men could be "considered in no other light than as *a punishment*," as an "excommunication," and therefore as a declaration, that those with whom they had refused to commune had "forfeited their right to spiritual privileges, and were henceforth consigned to the kingdom of Satan."*

4. No more erroneous statement can be made as to our course in regard to the Lord's Supper, than that which declares, that "it is unquestionably of the nature of *a punishment*" inflicted upon all others, unless it be that contained in the next paragraph, where it is supposed to be identical with "Excommunication." On the faith of this, we are charged, in regard to Pedobaptists, with "proceeding with a high hand and attempting to terminate the dispute by authority," after which we are earnestly reminded, that "the solemn decision of a Christian assembly, that an individual has forfeited his right to spiritual privileges, and *is henceforth consigned to the kingdom of Satan,* is an awful proceeding, inferior only in terror to the sentence of the last day."

* Works, vol. 1, p. 341.

This is all very true, but where is its application to the case in hand? It should be remarked, that although less in degree, yet of the same nature with the error of unwarrantably excommunicating, is that of unjustly implying such a charge as this upon a fellow Christian. How can it be pretended that we excommunicate? This would in the mildest terms be, to separate from Church relations those who had once sustained them. But the individuals in question are those with whom we never have sustained Church relations, who have not sought them, who would not be willing to comply with our terms of membership, and who have agreed upon terms of their own, with which they know we cannot comply. As we hold to the strict independence of all Churches, this does not imply anything like excommunication, or even unchurching, on the one part or the other. If it did, however, it would equally imply it on the part of Pedobaptist Churches, as of our own. Yea, on the part of Mixed Communion Churches also; since they profess that their terms of Church Membership are so "expressly commanded," that they will not dispense with them, they are as much the means of excluding us, as our requiring Baptism is of excluding Pedobaptists. But in truth, no Church can excommunicate another Church, nor indeed any members of another Church, nor any person, not of its own body.* Nor is it the duty of

---

* This, we are surprised to observe, Robert Hall, in his reply to Mr. Kinghorn, attempts to deny; perseveringly charging us with excommunicating, and stating that he "will not descend to a tedious logomachy, further than to remark that" Mr. K. "has fallen into an error" in saying "how excommunication can take place in [regard to] one who never was in a Society, we have yet to learn." Suffice it to say that the definition of *excommunicate*, in such dictionaries as Richardson, Johnson, Walker, and Webster, contains the words to "*eject*," to "*expel;*" yet who would think it possible to *expel* a young man from College who had never entered. (See Reply to Kinghorn, ch. 9, p. 475.)

a Church, presumptuously to sit in judgment upon all others, and pronounce whether they are or are not true Christian Churches.

5. What is essential to a visible Christian Church, and, when a Church so far apostatizes as to forfeit all claims to the title,—are questions, in their application to such bodies as the Church of Rome, the Greek Church, and many others, known only to Him who searches the hearts; but upon which no earthly tribunal is competent to sit in judgment, and from which we are entirely saved the unpleasant necessity of making a decision only by our position. It must certainly be as great a violation of Christian Charity to refuse to commune with other Christian Churches upon their invitation, as not to invite their members to commune with us. Hence it has always been the custom of Mixed Communion Baptists, to participate in the Eucharist freely in Congregational Churches. If then these same persons refuse to participate with Episcopalians or Roman Catholics, it must be because they do not esteem them true Christian Churches; and we see not why they must not in every case decide that the Church inviting them to its communion holds errors of such a nature, as "necessarily exclude them from being of the number of those whom Christ has received," or else we are "expressly commanded," for aught we see, on Mr. Hall's principles, to accept their invitation. The Presbyterians, we believe, have undertaken to decide for themselves that the Roman Catholic was a true Church, all through the dark ages, and up to the time of the Reformation, but that, since then, the candlestick has been removed out of its place. Unless we believe that our Churches are not only entitled, but bound, thus to assume the prerogative of Deity, and sit in judgment upon each body

calling itself a Church of Christ, (with the danger on the one hand of 'eating and drinking with the drunken,' or upon the other of 'smiting our fellow-servants')—unless we are prepared for all this, Robert Hall's plan is utterly impracticable, and ours the only consistent one. It is true, our Author seems to suppose that there is a distinction between communing in other Churches, and inviting the members of other Churches to commune with us. Speaking of the Church of England, he says, "our dissent from the Establishment is founded on the necessity of departing from a communion, to which certain corruptions, in our apprehension, do inseparably adhere; while we welcome the pious part of that community to the celebration of the Eucharist, which we deem unexceptionable; we recede from their communion from necessity, but we feel no scruple in admitting them to ours. . . . On him who has not discernment to perceive, or candor to acknowledge the difference between these methods of proceeding, all further reasoning would be wasted."

Notwithstanding some danger of being thought to possess so little discernment or candor, that argument would be wasted on us, we confess that we do not see all the distinction that Robert Hall would like to establish; especially, since he aims throughout to maintain the same terms of permanent and full Church fellowship that he does for occasional participation at the Lord's Table. The plan he proposes, must, as he admits, if carried out, do away the denominational character of every Church, so that all would be Christian, none denominational. To refuse therefore to commune with any Church, could only be justified by not considering it a Christian Church. To this there could be but two exceptions, 1st, when such was *the mode* of celebrating this institution, that some erroneous practice was required of the communicant in order to celebrate, and 2nd, where by partaking with a Church a general agreement with their errors would be symbolized by so doing. This last would however imply almost the views we are advocating, *i. e.*, that the Lord's Supper indicates such relations between those uniting in it, that the errors of the majority are considered as therefore acquiesced in by the rest. This indeed might lead to a *more restricted* than even a Church fellowship in the Lord's Supper.

6. There is another consideration, which our Author deems so important that, but for multiplying divisions, he would have treated it as a separate argument. "Are the advocates of Infant Baptism," he asks, "criminal in approaching the Lord's Table?" "Upon the principles of our opponents, their approach is not only sinful, but sinful to such a degree, as to communicate a moral taint, to what in other circumstances would be deemed an act of obedience." Against this he argues as follows: "Whatever blame we may be disposed to attribute to the abettors of infant baptism, on the score of previous inattention or prejudice, as there is nothing in their principles to cause them to hesitate respecting the obligation of the Eucharist, *it is unquestionably their immediate duty to celebrate it; they would be guilty of a deliberate and wilful offence, were they to neglect it.* . . . . If my reader be disposed to gratify his curiosity by making a collection of all the uncandid strictures which have been passed upon the advocates of Pedobaptism, it is more than probable the charge of profaning the Lord's Supper would not be found among the number." He admits that Baptists are not heard "to breathe a murmur against" Pedobaptists on

this account, but maintains that in all consistency they ought.

According to the principles we have laid down, there is no reason why we should "breathe a murmur" against others, because they take the Lord's Supper in their own Churches. We do not unchurch them. It is not our duty to decide for others, how many errors a religious assembly may hold, and yet be a true Church. All we say is, that such are their views and practices, that we cannot pronounce them prepared to unite in Church relations with us; that we only unite in Church relations with those who are baptized; that these, not being baptized in our view, we cannot unite with them. If we err in making baptism a prerequisite to membership in our Churches, we err in company with Christians of all ages. The not inviting them to our Communion, does not pronounce that those religious societies, not founded upon our views of Baptism, are not Christian Churches, any more than an Israelite pronounced all other families beside his own, in partaking the Passover, not true Jews.

7. On the other hand, it is the infelicity of the Mixed Communion scheme, that every individual embracing it must be prepared at once, and on every occasion, to pronounce against each Church professedly Christian, or else to express before all the world, the Church fellowship manifested by uniting with them in this ordinance. With regard to individuals, the case is worse. Either we must be prepared to exclude any person whatever, desirous of joining with us in the Lord's Supper, and pronounce that he has "forfeited his right to spiritual privileges, and is henceforth consigned to the kingdom of Satan," or else, on his claiming to be a Christian, we must be prepared to

express, not only our confidence in his piety, but our readiness to unite in full Church relations with him, by celebrating this ordinance. Yet who would be prepared to do this, in regard to all Pedobaptist Churches or individuals, unless he had a greater faith in infant baptism than even the Roman Catholic professes.

CHAPTER V.

ROBERT HALL'S FIFTH ARGUMENT CONSIDERED.

1. 'The impossibility of reducing Strict Communion to any general principles,' considered. 2. The Lord's Table to be governed by the same rules as our Church Membership. 3. Baptism a prerequisite to Church Membership, a rule *semper, ubique, et ab omnibus.* 4. Every visible Church must have some visible profession of Christianity. 5. Visible Churches aggressive in their nature. 6. The 'general principle' of Mixed Communion, considered. 7. The distinction between tolerating imperfection and endorsing it. 8. The distinction between errors fundamental and not fundamental, considered. 9. Baptism formerly deemed necessary to salvation, admitted by Mr. Hall. 10. A further difference as to Mr. Hall's 'general principle.' 11. Some visible profession must be necessary to Church Membership.

1. "ON *the impossibility of reducing the Practice of Strict Communion to any general principle.*" On this subject, Mr. Hall urges the following: "We both admit that some indulgence of the mistakes or imperfections of the truly pious is due, from a regard to the dictates of inspiration and the nature of man. The only subject of controversy is, how far that forbearance is to be extended: we assert, to every diversity of judgment not incompatible with salvation; *they* [the strict communionists] *contend that a difference of opinion on baptism is an excepted case.**
. . . . If it be found impossible to fix a medium between the toleration of all opinions in religion, and the restriction

---

* Works, vol. 1, p. 345.

of it to errors *not fundamental*, the practice of exclusive Communion must be abandoned, because it is neither more nor less than an attempt to establish such a medium. By errors *not fundamental*, I mean such as are admitted to consist with a state of grace and salvation. (Vol. I., p. 344–5.)

In considering this section, we will first of all show that our practice in regard to the Lord's Supper is reducible to a principle at least consistent with itself; and then venture to inquire how far the same can be said of that advocated by the Author of the Terms of Communion.

2. Whoever has attended to the former portions of this Essay, will, we think, be at no loss to discover, that we have all along attempted to reduce the rule, by which we make Baptism a prerequisite to uniting with our Churches in the Lord's Supper, to a general principle, simple and obvious to the last degree, (one not so ambiguous as the difference between errors fundamental and not fundamental;) *i. e.*, that our uniting with Christians at the Lord's Table, or as it is commonly called, our "Occasional Communion," *should be governed by the same rules as our Church membership.* Upon this we uniformly act. Those whom we invite to partake with us, we would be willing to see all of them, just as they are, members of our Churches. We arrogate not the superiority over those whom we invite, of refusing to accept the invitation of their Churches in return, but are happy to reciprocate upon perfect social equality in the ordinance. We draw no subtle distinction that enables us to "recede from *their* Communion" while pressing "them to *ours.*" (Works, Vol. I., p. 479–80.)

As we have already sufficiently reasoned in regard to this principle, and as it is so clearly based on the simple fact that this ordinance is a divinely appointed symbol of Church Communion as before explained, it is enough here that we have shown that our course in regard to it is based upon a consistent general principle.

3. But if it is intended that the practice in our Churches of making Baptism prerequisite to their *membership,* is based on no general principle, then we have to remark, first, that if so, we are at least in company with all Christian Churches of all ages, (save only our modern Mixed Communion brethren,) who have ever adopted the same rule: so that we should at least have the principle of *semper, ubique, et ab omnibus,* to fall back upon; one, if not infallible, of no little conservative value, when novel speculations are in question.

4. But this rule is based on the general and obvious principle, that *every visible Christian Church must, in the very nature of things, have some visible profession of Christianity, among the prerequisites to its membership.* Ours is, as Robert Hall acknowledges, the Scriptural profession prior to membership. Any other, therefore, in its place, must be admitted as an exception, not as the rule.

5. And further, as our visible Churches are organized by their Divine Founder, with special reference, not only to their own edification, but to the carrying out of an *aggressive spiritual warfare* upon the world, many of their requirements of membership must be supposed to be designed for that object. Hence some things, not necessary for personal salvation, are properly made terms of the membership of a particular visible Church. And as Churches are independent bodies, each of them is "entitled to declare for itself the terms of admission to its Communion;" and this both as to those things it deems essential to salvation, and those it regards as requisite to

its accomplishing all the ends of its existence as a visible Church, whether on account of its peculiar situation, and duties to the world, or the universal commands of the Word of God.

Enough this in reply to the alleged "impossibility of reducing the practice of strict communion to any general principle." Enough to show that every part of our course, in this respect, is reducible to principles so general, obvious, and fundamental, that it would be impossible to overturn them without uprooting everything like a visible Church on earth. Even could it be shown, therefore, that we erred, it would only be in the particular application of sound general principles; while, from the very independence of our organizations, we do not thereby unchurch, nor "infringe upon the liberties and rights of others." (See Presbyterian Form of Government, Book 1, ch. 1, sec. 1.)

6. Let us now turn for a moment to examine the nature and consistency of the principles on which are based those "Terms of Communion" proposed in lieu of our own.

That upon which Mixed Communion rests, is thus stated by our Author. "When the necessity for tolerating imperfection is once admitted, there remains no point at which it can consistently stop, till it is extended to every gradation of error, the habitual maintenance of which is compatible with a state of salvation. . . . . If we impartially examine the reasons on which we rest the toleration of any supposed error, we shall find they invariably coincide with the idea of its not being fundamental;" or, in brief, we have "no right to establish terms of Communion which are not terms of salvation."

7. If in the above extract, by "tolerating imperfection," not denying a man to be *a Christian* on account of

imperfection, were alone intended, we should have no controversy; but when by tolerating, is meant admitting him to all the privileges of full visible Church Membership, inviting him to the Lord's Table, and thus, before men and angels, *affirming our belief and confidence* that he is in all respects, both a Christian and duly qualified for visible Church Membership, it is a very different matter. And when we not only do this in an individual case, but lay down as the basis of a full membership in our own particular Church, the toleration of every error, the habitual maintenance of which, by any one individual, is *compatible* with his salvation, and that with the full right on his part of voting in favor of, and every way sustaining it,—then unless a Church should choose to think almost every error "incompatible with salvation," it must be prepared to see each peculiar and cherished doctrine of Scripture swept away from the number of those to be maintained by the Church. We are to tolerate in our Churches, we are told, every error "*not fundamental.*" Thus, we must admit it to be preached in favor of, and voted for, as much as our own distinguishing truths: for "there remains no point at which we can consistently stop," short of this, on Robert Hall's plan.

8. Wherein, however, consists this distinction, between errors fundamental and errors not fundamental, on which the whole Mixed Communion system is essentially based? If we mistake not, it will be found that the distinction lies not in the character of *the error*, but of the man who holds it. So that, in fact, there are few errors that can be pronounced to be fundamental, in all cases; and none that can be said not to be so in any. This distinction is precisely like the Roman Catholic doctrine in regard to mortal and venial sins. There is, indeed, this difference,

that as "errors" may take a wider range than "sins," it must be proportionably more difficult to decide between those that are fundamental or mortal, and those which are not. If nothing is to be thought a fundamental error which can be and has been habitually maintained, even for a whole life, by some truly pious Christian, then there is hardly a single error that is fundamental, in doctrine or in practice; and the Church must tolerate everything most pernicious in the former, as "a difference of opinion upon points not incompatible with salvation," and almost every vice and crime in the latter, because there have been pious men who have not thought it wrong. A Church could not take a firm stand against any prevailing sin, because doubtful if it might not be compatible with salvation; or boldly and unitedly advocate any duty, for fear of offending some weak brother. The same faltering and wavering course which Mixed Communion pursues in regard to Pedobaptism, must be extended to Universalism and Campbellism, Popery and Arianism, Polygamy and Divorce. (See Part III., ch. 2.)

9. Or, if to escape these consequences, the opposite ground should be taken, and every error be deemed fundamental, in doctrine or practice, which has occasioned the loss of any persons holding it; then, what error is not fundamental? Shall any one venture to say that the very point of a willingness to submit to the commands of God as to Baptism itself, may not often be the very turning-point on which man's salvation shall depend? Robert Hall himself, so far from denying this, says, "I embrace, without hesitation, the affirmative side, and assert that in the Apostolic age, baptism *was* necessary to salvation," although, in that connection, he says, that he thinks it needless to prove that "it is not necessary now." (Vol.

I., p. 417.) Elsewhere, however, he puts the case of a man, knowing it to be his duty to be baptized, but from indifference to the will of God, or some worldly motive, declining; in which case, he himself would refuse him the Sacramental elements. Here, then, is an instance, in which an error as to Baptism is fundamental, even now. Those who have tasted that the Lord is gracious, know that the point as to the rejection of, or surrender to Christ, generally turns upon embracing or rejecting some apparently trifling error in doctrine or practice, that, however harmless in its consequences to others, is a matter of life or death to him whose spiritual state is at a crisis. It is the last feather that turns the scale. It may seem a paradox, but it is not the less true, that the error which costs a man the salvation of his soul ever seems to him a small one.

Since, then, there is *no error* but what may be fundamental, none could be excepted from that class, according to the latter mode of computation. There is certainly no error that may not be fundamental. The refusal to be baptized, may be, and often is. Yet is Mixed Communion founded essentially upon the principle that it is not. In truth, the distinction between errors fundamental, and not fundamental, is an unreal distinction; and all calculations based upon it, must ever vary according to the circumstances of him who presumes to judge by it, and will often be erroneous, decide whichever way he will. Yet this very distinction is one of the radical terms of that "*general principle*" upon which Mixed Communion boasts of resting itself. Nor is it any small infelicity of this general principle, that it is not only erroneous, but essentially embraces one of the worst errors of Popery; one that, uprooted under its ancient form of the distinction between mortal and venial sins, has here sprouted anew with a deeper root, a firmer stem, and a broader leaf.

10. But further, were we to admit everything that Mr. Hall asks, in regard to this distinction between fundamental and non-fundamental errors, and that an error in regard to Baptism is never fundamental, then should we still have to inquire, if the rest of the "general principle" were correct, that in our own visible Churches, we are under the necessity of tolerating *every gradation* of error not fundamental, or, (since the term is so ambiguous in its general application,) that " does not necessarily exclude those who hold it, from being of the number whom Christ has received?" (p. 326.) Now, we maintain that this general principle, so far from being true, is utterly inconsistent with the very nature and objects of a visible Church.

To suppose, that because a thing is not universally necessary to salvation, it therefore cannot be made a prerequisite to visible membership, can only have any speciousness from confounding the nature of the Invisible Church and our Visible Churches. But as the latter are intended by their Divine Founder, to carry on the aggressive warfare of holiness, as one chief object of their organization, it must be presumed that those things required in order to its membership, must have special reference to this fact, and, consequently, that things not necessary to personal salvation may yet be properly necessary to visible Church Membership. Yet are Robert Hall's "Terms of Communion" based on the general principle, that in no case can anything be requisite for membership in a visible Church, that is not in the Invisible.

11. But, to exhibit this in a more obvious and unanswerable point of view still, if it be possible, it surely

cannot be denied that the very constitution of a Visible Church *must* demand as a prerequisite to its Communion, *some* visible profession of Christianity :—if not Baptism, something in lieu of it. Now, as this profession of religion, whatever its nature be, must properly come after the religion itself, it cannot be identical with, nor essential to it.* Consequently, a person may be in a state of vital piety, and yet not fit for membership in a Visible Church. Many, whose piety we cannot doubt, delay a public profession for years. Some, from an extreme modesty and doubts of their acceptance. The world, and perhaps the Church, and even the pastor under whom they sit, know not their true state. Here is an error,—one, however, not fundamental in these cases,—even that of not confessing Christ before men. But would it be right to admit these, or any others, to the Lord's Table, and into a perfect membership in a visible Christian Church, until they had first of all made *some* credible profession of having passed from death unto life? That would destroy the evangelical character of our Churches. Such are some of the "general principles" upon which Mixed Communion is essentially based. Such is their consistency. Is any one prepared deliberately and practically to adopt them?

* See Appendix J.

CHAPTER VI.

ROBERT HALL'S SIXTH ARGUMENT CONSIDERED.

1. 'The Impolicy of Strict Communion.' 2. How far policy should weigh, considered. 3. Mr. Hall's statement as to its impolicy. Effects of "party," considered. 5. The comparatively rapid 'extension of scientific truths,' considered. 6. Distinction between the extension of speculative and practical truths, considered. 7. The speculative preacher of Baptist sentiments described. 8. The Baptist reformer described. 9. The question at issue between Robert Hall and ourselves. 10. The peculiar power of social organizations. 11. Shall the power of the Churches be applied to restore the obsolete practice? 12. Singular shift of Mr. Hall. 13. Practical test of his views. 14. Comparative progress of the Baptists in England and America. 15. Effects of Baptist sentiments on other denominations in America and Europe.

1. THE last consideration which Robert Hall urges in favor of his views, is entitled, *"The Impolicy of Strict Communion."* It is but just to remark at the outset, that he is as far from mixing up prudence and duty, or supposing that because a particular course seems politic, it must therefore be right, as any advocate of Strict Communion could desire. It is only where it is acknowledged that we are at liberty to follow either of two courses, that he supposes policy rightly to be consulted.

2. But although we cannot say that a particular course is right because it is prudent, the course which is right, so generally, not to say universally, produces the most agreeable and useful ultimate results, that this fact, where it can be observed on a sufficient scale, often becomes a test of no little worth in doubtful matters. Thus, for instance, the amazing effects of Revelation upon society for

good, form one, and not the least evidence of its divine character and authority. It is not improper therefore to contemplate the comparative *effects* of the two systems of Mixed and Strict Communion, upon the promotion of Baptist sentiments.

3. Upon this subject, Robert Hall remarks in substance thus, that "whatever retards inquiry, is favorable to error; that nothing has a greater tendency to obstruct free inquiry than the spirit and feeling of a party, since it erects its peculiarities as a standard round which the adherents rally, and which it becomes a point of honor to defend. Scientific truths make their way in the world with more ease and rapidity than religious, owing to the comparative absence of this combination, and because there is no class of men who have an interest, real or imaginary, in obstructing their progress." "The inference we would deduce from these facts" he continues, "is, that if we wish to revive an exploded truth, or to restore an obsolete practice, it is of the greatest moment to present it to the public in a manner least likely to produce the collision of party. But this is equivalent to saying, in other words, that it ought not to be made the basis of a sect; for the prejudices of party are always reciprocal, and in no instance, is that great law of motion more applicable, that 'reaction is always equal to action, and contrary thereto.' While it is maintained as a private opinion, by which I mean one not characteristic of a sect, it stands upon its proper merits, mingles with facility in different societies, and in proportion to its evidence, and the attention it excites, insinuates itself like leaven, till the whole is leavened."

We do not know how such a plan as that proposed might answer to revive an "*exploded truth*," but it seems to us not unlikely that this would sometimes be the most insidious, and therefore effectual way to revive an exploded *error*, or propagate an imaginary system, that the least touch of experience would prove fallacious. Certainly it would not by such a course have the same scrutiny and opposition to face; its merits would not be so closely examined; and it might in some way be connected with other feelings and interests, than those strictly belonging to it, so as to obtain a currency, which its own merits would never have secured. It is thus, for instance, that Puseyism has been propagated in the Episcopal Church. Truth, however, on the other hand, having a solid basis, can resist opposition, and only demands vigorous investigation for its merits to be fully known. The efforts of its enemies to oppose, will only lead, first to its discussion, and then to its dissemination.

4. True, the spirit of *mere* party, is a base and blinding thing. But while, on the one hand, to love truth only for the sake of its bearing upon our particular party, shows both a narrow and immoral mind; on the other hand, to form a party openly, and exposed to the fire of its enemies, in support of some obsolete truth; to cheer its ranks, and head the column, and lead it onward through all discomforts, amid the frowns of its foes, and the lukewarmness and desertion of the timid, is truly noble. Much that is decried as mere party spirit is, after all, neither more nor less than that practical courage which results from a consciousness of truth, and produces changes, the most judicious and abiding. It prefers to encounter inquiry and opposition *at the outset*, rather than gain currency by more insinuating means. The progress thus affected is slow at first, but solid and progressive. If, by way of illustration, we should compare the national charac-

teristics of the French and the English, there is infinitely more of this spirit in the latter than the former nation; and correspondingly we find, that the political reforms of France are more scientific in form, and brilliant in theory, and remarkable for the insidious "ease and rapidity" with which they make their way. But those of England, having to be first sifted by all parties, and thus brought to the test of past experience, are the most durable and progressive. Hence it is that they are not attended with that same reaction, alluded to by Robert Hall, (Works, vol. I., p. 354) as "equal to action, and contrary thereto;" a reaction by which the reforms of France sweep to and fro, at the most rapid rate, over the whole ground between anarchy and despotism, as on a railroad constructed of human bodies and slippery with human blood.

Brilliant theories, proposing to reform the constitution of all the visible Churches of Christ, throughout the whole world, need at least as much sifting and testing by practical experience, before being universally adopted, as theoretic reforms of political constitutions.

Robert Hall was himself, it is well known, of a feeble organization. Bold in speculation, because there habituated to conquest, he was yet backward in all that required practical energy and action. Hence it was, possibly, in part, that he, unconsciously to himself, but unduly and improperly, disliked submitting his principles in regard to our distinguishing ordinance, to the sterner test of making them a term of visible Church Membership, and sought a more "easy and rapid way" by which Baptist sentiments, like "scientific speculations," should brilliantly mount, as rockets, at once to their perihelion, though carrying with them the materials of explosion and downfall. We wish rather to see our principles, like a star, in some remote portion of the heavens, which, though it less attract the momentary gaze of the curious, shines calmly, quietly and eternally above, guiding the far-off mariners, one after another, in their heavenly voyage over the stormy deep.

Every conceivable motion of mind has its corresponding motion of the body; every principle, its legitimate expression in action. It may be called party spirit, or anything else, but that spirit, which impels a man to act out a principle boldly to all its legitimate results, to remove it from the airy region of theory and speculation to the *terra firma* of practice, is one of the most noble and useful dispositions that can actuate any man. There is nothing more dangerous to the cause of truth in general, as there is nothing more perilous to the character of an individual, than to hold opinions speculatively, without reducing them to practice. The most decisive test of truth and error is, that the former is capable of being acted out to all its legitimate consequences, and can never lead the party doing so astray; while the other, the further it is pursued, conducts only to the more complicated and gross inconsistencies. If that shall be called a party spirit, which induces our Churches, as such, to make use of their influence, and engage actively in spreading, (in connection with other truths,) Believers' Baptism; which induces them to refuse being trammelled by subjection, even for an hour, to any compromise that shall tie their tongues, or prevent them from using the whole weight of their influence on this subject, just as earnestly as their consciences bid; such a spirit is right and proper none the less. But our Churches, as such, must bind themselves not to meddle with the subject of Baptism, or make use of an iota of their influence, as an organization in favor of it, according to the plan of Robert Hall. Baptist individuals, but not

Baptist Churches, is the beau ideal of Mixed Communionism. But how it ever can be a stroke of policy in favor of Baptism, for such powerful social organizations, as the Churches of Christ, to resolve not to favour or propagate it, is not easily perceived. Enough this, in regard to the charge of party spirit.

5. In regard to what Robert Hall says, as to the rapid extension of scientific truths compared with religious, and which he attributes to " the absence of combination, in there being no class of men closely united, who have an interest, real or imaginary, in obstructing their progress " —it is true that these combinations to spread particular opinions, may seem for a moment to confirm those engaged in spreading them, and so render them more difficult of conviction. But eventually, there is no way so certain to let all the world see that an error is an error, and a truth is a truth, as to bring it to the light. Free discussion must lead ultimately to the establishment of truth; but there will never be any discussion at all, when all the arguing is on one side, and no party thinks it worth while to oppose. Combination on the one side will be balanced by combinations on the other, and Truth will eventually turn the scale; for it will be sure to win the greatest number of adherents, and the most important combinations. It is chiefly by means of these very "*combinations,*" that what moral truth we have, is spread as widely and rapidly as it is, and thus forms the basis of advancement to higher degrees of light and knowledge. The more "easy and rapid extension" of scientific than moral truth, to any degree that such is the fact, may therefore be traced to more natural causes, than the absence of a class of men to oppose progress of the former.

To some of the causes we will advert:

Scientific truth requires only a lower and more generally diffused class of mind and knowledge to be appreciated, and is capable of a more exact and obvious demonstration. It needs only correct *intellectual* perceptions; and is, by the aid of these, more easily reducible to indisputable facts. The latter requires, *in addition to the above*, correct moral perceptions, possessed and cultivated only by the few. Hence, as there are here more sources of error, the progress of this kind of truth must be slower, to be safe.

6. It is proper to remark, however, that the chief difference, as to rapidity of adoption, is not between *scientific* truth and *moral,* but between scientific or *speculative* truth and *practical*. It is not so difficult to spread moral and religious *opinions* as *practices*. That opinions do eventually show themselves in action is unquestionable, but not immediately; often very slowly. Account for it as we may, the fact is certain, that it is easier to change twenty of the current opinions of a people, than to reform one prevailing habit. One popular preacher, one book full of curious speculations on matters of religion, will win thousands of theoretical converts. Religious *opinions* ebb and flow like a tide, or like a current at sea, which, sweeping with an unseen and incalculable force, bears the mightiest navy, with its ponderous burdens, easily and smoothly on its surface. But while it is not difficult for a popular preacher to change a whole congregation from one set of *views* to another,—to alter a custom, whether it be the posture of the congregation in prayer or at the Lord's Supper, to change the order of services, to introduce or exclude an organ from the choir, or a gown from the pulpit, is often an occasion of schism or revolution.

7. To apply now these remarks to our present case. If

we *merely* wished to change the speculative *opinions* of the Christian world upon the subject of Baptism, to make them believe that nigh two thousand years ago, Baptism was administered only on a profession of faith, and always by immersion, then, in certain circumstances, Robert Hall's plan would be the most "politic" way to revive the obsolete opinion.* Let a few influential and popular preachers introduce it occasionally into their sermons, never controvert, but exhibit perhaps a vivid picture of Christ descending into the plastic tide, the swelling water of the sacred stream yielding to Him a liquid and emblematic grave. The scene of Phillip baptizing the Eunuch might even be dwelt on; and the preacher occasionally declare, that he would even baptize those who wished it in the same way; but that whatever might be their differences of opinion or practice, the whole subject of Baptism was one of indifference, a non-essential; and therefore its performance in any way, or its total neglect, made not the least difference as to all the privileges of full Church Membership or Ministry. Few would question, and none would oppose, what practically affected them so little, and without opposition or discussion, a verdict might in time be obtained in favor of this speculation from any and every congregation. If few had sufficient knowledge to assent, fewer still would have inclination to deny; so long as it was conceded that either sprinkling or immersion were enough to admit to full Church Membership, and they were permitted to infer, that whichever was most customary and convenient should now be followed, to avert controversy.

8. But if the object proposed be, to change the *practice*

---

* In fact, to this extent our views are already received by men of science. Any standard work on Christian Antiquities, Church History or Encyclopædia, will show this. J. N. B.

of Christians in regard to Baptism, then the more proper, candid and successful mode will be, not to profess neutrality and indifference, but openly to form our Churches upon the basis of their being distinctly Baptist, and the members pledged to uphold and spread, and act up to Baptist sentiments. *Action alone produces action.* It alone produces a deep conviction of the sincerity and earnestness of those who undertake any reform, as well as of the importance of the reformation itself.

The preacher who would produce a practical alteration upon the subject of Baptism, must come like a second John the Baptist, not with an effeminate softness and timidity, but with a certain roughness and uncompromising sternness to those who are indifferent to what they know or might know, if they would, to be the will of God. He must be prepared to stand aloof from the sympathies of the world, and even of the religious world. He must tell men, that the time for controversy on such a subject is past; that it is really a very plain matter for him who takes the Bible alone for his guide; that, prejudice apart, few things can be more clear; that when God has called a man's attention to the subject, real doubts can alone remain, either from regarding the opinions of Christians as a more authoritative guide than the New Testament, or from not having examined the matter carefully, and in an unprejudiced manner; either of which, in regard to Baptism, cannot be presumed to be a matter of indifference, even as to visible Church Membership. He must tell them that this is not a mere speculation, but a practical matter, one that requires action, reformation; that infant sprinkling is not Christian Baptism; that those who have received no more than this, have never been "buried with Christ by Baptism;" and that however excellent their piety may be in other respects, they are in fact living unbaptized.

He must assure not only Christian individuals, but Churches, that it is *their* duty as such,—even as bodies to whom the ordinances of Christ's house are solemnly given in charge,—to make use of their influence not as individuals alone, but as *organizations*, as Churches, to promote this reformation. He should propose to form Churches upon the primitive basis, each individual being prepared to exert his active influence and example, in favor of restoring Baptism to the position, in every respect, which it originally occupied.

9. The question at issue between Robert Hall and ourselves in this chapter is, in substance, neither more nor less than this; whether the former or the latter of these preachers would be the more successful in " restoring the obsolete practice " of Believers' Baptism? Who sees not that indifferentism in a reformer, never yet roused the sluggish and torpid mind into action. If the question were to be settled by a mere intellectual acquiescence in a metaphysical truth, the plan of the first preacher might succeed, in those few cases where the mind was already sufficiently interested to pursue the investigation. But where most are too indifferent to examine; and where the course of duty will often be contrary to relatives and friends, to the religious as well as the sinful world; and will perhaps awaken hostility and persecution, as the practice of Believers' Baptism has often done; then one would suppose, that a decided and constant course in the Church, would be most likely to give firmness to the timid and resolution to the wavering. In such case the sympathy of a Church, united and warmly interested for their sufferings, would strengthen them, and the example of breth-

ren who have gone through the same struggle, would decide them in favor of action. It is an unquestionable fact, and one that the present general decline of Infant Baptism in Pedobaptist Churches abundantly proves, that it is not so much want of light, but the want of a proper feeling of the importance of living up to the light they have, that makes a very large proportion of our brethren in Christ live without true Baptism; and were they only to step forward and pursue a decided course, according to their convictions upon this point, it would occasion such inquiry, that even the most indifferent would be awakened, and the most doubtful see it clearly. To accomplish this, the importance of personal action must be enforced.

We have admitted the evil of a *mere* party spirit. But the power of organized party action is immense, and where only used to produce truth, proper; and not only proper, but imperatively demanded. It is the great fulcrum by which a truth, downpressed and crushed by the masses, is elevated by its few friends to its just level. Surely every member of a visible Church of Christ is specially bound to throw the weight, not merely of his individual, but of all the social influence he possesses from the organization of the Christian Church, in favor of an ordinance, especially committed to the care and maintenance of the Churches.

The peculiar power of a social organization arises from two sources. First, that it is truth *in action*, not in theory; an opinion reduced to practice, not resting in vague, untested speculations. Second, from the *combination* of effort and influence on one point, many persons acting in concert. It is from the first of these causes, that one drunkard signing the pledge, will often do more to convince the enemies of Temperance, than a hundred lectures or arguments. It is from the second that in a Temperance Society each member strengthens the other.

11. This two-fold power of social organization is sanctioned in its proper use, and was indeed originally applied by Divine inspiration in the formation of Christian Churches. Baptism is the peculiar pledge to a Christian life, administered by the Divine command and sealed by the Holy Spirit. Herein is one great source of power in every Christian Church, *i. e.* the moral force which it possesses as a social organization, over and above the strength of the individuals; the whole bound together and actuated as one living body, by the indwelling presence of the Holy Ghost. The nature of our inquiry at the present moment precludes us from asking if it be *right* for such a body as this, to whom and to whom alone on earth the ordinances of the Gospel are committed, to enter into such a compact of indifference in regard to one of these, that "the appellation of Baptist shall not be so properly applicable to Churches as to individuals." But strange to say, the question we have to settle is, whether such withdrawal of its whole social influence by the only body to which the support of these ordinances is committed, is not "*politic*," as the most effectual means of "restoring the obsolete practice" of Believers' Baptism. This is the very point which Robert Hall labors throughout the whole of this section to prove.

12. It is indeed singular at times, to see the shifts to which the author is driven, in some of his attempts to support this position. For example, he paints in very strong language the unfair attacks of other denominations upon us, and speaks of "the prejudice displayed by that class of Christians, to whom we make the nearest approach," but attributes all this to the want of Open Com-

munion. He complains, that "*a disposition to fair and liberal concession on the point at issue, is almost confined* to the members of Established Churches;" but that " our dissenting brethren are displeased with these concessions, deny there is any proof that immersion was ever used in primitive times, and speak of the extension of baptism to infants with as much confidence, as though it were among the plainest and most undeniable dictates of Revelation." "To such a height," he proceeds, " has this animosity been carried, that there are not wanting persons who seem anxious to revive the recollection of Munster, and by republishing the narrative of the enormities perpetrated there, under the title of the History of the Baptists, to implicate us in the infamy and guilt of those transactions. While we must reprobate such a spirit, we are compelled to acknowledge, that the practice of Exclusive Communion is admirably adapted to excite it in minds of a certain order."*

This picture is drawn, not by us, but by the champion of Mixed Communion. We could not have drawn it. But what is the remedy he proposes for this slander, by which he complains that our Churches are assailed? To put all the power of our Churches into the hands of those who assail us. Only let these persons commune, and vote, and manage everything their own way, and then we shall see the obsolete practice of Believers' Baptism restored! This would surely be like giving the lamb to the wolf to suckle, that she may learn not to devour it.

13. But it is needless to spend time on such theories, while facts invite our attention. The point to be ascertained, is, which practice is most favorable to the spread

---

* Works, vol. 1, p. 356.

of Baptist sentiments,—open or strict Communion; the plan adopted in this country or that proposed by Robert Hall?

14. If we should decide this question by the comparative increase of the Baptist denomination in Great Britain, where Mixed Communion generally prevails, and in this country, where the opposite practice is almost universal, we shall find such facts as the following: There are 982,101 members of Baptist Churches in the United States to 148,179 in Great Britain, or nearly seven to one. Or if we compare the number of Churches, we find in the United States 14,078, in Great Britain 1,881. If we contrast the number of ordained Ministers, we find in the United States 8,826, in Great Britain 1,382.*

This comparison of present numbers appears to us a fair test. The rise of the Baptists as a denomination, in England and in this country, was at about the same time, under circumstances even much more favorable to their progress in the old than in the new country. On the one hand it is true, that the more free toleration of religious opinions, and the absence of an Established Church, might seem most favourable to their increase in this country; but on the other, the comparative smallness of the population, until within a few years, the difficulty of changing the sentiments of a nation scattered remotely, the poverty of a young people, all make it a matter of surprise that Baptist sentiments should have spread as they have. Under God, this has originated in their assuming an independent and uncompromising basis;—in their Churches being formed, not on Robert Hall's plan of Mixed Membership, but upon that derived from the Apostolic practice, of

---

* The figures are taken from the Baptist Almanac for 1849.

making Baptism a prerequisite to membership in their Churches.

It might at least have been expected that, owing to the disadvantages of the Baptists of this country above alluded to, that our denomination, here at least, would have been far behind it in England, in point of Ministerial education. The reverse however is the fact. Such is the effect of habits of self-reliance and independent energy, fostered, in part at least, by the principles upon which the denomination in this country has acted in regard to their Church fellowship, that instead of five Colleges, with seventy-eight students, which they have in Great Britain, there are in the United States fifteen Colleges, with 1,409 students, and seven Theological Institutions, with 152 students.

If we compare the active piety of the Baptists of England and of the United States; while owing to the comparative poverty of a new country, the greater demands for the supply of destitute sections at home, and other causes, American contributions for Foreign Missions are not all that might otherwise have been expected from our large number of members; yet in active piety and benevolence, fairly computed, they perhaps hardly come behind any denomination in any country. That inertness, which is the characteristic symptom and ultimate destruction of all bigotry and narrowness, certainly fails to show itself. Let the traveller go into the most remote settlements of the far West, and as he passes along, he will every now and then meet with a Baptist house of worship. It may be of rude construction, a log hut perhaps, but this is as good as the surrounding houses. Let him go into the cities of the New Continent, and he will find costly houses of worship, which in point of comfort, neatness, architectural beauty, the respectability of the worshipers, and excellence of the arrangements, will compare favourably with those of our denomination in the older and wealthier cities of the Mother Country.

15. If now we consider the hold which Baptist sentiments have taken upon the mind of the public at large in this country, even upon other denominations of religion; we shall find the most striking proof of the fallacy of Robert Hall's opinion, that it is only by mixing in all Church relations with Pedobaptists, that our sentiments would ever find their way to their hearts, or even attract their attention. The practice of immersion in the Methodist Church has become quite common. The disuse of Infant Baptism by Presbyterian and Congregational members is now so general, and the decline of it every year becoming so much more rapid, that it is evident, the system is fast losing its hold upon the faith of those denominations. In the Episcopal Church in Kentucky, a section of country where our mode of Baptism prevails extensively, the Bishop of the Diocese has publicly acknowledged immersion to have been universal (*semper, ubique, et ab omnibus*) in the earlier ages of Christianity, and has strongly urged a return to that practice.

Indeed, there is hardly a denomination in the United States, that has not been powerfully impressed by Baptist sentiments. Even the vagrant Mormons have found it politic to institute a counterfeit Baptism like ours. If we look forward to the future, there appears every probability of a very general, if not universal spread of our views of this ordinance, both as to its mode and subjects. Under God, this seems to have been brought about by the decided stand taken by the denomination. To have been less uncompromising, would have diminished the importance and prevalence of Baptist sentiments.

The question to be discussed in this chapter, was as to *Policy alone;*—which was the most successful method of reviving the true but obsolete view of Baptism, which is characteristic of our denomination? We conceive that no doubt upon this subject can rest on any mind.

CHAPTER VII.

REVIEW OF PART III.

1. Review of Robert Hall's first argument. 2. Of the second. 3. Of the third. 4. Of the fourth. 5. Of the fifth. 6. Of the sixth. 7. Of Mr. Hall's 'leading principle.' 8. Mr. Hall's leading position clearly traceable back to the fundamental error of the Papacy. 9. Counsels of Sir James Mackintosh to Robert Hall.

1. WE have thus examined, argument by argument, all that has been brought against our practice in regard to the Lord's Supper by the ablest of our opponents. We have endeavored to omit no idea advanced by him, that could affect the conclusion. If we mistake not, every candid reader will perceive, that his arguments utterly fail to prove anything against our principles in regard to that ordinance. Indeed, these very arguments are many of them capable of being turned with the greatest force against his own positions.

He urged *the obligations of brotherly love, as a reason for Free Communion.* We have shown that the word Communion may be used either literally or figuratively; that literally we do hold Christian Communion with all whom we consider Christians, of whatever denomination. But it is obvious, that no argument can be derived from the general obligations of brotherly love, to extend the symbols of Membership in a particular Church, to those to whom the relations symbolized do not apply. On the contrary, Christian faithfulness and candor, indeed a common regard for truth, would seem to dictate an opposite course. In fact, the whole of this argument derives its plausibility from an ambiguous use of the term Communion.

2. He urged the obligation, to receive into the Membership of our Churches all who give credible evidence of piety, *from the express injunction of Scripture, to tolerate those errors not inconsistent with salvation*, on the ground that Christ had received those who held them. We have shown, that the injunction to toleration in question, was expressly based on *two* conditions, first, that they should be such persons as Christ has received; and secondly, living in compliance with all the revealed will of God, in regard to the points as to which special forbearance is urged. Every inference drawn from such passages, must be adverse to receiving into the full membership of our own Churches, those persons, who are avowedly living in the neglect of so conspicuous and plain a part of the revealed will of God, in regard to Church Membership, as Baptism.

3. He argued that *Pedobaptists being a part of the true Church, their exclusion was on that account unlawful.* We have shown that there is here an ambiguous use of the term *Church*. It is, indeed, as he rightly allows, used in two senses; either to denote the whole family of the redeemed, in heaven and on earth, which is a *spiritual* body, or particular organizations of Christians, which are *visible* bodies. From membership in the Invisible Church, we do not, by thought, word or deed, exclude any Christians. This, however, is quite distinct from inviting all such to membership in our particular Church, which is a local matter. It is indeed impossible, in the very nature of things, that a visible Church should not embrace at least *some* things

in the terms of its membership, not embraced in those of the Invisible Church. A credible and visible profession of faith must belong to the former. This being essentially distinct from that faith, which alone is essential to membership in the Invisible Church, makes the terms of membership, in the two bodies, necessarily different. Hence it follows, that the whole of this argument, being founded on an ambiguous use of the word Church, or rather on confounding the terms of membership in two distinct bodies, falls to the ground.

4. He argued, that the exclusion of Pedobaptists from the Lord's Table, could be considered *only as a punishment*, as tantamount to excommunication. Here again we detect a fallacy in principle, as well as in the use of terms. We have shown, that by not inviting those who are not members of our Churches, to participate *with us* in the symbols of such membership, we do not exclude them from participating, and least of all do we excommunicate persons who never belonged to our body. That the non-extension of this invitation is not *intended* as a punishment, and has no more right to be considered such; than the non-extension of an invitation by every Jew to every other, to participate with him in the Passover; or, than the course of the Methodists in regard to their Love Feasts; or, than the course of all other denominations, in not inviting to their Church Membership those Christians who are unwilling to comply with their articles of Covenant.

5. He urged *the impossibility of reducing the practice of Strict Communion to any general principle.* We have shown that it is reducible to the very simple and obvious principle, that our "Occasional Communion," or participation at the same table, should be governed by the same rules as our Church Membership. We further showed

that the general p'inciple on which Mixed Church Membership and Communion are together based, *i. e.* that the visible Churches ought to tolerate all " those diversities of opinion which are not inconsistent with salvation," or that the " Visible Church differs from the Invisible *only* as a part differs from the whole," and consequently, that the terms of admission to the one were properly the same as those of admission to the other, overlooked and denied the obvious fact, that every visible Church must, in the nature of things, have some visible profession of Christianity among the prerequisites to its membership; and that any other plan is contrary to the principles of all Christians, of all ages and of all climes, and one impossible to be acted upon.

6. He urged *the impolicy of Strict Communion,* contending that it retarded the progress of Baptist views and practices. In opposition to this, we have shown that whatever may be the case with mere airy and impracticable speculations, that the energies of voluntary organizations are among the most powerful means by which the erroneous practices of society are reformed and obsolete virtues revived; that to the visible Churches of Christ the custody of the ordinances is specially committed, and consequently the duty of using their energies and influence to restore them to their primitive position and lustre. We have shown what would naturally be the effect of such organizations as Christian Churches using their energies to reform the abuses of the ordinance of baptism, and to revive the primitive method of its observance. We have also shown, from the comparative progress of the denomination, not only in numbers, but in everything which evinces true denominational prosperity, that where the results of Mixed Communion and our own practice are

capable of being fairly compared, the results show, as clearly as statistics on the largest scale can show anything, that the plan of Mixed Communion palsies the strength, and prevents the growth of our denomination, and even retards, as in Great Britain, the spread of our principles.

The plan which we follow is avowedly the primitive plan. It is in all respects consistent for ourselves, respectful to our opponents, and best calculated to subserve the cause of truth; by throwing open our principles in regard to Baptism, without reserve, to the gaze and scrutiny of the whole Christian world. By such means they would the sooner be discarded if they were erroneous; and by these means, being confident of their truth, we feel sure they will be most rapidly extended.

7. With regard, therefore, to that system for which Robert Hall contended, as a whole, (and especially what he calls his "leading position," *i. e.* that " no Church has a right to establish terms of Communion [in the Lord's Supper] that are not terms of salvation,") whether this be considered as a theory or a rule of practice, a divine command or a human expedient, it is novel, visionary, and quite unsatisfactory. While we must admire the sincerity and ability of the author, we cannot hesitate in pronouncing the theory he proposes a sophism. The plan, if it were applicable to *our* denomination, would equally require the most complete revolution in all others; but as yet no other body of Christians has for a moment thought of adopting it. That it is based upon an error we think incontrovertible. At the same time, whether we consider the exalted sentiments to which it appeals, or the brilliancy and piety with which it is maintained, it must be pronounced the most enchanting of all visions that are mere visions. The practical Christian, when he remem-

bers that he is at present placed at an appointed post of duty and of usefulness in the militant, and not the triumphant portion of the Church, is forced to lay these terms aside, as incompatible with the orders of the great Captain of our salvation; as sublime, but unsuited to the present state; as affording elevated contemplations, too elevated to be realized on earth; or, to express ourselves as briefly as possible, he is forced to regard the whole scheme as a *splendid fallacy.*

8. All the most pious and elevated of mankind have, indeed, sighed over the divisions of Christians, longed to see the whole family of believers more fully and completely united; and some, perhaps, have formed projects for the accomplishment of so desirable an object. Their visions, however, have generally subsided into an anticipation of that period when in a future state these most elevated aspirations would be fully satisfied. But the attempt too suddenly to realize these hopes on earth, has led most who have attempted it, to seek some shorter road than that appointed by God, and to overlook and overleap barriers which He has planted. Who shall tell how much all true unity has been defeated thus far, by the errors of the very persons who have made the greatest efforts to promote it? Anciently, it was sought to be attained by that most splendid of fictions, as it lay in the visions of the early Fathers, a visible Catholic or Universal Church. And yet to this all the most conspicuous features of the Popish system are easily traceable. It would not be difficult to show that the fallacy of the Romish plan for uniting all the members of the Invisible Church in one Visible Communion, is traceable to the same original source as that of the more modern one of Robert Hall, *i. e., confounding the terms of invisible and visible Church*

Membership. They are, indeed, both counterparts of the same error. The extremely opposite tendency which they exhibit practically, arises thus. The ancient theory alters the terms of Invisible Church membership, to make them correspond with those of the Visible. The system of Robert Hall, commencing at the opposite point, and with true views of the only prerequisites of membership in the Invisible Church, alters the terms of Visible membership, to make them coincide with those of the Invisible.

9. It is dangerous for any man to live too exclusively in the world of imagination. "Nothing," says Sir James Mackintosh, in one of his letters to Robert Hall, " is so difficult as to decide, how much ideal models ought to b combined with experience ; how much of the future should be let into the present, in the progress of the human mind, to ennoble and purify, without raising us above the sphere of our usefulness." A man's writings reflect his own character. Nor can we close this section of our work better, than by quoting, for the study of those whose tendency is to frame ideal churches, or ideal worlds, the judicious remarks made to this great author himself in regard to the tendencies of his noble mind, by perhaps the only human being who knew him through life, with the ability rightly to estimate his exalted character.

"I exhort you, my most worthy friend," he says, "to check your best propensities, for the sake of attaining their object. You cannot live *for* men, without living *with* them. Serve God then by the active service of men. Contemplate more the good you *can* do, than the evil you can only lament. Allow yourself to see the loveliness of virtue amid all its imperfections ; and employ your moral imagination not so much by bringing it into contrast with the model of ideal perfection, as in gently blending some of the fainter colors of the latter, with the brighter hues of real experienced excellence; thus heightening the beauty instead of broadening the shade, which must surround us, till we awaken from this dream in other spheres of existence."*

* Robert Hall's Works, Vol. 3, p. 51.

PART IV.

THE ARGUMENTS OF REV. BAPTIST W. NOEL ON FREE COMMUNION, CONSIDERED.

INTRODUCTORY.

REASONS FOR REVIEWING MR. NOEL'S REMARKS.

1. Recent appearance of his book on Baptism, and its claims to general regard. 2. Shortness of the section on Communion. 3. Not many new ideas, but in general follows Mr. Hall. 4. Yet some differences in method and spirit. 5. Analysis of his remarks.

1. SINCE the preceding pages were completed, the work of the Hon. and Rev. Baptist W. Noel, on Christian Baptism, has been published in this country. This respected Author, and admirable Christian, devotes the second Section of Chapter V. of his volume, to the discussion of "Free Communion," arriving at a conclusion exactly opposite to that to which we have been led. The deserved reputation of Mr. Noel; the extent to which his opinions will be circulated; the earnest Christian spirit which guides his pen; and above all, the publication of these sentiments, in connexion with his manly and decided views on Baptism, make it appropriate to add a few remarks, showing how far the principles we have laid down apply to his arguments.

2. The observations of Mr. Noel, on the subject of Communion, do not occupy a twentieth of the entire work, and are comprised in less than fifteen pages—*i. e.*, pp. 287—301 of the Harpers' edition. To this edition, for convenience, the pages being the same as in those of Mr. Colby and Mr. Fletcher, reference will be made in the following remarks.

3. No person, who has studied Robert Hall's writings on this subject, will find in the pages of Mr. Noel many new ideas or illustrations. He makes the same concessions, urges the same arguments, and arrives at the same conclusions, even on points in regard to which open Communionists disagree among themselves. Consequently, his section on Communion has far less the air of his own individual thinking, than any other part of his work. The problem of Christian Baptism, he has evidently wrought out for himself; he has "not received it of man." But in his views on Communion, he has followed others.

4. In one or two respects there is a difference. We see less of that lucid arrangement of ideas, which so eminently characterizes Robert Hall, and makes his arguments perspicuous, forcible, and easy to be weighed. On this account, it is a more arduous task to reply to Mr. Noel in any consecutive order. The observation which Mr. Hall made, as to the difficulty of answering Mr. Kinghorn, is in no small degree applicable here. "The perpetual recurrence of the same matter, the paucity of distinct and intelligible topics of argument, together with an obvious want of coherence and of dependence of one part upon another, render it difficult to impart that order and continuity to a reply, in the absence of which, argumentative discussions are insufferably tedious."

But, on the other hand, the spirit in which Mr. Noel writes, is certainly less that of an intellectual combatant, and more eminently that of an earnest follower of Christ, than Robert Hall's. He gives the reasons which have induced him to embrace lately acquired knowledge of Christian truth, so far as he has received it, prayerfully and affectionately. It is this which imparts the chief interest to our Author's character, and to his views on all subjects.

5. In the pages we are now reviewing, Mr. Noel *first* states, (p. 287), what he conceives to be the question at issue, between the advocates of Free Communion and those Baptists, who hold the same views in regard to the rightful priority of Baptism to the Lord's Supper, which all other Christians entertain. He then advances two arguments in favor of his own opinions; one from the nature of things, the other from Scripture. (pp. 288—290.) The remainder of the Chapter is devoted to the consideration of arguments, sometimes used on the other side. (pp. 290 to 301). This last part occupies eleven out of the fifteen pages, and exhibits but little system.

We will follow our Author, as nearly as possible, in his manner of treating the subject.

CHAPTER I.

MR. NOEL'S STATEMENT OF THE QUESTION.

1. In this he agrees with Robert Hall—Regards Pedobaptists as unbaptized, pleads for their admission as such. 2. Tendencies of this course—Mr. Noel's inconsistency. 3. Concedes too much to the sincerity with which Pedobaptism is upheld. 4. Yet in effect yields the very point at issue.

1. *As to his Statement of the Question.* In this he precisely concurs with Robert Hall, and thus narrows the point at issue. Pedobaptists seem usually to suppose, that where persons *sincerely think* they have been baptized, it is the same as though they had been. On the contrary, our Author saves much trouble here by admitting, (p. 287) " Like the strict Baptists, I believe, each person, who has been merely sprinkled in infancy is unbaptized, because the external act of Baptism is immersion, and that act is meant to be a profession of repentance and faith in the Lord Jesus Christ. The person sprinkled in infancy has neither been immersed, nor has he made, through his reception of the sprinkled water, any profession whatever, of discipleship; he is therefore wholly unbaptized; and it is regarding him simply as an unbaptized believer, that I advocate his right to a place at the Lord's Table, in a Baptist Church."

2. His argument, therefore, would lead to the extinction of *all* Baptism, as a term of Church fellowship or Communion, even in what he still, (unlike Robert Hall,) would

call a "Baptist Church." Indeed, at the close of his remarks, (p. 301,) he appears to deny the right, to require "other terms of Communion than such as are terms of salvation, and to consider this the more brotherly course, demanded by the plain precepts of Scripture." Unless he were to suppose Baptism essential to salvation, we do not see, how Churches formed on such principles, could be in any sense "Baptist." But it is not our duty to reconcile these statements, only impartially to record them. Churches formed throughout the whole Christian world on such a basis, would contain at present so vast a numerical majority of Pedobaptists, that it would be absurd and arrogant in us to claim them.

3. On page 288, however, Mr. Noel concedes too much in regard to the spirit in which Pedobaptism is upheld by those who practise it; and as the same sentiments are even more strictly implied and asserted on another page, we notice it at once.

He is indeed correct, in saying of all pious persons, that they are the "servants, soldiers and friends" of the Lord Jesus Christ, and as to everything beside Baptism, it may also be the case, that they "copy his example and obey his precepts," (p. 288); but this certainly is not true in regard to that ordinance, according to the whole tenor of Mr. Noel's work. In this respect they certainly do *not* "copy the example" of their Saviour, and they certainly *do* disobey his precepts; some by severing the ordinance from the profession of faith, some by substituting sprinkling for immersion, and some, like John Joseph Gurney, by treating all Baptism with open and utter neglect. Yet, on page 294, Mr. Noel carries his language so far, as to declare, that these very persons (he probably has special reference to Pedobaptists) are admitted by the Churches which practise Free Communion, on the ground that they are "believers *who keep the commands of Christ, honor Baptism, and believe that they have been baptized.*" Does a Quaker honor Baptism and believe that he has been baptized? Or, with what consistency can Mr. Noel say, that he admits a Pedobaptist to the Lord's Table, "because he honors Baptism?"

4. Indeed, unconsciously to himself, he shifts his whole statement of the question, or else concedes the very point at issue, when he says, "If indeed to admit him [a Christian] to the Table, were to dispense with the command of Christ, and to sanction the neglect of Baptism, he must not be admitted; but this cannot be, *because* he is admitted by the Churches who practise Free Communion, on the ground that he is a believer "who keeps the commands of Christ, honors Baptism, and believes that he has been baptized."

CHAPTER II.

MR. NOEL'S ARGUMENTS CONSIDERED.

I. *Argument from the nature of things.* 1. Error in illustration. 2. Confounds the Visible Church with the Invisible. 3. Assumes identity of qualifications. 4. Pedobaptists are not disowned as brethren, but as unbaptized. 5. The Lord's Supper belongs to visible churches. 6. The question resolves itself into this, Is it the duty of Churches, *as such*, to uphold Christian Baptism?

II. *Arguments from the Scriptures.* 1. The main reliance here. 2. (*a.*) John 13: 35, and 17: 20, considered. 3. Nature of Christian union. 4. On whom rests the blame of breaking the Visible Church fellowship. 5. (*b.*) Rom. 14: 1—7, and 15: 7, considered. 6. Mistakes and their consequences. 7. The proper grounds of Church toleration. 8. The proper grounds of exclusion. Gal. 5: 12, 1 Cor. 5: 11—13, Rom. 16: 17, 2 Thess. 3: 14, compared with v. 6. 9. Result—There are other terms of communion than such as are terms of salvation. 10. Practical importance of this principle. 11. A fundamental distinction explained. 12. (*c.*) Mr. Noel's concessions;—1. Of an instituted connection between Baptism and the Lord's Supper. 2. Of the close Scriptural connection between Regeneration and Baptism.

We now proceed to consider the Arguments by which our Author sustains his position. They are two; first, from the Nature of Things; and secondly, from Scripture.

I. The reason for Free Communion drawn *from the Nature of Things.* "It is according to nature and grace too, that the sheep of the same flock, under the same shepherd, should walk together, and feed together in the same pasture," (p. 288). It is seldom safe to argue very closely from an illustration. If it were allowable here, we should reply, that in precisely the same sense, in which all evangelical Christians are sheep of the same flock, and under the same shepherd, they *do* feed in the same pasture. Do not all the various evangelical denominations of Christians feed upon the same spiritual food, upon the same great truths of the Bible? Is not Christ the one shepherd of all? What does our Author mean, when he speaks of sheep of the same flock?—Members of one Church? But the term Church, in Scripture, is used in two senses;—sometimes for the One Universal Church, which is invisible; sometimes for any single congregation of professed Christians, in the habit of assembling for worship, and for the maintenance of Christian ordinances, as the Church at Antioch, Smyrna, or Rome. Mr. Noel does not mean to say, that all Christians are, or ought to be, members of the same flock or Church in this latter sense, nor that they ought to be all united under one earthly pastor. But where then is the value of his illustration? What would he show by it? Ordinances belong clearly to visible Churches, not to the One Invisible Church of all Earth and Heaven. Christians are not, and are not intended to be all of the same visible Church or flock. They are under different earthly shepherds, and this arrangement is of God and not of man. Each Church is an independent body; and according to our Author it would seem (p. 295) that each "Church must be the ultimate judge of the qualifications of all who seek communion with it."

2. The illustration, we believe, would rather militate against our author's views than in favor of them, unless it should be first proved, that the terms of Invisible and of Visible church membership are necessarily *the same*, so that the qualifications which are sufficient to admit us to the former, entitle us without *anything further whatever* to the latter. This he quietly takes for granted without the

least warrant, and contrary to all just views; for while the *disposition* to confess Christ may be and is essential to true piety, and to invisible membership; the *actual confession* of Christ, which in some way must be a prerequisite to visible church membership, never can be essential to membership in the Invisible Church, since properly it can only take place after true piety. To assume, therefore, that membership in the Invisible Church alone, necessarily implies a perfect title to all the peculiar privileges of each Visible Church is quite unwarrantable and erroneous.

3. And yet Mr. Noel accusingly asks, (p. 288,) "Why ought not Baptists to own them [evangelical Pedobaptists] as brethren? All who are the servants of Christ ought to be owned as such. If he honors and loves them, it is not his will that their fellow-servants should dishonor them. God has made them His children by adoption and grace, and cannot be pleased to see that while they are owned by Him, they are disowned by their brethren."

4. The answer to such an accusation is obvious. We do not disown them as Christian brethren. We do not own them as *Baptists*. They do not even wish to be so considered. All Christians we are willing to own "*as such*," that is, as Christians, but not as members of Baptist Churches.

5. The Lord's Supper is *not* only the symbol of our Communion with Christ, or with Christians as such, but also of *Visible Church fellowship*, among those who thus unite, for as we have said, this being a visible ordinance belongs to visible Churches as such, and not to the Universal Church. If this were not so, we ought like the Roman Catholics to celebrate Communion Service, (*i. e.* Mass) with departed saints.

But if the Lord's Supper is an ordinance belonging to

visible Churches as such—so is the other great ordinance, Baptism. Hence it must follow that to the Visible Churches of Christ in that capacity, is specially entrusted the duty of upholding Baptism in its primitive mode and position. If they neglect, who shall preserve it?

6. And the question of Communion really resolves itself into this, whether it is the duty of the Churches of Christ *as such* to uphold baptism. If Pedobaptists are to be admitted to perfect membership; if there is to be no distinction between their churches and ours, if their ministers are to be ordained over Baptist Churches, and Baptist Ministers over theirs, as it may happen; in fine, if, as Robert Hall contended, " the mixture of Baptists and Pedobaptists in Christian societies should be such that the appellation of Baptist might be found not so properly applicable to Churches as to individuals," then we submit that Baptism would thereby be declared not to be an ordinance belonging to the Visible Churches at all. Quakers or Pedobaptists might be the only officers to administer it. In fact, it would be obviously improper that it should be performed *in the Church* in any case, as all the Church, often a majority of the members, could not unite in it. But if Christian Baptism is to be driven out of these bodies, where is it to be upheld? If not by their Pastors, by whom can it be administered? The Saviour committed it in charge to his visible Churches, and to *them alone*. If they refuse to celebrate it, it *must become extinct*.

The question is, therefore, really not so much one of Communion, as of Baptism; whether there ought to be Churches in which Baptism is administered; whether the ministers of Christ's visible Churches on earth have any right to practise or to preach upon Baptism. In admitting, (which Mr. Noel does frequently,) that there rightly are and ought to be Baptist Churches; in being, as Mr. Noel declares himself, ready to administer the rite of Baptism, as the Pastor of a visible Church, he virtually overturns Robert Hall's theory. Thus much in regard to the argument drawn from the Nature of Things.

II. We now turn to consider Mr. Noel's appeal to *the Scriptures*. It is on this that he seems mainly to rely, and on this we also are willing to rest the decision of the whole case.

2. (*a.*) He first quotes John xiii. 35, and xvii. 20, passages in which Christ enjoins and prays for the mutual love and union of all his followers. On these texts, he justly remarks, that "their union must be so manifested by brotherly fellowship, that the world may see and be converted by it." (p. 289.)

3. Our first remark is, that the Saviour could not have intended this union for which he prays, to extend so far as to bring all Christians into one Visible Church. If he did, the Roman Catholics are right, and we are all wrong; for this is their boasted Unity. But it has ever proved the most deadly enemy to that union which Christ inculcated. The Apostle established hundreds of distinct visible Churches. The oneness which these injunctions and prayers inculcate, so far as relates to Church fellowship, must be a felt and acknowleged union in the One Invisible Church. Now we are as ready and forward as other denominations, to testify our regard, by all consistent means, for pious Pedobaptists, as members of the Universal Church. We unite with them in prayer, in great moral and religious enterprises as freely as do Methodists, Episcopalians, and Presbyterians of the Old and New School do amongst themselves.

4. But if it should be urged that it would add greatly to

the obvious union and brotherly fellowship of all true Christians, if they were to celebrate together the symbols of visible Church fellowship; then obviously the fault of not doing so must rest with those who by their wrong views of the nature, duties, and sacraments of visible Churches, render such symbols inappropriate. The blame cannot fall upon those who "keep the ordinances as they were delivered." It may also be remarked, that Pedobaptists could certainly conform to our mode of baptism, which they all admit to be valid, and which would do much to settle this difficulty; but we could not adopt their mode, not esteeming it lawful. No Pedobaptist, therefore, while unwilling to make this concession to charity, can, with any show of consistency, adduce these passages against our practice in regard to Communion. Indeed, if all Pedobaptists were but to defer baptism until their children were old enough to judge for themselves, and were to adopt our mode, this source of vexation would die away without any further agitation.

5. (*b.*) From these general passages, Mr. Noel proceeds to those more specific injunctions as to the treatment of our fellow Christians, contained in Rom. 14: 1–7, and 15: 7, "Him that is weak in the faith receive ye," &c. On these, (p. 289,) he argues thus: "If likewise the Pedobaptist has not light enough to throw off the Jewish ordinance of infant circumcision, but must revive it in infant baptism, he is not to be repelled from communion with those to whom God has given more knowledge in this matter." We presume the Author means, that he is not to be repelled *on account* of infant baptism; a question, in regard to which we are saved from the necessity of any discussion; as it is not on that account that we decline receiving Pedobaptists as members of our Churches, but

simply because *they themselves are unbaptized*,—a very different matter.

6. But, argues Mr. Noel, "we are called to receive all Christ's disciples, notwithstanding their errors, as Christ has received us, notwithstanding ours." Rom. 15 : 7. We reply that we do receive them as Christ's disciples, and have for them a warm and sincere *Christian* fellowship. But it is urged, that Paul must be understood here to enjoin the reception of all such persons into a visible *Church* fellowship. Allow this, and we must be willing to receive into the full communion and membership of every Baptist Church, Episcopalians, Quakers and Roman Catholics, members of the Greek Church or other Pedobaptists, with all their various notions of ecclesiastical government, modes of worship, their saints and images, crucifixes and beads, celibate clergy, masses for the dead and prayers to the Virgin. We must tolerate all these things in our Churches, unless we are prepared to assert that there are no true Christians among those who hold them; and we must not inculcate Believers' Baptism in the Church a whit more strenuously than infant baptism, or than any of the above dogmas. They must either all be promoted by us equally, as majorities happen to sway the scale, or all be neutral and forbidden subjects.

7. Still, by whatever the word of God says, we must abide, and Mr. Noel quotes Rom. 14 : 3. "Let not him that eateth not, judge him that eateth, *for God hath received him.*" The great question is, whether this passage teaches that we are bound to receive into our *visible* Churches, every one of those whom Christ has received as members of the *Invisible* Church; to receive them, whatever may be the nature and tendency of their errors, and whatever the results which might ensue from countenancing sys-

tems, subversive of the faith of thousands, though perhaps not excluding from salvation every individual holding them. This, which Mr. Noel seems to think, "demanded by the plain precepts of Scripture," (p. 301,) we do not hesitate to assert, finds in it no countenance whatever, and least of all in the 14th and 15th chapters of Romans. Whoever examines these passages will find that the Apostle Paul proceeds throughout in his argument for the reception of those scrupulous brethren, on the expressed ground, that they were complying with *the whole revealed will of God*, in regard to those matters which occasioned the doubt as to their reception. "One man believeth that he may eat all things, another who is weak, eateth herbs;" but both fulfill all that God *requires* in this matter. "There is nothing unclean in itself," except to him who believes it so. "One man esteemeth one day above another, another man esteemeth every day alike," but neither in any manner violates the revealed will of God. Such was the obvious train of the Apostle's thought. And hence he argued, that since the individual was one whom God had received as a Christian, and who, as to the doubtful point, complied with the whole revealed will of God, and therefore clearly received His approbation in regard to these very matters, he was to be received in the same way by the Church at Rome. Here, therefore, were two conditions on which the Apostle argued for the reception of doubtful persons; first, because Christ has received them into the invisible Church, and secondly, because they have complied with all the requirements of the New Testament, in regard to the questionable point. It is difficult to see, how from such a passage, the admission of persons, who, it is acknowledged, violate one of the conditions, can be "demanded."

8. Such is the amount of the argument from Scripture, as offered by Mr. Noel. At the close of his remarks, (p. 300,) the author does, indeed, introduce other Scriptural considerations, thus. After charging us, (p. 292,) with expelling pious Pedobaptists, he returns (p. 300) to this topic, and thus depicts the "odiousness" of so doing. "For, consider," he says, "the real nature of this exclusion. Those *only* are ordered in the Word of God to be excluded, who are heretical in doctrine, (Gal. 5 : 12,) who are vicious in practice, (1 Cor. 5 : 11, 13,) who are schismatical in temper, (Rom. 16 : 17,) who injure their brethren, (Matt. 18 : 17,) or who are openly disobedient to the commands of Christ, (2 Thess. 3 : 14)." Now we might ask, if the whole of Mr. Noel's book on Baptism is not intended to prove that all Pedobaptists are, however ignorantly, openly disobedient to a command of Christ. But not to dwell on that, we join issue with our author, on the fact which he asserts. The passages he quotes, and the remarks he makes, do not fairly exhibit the *only* ground on which, according to the New Testament, persons were to be excluded from the fellowship of a Visible Church; unless, indeed, the last specification is intended to include every departure, however trifling, from the revealed will of God. If 2 Thess. 3 : 6, had been referred to, as well as 2 Thess. 3 : 14, it would have been but proper. "Now we command you brethren, in the name of the Lord Jesus Christ, that ye withdraw yourselves from every brother who *walketh disorderly*, and not after the traditions which he received of us." From verses 8 and 10, we learn that *idlers* and *busybodies*, for example, were to be excluded. This passage has been so commonly alluded to, in this connection, that we are surprised our Author should not have noticed it. While it is, therefore, unquestionably the fact that

persons of immoral lives, and guilty of such crimes as exclude men from all hope of heaven, are to be separated from the Church; yet it is also true that errors, not involving such fearful and eternal consequences, but subversive of Church discipline or order, may form a sufficient reason for exclusion from a Visible Church. The interests of the Society, as a whole, and not those alone of the erroneous individual, are to be considered in this matter. How then can such Scripture, fairly weighed, be urged as proof that "*all* true believers are to be admitted to Communion" with us,—or that we have a right to demand "no other terms of Communion than such as are terms of salvation." It might as well be contended that in an army no man should be excluded from the ranks, who was a good, pious man, though he might be destitute of courage, discipline, or strength.

9. It is an unquestionable fact, that their views of Baptism have made Baptists the only denomination in all Christendom, that has uniformly considered a credible profession of piety, a prerequisite to full Communion and Church Membership. Those bodies of Christians that now uphold this view, are much indebted to them for its preservation, vitally important as it is to evangelical piety. Infant Baptism may be merely an insipid and harmless thing in individual cases; but as a system, its tendency is to break down that great bulwark of Christian piety in a converted Church Membership, and even a converted ministry.* This cannot be a matter of indifference, therefore, in the constitution of our Churches, much less in the official character of Church Officers.

10. Other evangelical Christians possess a vast numerical

---

* ppendix M.

majority over persons of Baptist sentiments. To tolerate the various opinions of all these, must eventually break down those distinctive features of primitive doctrine, that have enabled us to do good to the world, to other Churches, or even to maintain a simple existence. It would prevent Baptism from ever being treated as a Church ordinance, and alter our form of government and mode of worship, according to the caprice of fluctuating majorities.

11. But we have one further and more fundamental remark in regard to the passages quoted by Mr. Noel, as showing who ought and who ought not to be expelled from the Church. There is a vast deal of difference between expelling persons once regularly received into any voluntary society, and not being willing to admit them to membership. The former can only be done on the ground of some change on their part; usually some grave overt act; but negative considerations, and even a simple want of sufficient favorable evidence, fully justify the latter as a precautionary measure. Now we never expel, or in that sense exclude any persons for not being baptized; they never being members of our Churches. It is conceded by all, that in this we act precisely as did the primitive Christians. They never admitted the unbaptized into their Churches. Now it is doubly unfair to charge us with expelling persons because we decline to admit them, and to turn round and say, the Apostles never excluded, except for heretical doctrine, vicious practice, schismatical temper, &c. The answer is obvious; the Apostles never had occasion to expel for any but these things, because they took precautionary measures, and never deliberately received in those who were doubtful characters. But if the word exclude is to be used in the sense of declining to receive, then the Apostles *did* exclude for the simple want

of baptism, just as we do; and this should have been added to Mr. Noel's list of causes.

12. (c.) We have thus considered the whole amount of Mr. Noel's argument, drawn from *Scripture*, upon which he chiefly relies. But we may here notice some *concessions* which occur in the course of the work, as to the teachings of the Word of God, on the connection between Baptism and the Lord's Supper. On pp. 280, 281, he admits and urges that, "As there is no instance in the New Testament of any person who was converted to Christ, after he commissioned his disciples to baptize, coming to the Lord's Table unbaptized, a person who should do so now, would place himself in a situation unlike that of all the Christians during the ministry of the Apostles. It is safer to conform to the Apostolic custom, and to attend the Lord's Table as baptized, rather than as unbaptized. A person sprinkled in infancy may, indeed, have professed his faith in Christ by coming to the Lord's Table, and in other ways, but he has never made a baptismal profession of faith, according to Christ's commands, both implied and expressed, Matt. 28 : 19 ; Mark 16 : 16 ; John 3 : 5 ; Acts 2 : 38." He even admits, (p. 292,) that there is an *instituted* connection between Baptism and the Lord's Supper. "That there is an instituted connection between Baptism and the Lord's Supper, I freely admit, and it is no less clear that after the institution of Baptism by our Lord, no person who refused to be baptized was ever admitted in any Christian Church to that Supper." We will hereafter notice the special analogy by which he apologizes for a departure from this rule. To us, it appears, that in admitting an "instituted connection," he admits everything. For an *instituted* connection must mean just the opposite of an *accidental* connection. The word from *in* and *statuere*

has primary reference to *laws,* which are said to be instituted or *in-statuted*—fixed, made to stand, "established," "enacted," "prescribed," "appointed." (See Webster's and Richardson's Dictionaries, and Crabbe's Synonymes.) If, then, the connection between Baptism and the Lord's Supper is not an accidental one, but one enacted, *in-statuted* by the very Head and Lawgiver of the Church, into the laws of administering these ordinances, what room is there for further argument as to inviting those to partake with us in the second ordinance, who have not and never intend to partake of the first? The only question that could be raised, is, whether in a Christian Church, we are bound to be governed by the laws of Christ.

13. To prove still further how freely Mr. Noel concedes this instituted connection between Baptism and the Lord's Supper, and how strong a hold it has obtained over his mind, we quote from the published account of his address at the water's edge, which has every appearance of being verbatim. In giving his reasons for submitting to Baptism, he is represented to have said: "In the first place, there is no instance in the New Testament, of any person unbaptized, after the institution of Christian Baptism by our Lord, coming to the Lord's Table; and, therefore, if we should continue to attend the Lord's Table without being baptized, knowing that Pedobaptism is not the Baptism appointed by Christ, we *should be doing contrary to all the precedents of the New Testament.*" This language seemed so strong, and its whole bearing so entirely against open Communion, that it at first led many Baptists in this country to the premature conclusion that Mr. Noel's views of the Lord's Supper were more akin to those of the Baptists in this country than in England. Indeed we believe that this is the case, so far as his personal duty is con-

cerned. It is true, he does not here use the words "instituted connection," but why did he put the two ordinances together in so remarkable a manner, unless he intuitively felt that there was an appointed and special connection between them?

14. The very strong view which the Author takes, of the Scriptural connexion between Baptism and Regeneration, render his *practical* denial by free Communion, of the instituted connexion between Baptism and the Lord's Supper, which he verbally admits, still more surprising. In commenting on Titus 3: 5, he explains "the washing of regeneration," by which, with the renewing of the Holy Ghost, we are saved—to mean Baptism. "The Spirit," he says, (p. 113,) "imparts new life, Baptism manifests it; and both complete the new birth. As a child first lives, and then comes into the world, and thus is born; his entrance into the world not giving life, but manifesting it; so the child of God receives life, and then is baptized, and thus is new-born, his baptism not giving spiritual life, but manifesting it; and therefore Baptism is the washing of regeneration, or the washing, which is the manifestation and completion of regeneration. By these two things, the washing and the renewing, the spiritual renovation, and the Baptism which manifests it, God saves His people. All the passages respecting Baptism are exactly in harmony in this matter." Now if Baptism is "the manifestation and completion of regeneration," then in Free Communion, we invite to the Lord's Table those, not manifestly or completely regenerated! And with a full consciousness, that he could not himself approach the Lord's Table unbaptized, without "violating all the precedents of the New Testament," even believing Baptism necessary to "the manifestation and completion of rege-

neration," and freely admitting, that "there is an instituted connexion" between it and the Lord's Supper, Mr. Noel yet contends, that we ought to admit to the latter, and this even in Baptist Churches, those who reject the former. Is it not at least plain, that such a course must destroy them as Baptist Churches, especially, as neither he, nor Robert Hall, ever pretend to draw any distinction between admitting to the Lord's Table, and to full Church Membership. That Mr. Noel is sincere, none can doubt; but when he proposes to form the terms of fellowship for Baptist Churches, upon supposed possible exceptions, in direct opposition to "all the precedents of the New Testament;" he exhibits a spirit of extreme concession—an excessive generosity to those who differ from him, utterly subversive of instituted ordinances.

CHAPTER III.

MR. NOEL'S OBJECTIONS TO STRICT COMMUNION CONSIDERED.

1. These might be passed over. 2. State of the case.
I. *Prohibitory aspect of the system.*—1. Each visible church independent. 2. No conscientious Christian is forbidden to commune at the Lord's Table with those who hold similar views.
II. *Implied usurpation over conscience.*—1. Peculiar impropriety of this objection from Mr. Noel after his concessions. 2. Supposes two serious misconceptions. 3. Singular reasoning. 4. Results to which it tends.
III. *Apparent inconsistency.*—1. It is not *real.* 2. Evidence of this. 3. The first Christians worshipped with the Jews in the Synagogues. 4. Unique relation of Baptism and the Supper, intuitively felt. 5. The alternative forced upon us. 6. Acknowledgment of Drs. Ypeij and Dermont of Holland. 7. Remark of Andrew Fuller. 8. Illustrations.
IV. *Impolicy of exclusiveness:* especially where a doctrine is unpopular, though true.—1. The Author's theories. 2. They strike at the root of *investigation,* by denying its necessity. 3. Action is here more necessary even than investigation. 4. Action produces action. 5. Such exemplary action does not diminish *spirituality.* Comparison of United States and England shows this. 6. Mr. Noel's grand concession. 7. It amounts to the surrender of his whole argument.

1. WE have now only to review that portion of Mr. Noel's remarks, in which the arguments of Strict Communionists are discussed. But as we have not professed to urge all that can be said in favor of strict communion; but merely to carry out a single consistent line of argument to its legitimate results, we might here with propriety conclude; not being necessarily required to notice any remarks which do not bear upon the particular train of thought to which we have confined ourselves.

2. The state of the case so far is in brief this. Mr. Noel admits that the system of inviting the baptized alone to our Church membership and its symbols, is by virtue of an instituted connexion, the only plan "conformable" with "the instances of the New Testament;" but he puts in a plea of special exceptions to the letter, in favor of what he considers the spirit of Scripture. This he attempts to support by an appeal, first to the nature of things, and then to the Word of God. We have considered his reasoning in favor of both these appeals. It has, we submit, utterly failed to establish what he proposed. All his objections, therefore, to arguments sometimes urged on the other side, whatever their value, could not make good his side of the question. Objections can only demolish; they establish nothing.

We touch, however, upon a few points, though at the hazard of prolixity.

I. On p. 291, commenting upon some statements of Mr. Fuller and the Primitive Church Magazine, Mr. Noel objects to our plan of Communion, that thus "the saints of Jesus are put out of Communion with any of His Churches." So also (on p. 294) he urges that it says in effect, "Because you cannot confess Christ in one way, we will hinder you from confessing him in another."

1. There certainly is nothing in our plan of Communion that involves any such consequences. Mr. Noel, in common with ourselves, considers each Church a perfectly independent body. Not to receive a person into a Baptist Church does not prevent his reception into any other, regulated by different principles. But it may be urged that if all Christian Churches were founded upon our plan, large numbers of the professing saints of Jesus would be put out of Communion with any of them. By no means.

In that case, no professing Christian would, upon this account, be put out of communion with any Christian Church. For then, all such persons would be baptized. Unquestionably it would produce confusion to adopt half our plan, but not the whole; Strict Communion, but not Baptism. For such confusion, those must be answerable who occasion it. But it is not to be supposed that those Christian Churches that dispense with what we consider Baptism, everywhere else but at the Communion Table, will yet require it there. Such a course would assuredly be inconsistent and absurd. We do not hinder those who disbelieve in our Baptism, from joining or forming Churches not requiring it. Our principles, then, ever so fully carried out, if fairly acted upon, could never lead to the exclusion of any of the professing saints of Jesus from Church Communion. We do not, therefore, "hinder them" from confessing Christ in the Lord's Supper, because they do not in Baptism.

2. How inappropriate, then, to use the mildest term, is the language in which Mr. Noel characterizes our views of Communion, (p. 297,) where he says that by us, "eminent Christians are treated as heretics, disobedient to the law of Christ, and aliens from his Church." Disobedient to the law of Baptism, Pedobaptists certainly are, if our views are correct; many of them ignorantly no doubt, but many more from purposely avoiding the study of the subject, like Mr. Noel. (Pref. p. 1.) But our views of the independence of Churches would alone be sufficient to prevent us from treating such persons as "heretics;" least of all from regarding them as "aliens" from the Church of Christ. There is but one body in all earth and heaven, entitled to the appellation of *The* Church or "*His* Church," *i. e.* The Universal Church, which is invisible. There is,

a wide difference between the proper terms of Visible and Invisible Church membership. That is implied in the distinction of the names. The Lord's Supper is a symbol of *Visible* Church membership. Not partaking of it together, therefore, implies no want of fellowship in the Invisible Church.

II. Mr. Noel, (p. 291-2,) quotes the following as a statement of our sentiments: "We are willing to receive all who appear to have been received of God to the ordinances of Baptism and the Lord's Supper, but we cannot divide the one from the other." This he declares to be no reception of them, but as saying in effect: "Unless you will forego what you believe to be a duty,—the baptism of infants, and accept us as authoritative expositors of Christian doctrine, we must expel you from our Society, when we commemorate the dying love of our Lord."

1. These remarks refer to a course of reasoning, not strictly within our line of argument. But the objection seems to come with peculiar impropriety from one, who, in the next sentence, "freely admits" that there is "an instituted connection" between Baptism and the Lord's Supper; for how then can we divide them? But he says he does not wish to divide them himself, but only to permit Pedobaptists to do so if they will. This is just what we do; allowing all other Churches the same liberty that we use, but wishing ourselves to "keep the ordinances as they were delivered unto us." Hence we cannot constitute our own Churches upon the basis of separating those two ordinances, which appear in all Scripture precedents to be connected. Each Church is the authorized expositor of Christian doctrine for itself,—it has to decide what is Christian Baptism; whether there is, according to Scripture, an instituted connection between Baptism and the Lord's Supper; or in Mr.

Noel's own words, it must be the ultimate judge of the qualifications of those who seek communion with it. We concede to others the same right to judge for themselves; but it seems to us utterly incongruous for Mr. Noel, after freely admitting that there is an instituted connection between Baptism and the Lord's Supper, to complain because we simply act upon the principle of not dividing them in the constitution of our Churches.

2. So obvious is this fallacy, that we think it could not have imposed upon Mr. Noel, long enough to have written it down, had it not been coupled in his mind, as it is in the passage we have quoted, with one or two misconceptions of so serious a character, that we cannot even, at the risk of repetition, pass them without notice.

(*a.*) He speaks as though we first received pious Pedobaptists into our Churches; and then, "when we commemorate the dying love of our Lord," "*expelled* them from our Society." To *expel* is to *drive out*. It is impossible to drive out of a Church those who never were in it. But we have already discussed this point.

(*b.*) But the cause for which we are represented as *expelling* those who do not and will not join us, is as erroneous as the charge itself. We are represented as saying, "Unless you will forego what you believe to be a duty,—the baptism of infants, and accept us as authoritative expositors of Christian doctrine, we must expel you." But it is not for anything which Pedobaptists feel called upon to *do*, not even for baptizing infants, that we refrain from inviting them to visible Church membership, or its symbols. It is, because they do not submit to Christian Baptism.

3. And yet the same sentiment is repeated (p. 300) even more strongly. "You do this," says our author, speaking of our not inviting Pedobaptists to commune, "because

they do just what you do yourselves, since you will baptize believers alone, because you think that Christ requires it, and they will baptize infants, because they think that He requires it. You do this, therefore, on a principle that would justify their exclusion of you, which proscribes all communion among believers," &c. This is truly singular reasoning for a man like Mr. Noel. He first assumes that it is for baptizing infants, that we do not invite them to our Communion Table; and then, by a most unheard of logic, would prove that in this, they only do just what we do ourselves, because they are sincere, and so are we.

4. According to this, *anything* which a person erroneously *thinks* to be the will of Christ, is just as acceptable as if it actually were his will. The Roman Catholic thinks that the worship of the Virgin Mary, and prayers and masses for the dead are the will of Christ; yet does the sincere but idolatrous worshipper of the Virgin, when he prostrates himself before her image, "only do just what we do," when we baptize or are baptized as believers, because we both think that Christ requires our respective acts of worship. What kind of reasoning is this, by which idolatry and Christian Baptism are placed upon a moral level; each represented as equally agreeable to Christ, because both are sincere. Carry this a little further. The Hindoo, as he lays his head beneath the rolling car of Juggernaut, and the mother, as she smothers her child in the mud of the Ganges, are also sincere, and think themselves performing the will of heaven. Shall we then say that they only do "just as we do ourselves," because they think they are performing the will of heaven in murder and suicide, and we can do no more in Christian Baptism? He erroneously complains that our plan "proscribes all communion among believers." His would assuredly embrace idolaters, mur-

derers and suicides as " doing just what we do ourselves," acting sincerely. According to this reasoning, Paul, when he persecuted the saints of God, and imbrued his hands in their blood, " only did just what we do," because he " verily thought" that God required it: and this is, why we baptize.

III. On pp. 292–3, after admitting that originally "no person who refused to be baptized was ever admitted in any Christian Church to the Lord's Supper," he wishes to show that this can be no guide for us now, because the same was then as true of preaching or leading in public prayer, as of the Eucharist.—We shall not here particularly inquire how early and to what extent the Christians separated themselves from those Jewish synagogues that did not exclude them; though until that period they did sit under the preaching and prayers of unbaptized persons.

4. It is sufficient to remark that his parallel does not hold good, because these two special ordinances of Christianity sustain a unique relation to each other. It is but consistent, therefore, that there should be prior ceremonial agreement, where there is ceremonial communion, as there must be prior spiritual agreement where there is spiritual communion. We need not here recur in proof of this, to our author's admission not only of a natural, but of an " instituted connexion" between these two ordinances, nor to the fact that he seems in his own case to *feel* the connection to be very strong. On p. 280 he says, that " a person who should come to the Lord's Table unbaptized, would place himself in a situation unlike that of all the Christians during the ministry of the Apostles." Now, why does he intuitively speak of the Lord's Supper so particularly in connexion with Baptism? That occurs but occasionally,—worship to God. daily. Why did he not

say that for a person to come daily to God in prayer, or to preach in his name, and yet remain unbaptized, would be to place himself in a situation unlike that of all the primitive Christians during the ministry of the Apostles? Plainly, because he instinctively felt that there is a natural connection in the one case, that there is not in the other.

5. But from these germs in p. 292, a plan of communion is developed, (p. 293,) upon which it would be impossible to refuse Roman Catholics as such, the right to flock in any numbers to our Churches, and alter them by their votes to whatever shape they please. " What upright and earnest believer was ever in those days excluded ?" asks our author. Must we then be driven to the extremity of either denying that there are any upright and earnest believers among the Roman Catholics and the Puseyite Episcopalians, or else be forced to receive all such into full membership, and to the Communion Table, its chief symbol,—permit them to come in as equally entitled to all the privileges, and even direction and offices of our Churches; confer on them the right to preach their doctrines, to worship after their forms, to introduce their system of Church government, to baptize those whom they see fit, yea, to celebrate masses for the dead, and the worship of the Virgin, provided they could once secure a majority of a single Church in their favor? Whole denominations often alter radically in a few years, even where the forms of their government and worship are far more studiously conservative than our own. Look at the revolutions which the Episcopal Church has undergone, owing to its lax notions of Communion. Fifty years ago it was mostly Arminian; twenty years ago it had become largely evangelical; now it is full of the worst errors of Rome. We are quite willing that the government of our Churches should be in the hands of the

Communicants so long as the New Testament requisitions are complied with; which make necessary a certain union of objective Christianity, in connexion with its subjective basis. Free Communion presupposes a religion *entirely* subjective; which is as certainly, though not perhaps as mischievously a departure from the original principles of the Constitution of Visible Church Membership, as the Roman Catholic system, which makes objective Christianity alone requisite without any mixture of the subjective element.

6. If it is desirable to preserve to future ages one denomination upholding the doctrines and principles of Christianity, as exhibited in the New Testament, it must be by keeping these two elements in their proper mutual relation. A denomination doing this, will preserve its characteristics, but no other. A distinguished German Professor of Theology has borne an appropriate testimony to the manner in which Baptists have fulfilled their part thus far. To quote this will probably be the most effectual warning against an innovation so radical in its nature, as that advocated by Robert Hall and Mr. Noel; one which, by dispensing with *objective piety* from the prerequisites of Communion, must essentially alter that Church Constitution which is the most perfect embodiment of New Testament Christianity. The extract is taken from a volume, entitled "An Account of the Origin of the Dutch Baptists," published in 1819, by Dr. Ypeij, Professor of Theology, at Gröningen, and Rev. J. J. Dermont, Chaplain to the King of the Netherlands. "The Baptists may be considered as the only Christian community which has stood since the days of the Apostles, and as a Christian society has preserved pure the doctrines of the Gospel through all ages. The perfectly correct external and internal economy

of the Baptist denomination tends to confirm the truth disputed by the Romish Church, that the Reformation was in the highest degree necessary; and at the same time goes to refute the erroneous notion of the Catholics, that their communion is the most ancient."

7. The language of Andrew Fuller, which Mr. Noel quotes, (p. 294,) as exceptionable, seems to us to contain an important truth, couched in the most exact and appropriate language. "The Scriptures lay great stress upon confessing Christ's name before men, (Matt. 10 : 32,) and baptism is one of the most distinguished ways of doing this. When a man becomes a believer in Christ, he confesses it usually in words to other believers, but the appointed way of confessing it openly to the world, is by being baptized in his name. If, therefore, we profess Christianity only in words, the thing professed may be genuine, but the profession is certainly defective."

8. Mr. Noel's illustrations are not more fortunate than his arguments on the point. Speaking of Baptist and Pedobaptist members in the same Church, he says, (p. 294,) "Both wear the King's uniform, but the one assumed it at the earlier rite; the other more irregularly at the latter rite. If the one in Baptism professed to die with Christ, the other in the Supper showed forth the Lord's death."

Were we to form a figure to express our views, it would be somewhat different from this of our author's. Though we would not, for fear of misapprehension, compare unbaptized communicants to guests at the marriage feast without a wedding garment, yet we would liken them to soldiers, brave men, and zealous in the Christian warfare, but still out of uniform, and refusing to put it on. "So many of you," says Paul, "as have been baptized into Christ, have *put on* Christ." Good soldiers and true they are, but, in the matter of apparel, like Falstaff's regiment. To mix up such in the very same company with those regularly equipped (baptized and unbaptized in the same Churches) and then boast of the motley and speckled appearance of the regiment; what is it but the surest method conceivable of destroying all respect for the uniform. It would be impossible that any regard for soldierly equipment should survive such a shock. It would then appear that Free Communion principles must give the death blow to all respect for Baptism, of every form and kind; a result quite as erroneous as Infant Baptism itself.

IV. 1. After what has been said, it seems almost unnecessary to touch upon Mr. Noel's remarks in regard to the *policy* of Mixed Communion. He argues (p. 297) thus. "When any doctrine is at once popular and false, an exclusive policy upholds it. . . . But exclusiveness is extremely impolitic, when a doctrine is unpopular and true. Nothing is more favorable to the progress of such a doctrine than investigation. . . . Which course, then, tends most to encourage investigation, close Communion, or open? . . . The former must irritate and repel; the latter cannot but attract regard." We have not space here to examine all the theories by which the Author attempts to prove his point. It must suffice to remark,

2. That Free Communion cuts at the root of investigation *by denying all necessity for it*. By admitting both parties to be sufficiently correct, it practically says that there is nothing requiring investigation. It discourages all discussion. It has often tied the hands of pastors, forbidden them to discuss the subject from their pulpits, or in private; prevented them from administering the ordinance of Baptism in the Church on the Lord's Day; and made it now quite customary, in England, to prefer a

week-day evening, when the Church is not officially convened.

3. But waiving that, we ask if investigation is the only thing required, in the present age, on the subject of Baptism? It is not even the chief thing. It is *action* that is needed. Our views lie on the very surface of the New Testament. It does indeed require a great deal of investigation for a Christian to find a plausible excuse for *not* being baptized. But while we never fear it, it cannot make our views more certain than they are. Probably half the members of Pedobaptist Churches at this moment, have searched the Scriptures far enough to *drop* Infant Baptism, as useless and unscriptural. Were they only to act consistently with what they already know, it would soon produce investigation enough to enlighten the other half, and baptism would be restored to its original position in all evangelical Churches.

4. Now it is action that produces action. To tell a person that he is in error, but that it is of no importance, will rarely incite investigation, but never rouse the sluggish conscience to action, which is what is here chiefly requisite. Pure self-denying example is all important.

5. Mr. Noel is afraid of our views of Communion "injuring the spirit of the Churches which practice it." (p. 298.) "At least, they must be tempted to overvalue the form of religion, and to undervalue the reality; to pay tithe of mint, and anise, and cummin, and to omit the weightier matters of the law, judgment, mercy and faith,"—"to overvalue themselves on account of baptism, and by impairing the spirituality of the Church, *hinder the conversion of sinners.*" This would be a serious charge, if true. But look at facts. In this country, for instance, where Baptist Churches are founded upon our principles; are

revivals less frequent, are professed conversions more rare than in England among the Open Communion Churches? Compare the statistics of our denomination in this country and in England. In every respect that marks a growing, healthy body of Christians, will it be found that the views of Communion current in this country have exerted a baneful influence? Compare the Baptists of this country with any other evangelical body of Christians, and statistics will show as healthful and extensive a progress over all parts of the country as in any other denomination.

6. Towards the conclusion of the chapter, Mr. Noel, in reply to an argument of Andrew Fuller's, makes concessions which virtually overthrow the whole principle for which he has been contending. Speaking of the admission of Pedobaptists to Communion, (p. 299,) he says, "Nor could their presence injure these churches; and with respect to members, each Church has the means of preventing the alleged evil in its own hands; for although it may not repel from its communion Pedobaptists, as such, it has yet the right to ask from all who are candidates for communion, *credible proofs* that they are true disciples. . . . Each Church may, if it will, require from candidates the profession of this faith, and *testimonials* to their conduct. The profession thus required may be *exactly that which would be made in baptism;* and if the Church dread the appearance of sanctioning disobedience to a command of Christ, each Pedobaptist candidate may be required *distinctly to profess* that he refuses to be baptized only in obedience to what he believes, *after examination*, to be the will of Christ." Here, in the shape of "credible proofs," "testimonials," and "professions," "*after examination*," a great deal more is admitted, and proposed to be required of candidates for Communion, than

is essential to salvation; a great deal more than he himself, pious, excellent, and able minister of Jesus Christ, as he has been for more than twenty years, could have answered two years ago. (See his Preface, p. 1.)

7. And yet, after all this, he tells us, (p. 301,) that the whole point at issue between the Free Communion and other Baptists, is that the former contend that we have a right "to demand no other terms of Communion than such as are terms of salvation." If that, indeed, be a fair statement of the case, then we submit that he has here conceded the very point at issue.

CONCLUSION OF PART IV.

We had intended only to make a few observations, in regard to the latter part of Mr. Noel's remarks; but have been led on from one page to another, until there is hardly a sentence, and not an argument which we have left unconsidered. In view of the whole, we think it will be evident to every reader, that Mr. Noel has certainly failed to produce any just reason for departing in the constitution of our Churches from the Primitive order. Least of all, has he proved the point he undertook to demonstrate, and which is the only alternative from our plan, that no other terms of Church Fellowship and Communion are admissible than such as are terms of salvation.

The object of this review of Mr. Noel's remarks has been simply defensive; not to exhibit the positive arguments in favour of our system of Church Fellowship, but simply to defend our course against the strictures of one whose excellence of character makes it painful to differ from him, even in matters that, compared with the great points on which he is so admirable, are but of trifling importance.

Indeed, it is but justice to add, that throughout the whole course, not only of these pages, but of his public life, the Author has exhibited the most earnest love of truth, and the most elevated and disinterested readiness to sacrifice everything for its promotion. The Christian reverence for the will of God, and love to all who love Christ, exhibited in the pages of his entire work, will do more, by the holy example it sets, to diffuse the spirit of charity into all parts of the controversy of Baptism, than any arguments for particular modes of exhibiting it. His address, delivered when about to be "buried with Christ by baptism," must win for his course, the respect and love of all who love Christ. Let us close these observations, by expressing the hope that a new day has dawned upon Christendom, and that not only in their more social intercourse, but even in their controversies, our religious leaders will exhibit more of the meekness and gentleness of Christ, by speaking the truth in love; and that the day will soon arrive when "Ephraim shall not envy Judah, and Judah shall not vex Ephraim."

GENERAL CONCLUSION.

1. The bearing of these views on the Churches. 2. The power of the Churches, to spread right views of the ordinances. 4. The ordinances specially committed to the Churches. 4. The relative position of the Church and the Bible to the world. 5. Duty of the Churches in view of the corruption of the ordinances. 6. Objection—part to be sacrificed to the good of the whole. 7. The duty of Pedobaptist Churches—their Baptism a nullity. 8. Position of the Baptists towards them—we ask them to defer Baptism to believing. 9. The duty of such Churches. 10. The duty of such ministers. 11. Why we offer these remarks. 12. All Christians love Christ better than any symbols. 13. Fate of Sects. 14. Prevailing ideas of this age—*Voluntariness.* 15. *Self-government.* 16. Baptist sentiments embody these. 17. Changes progressive. 18. The Home of the Christian. 19. It embodies the results of all the changes of Time.

1. HAVING now considered the great principles upon which our views of Communion are based, we venture to offer one or two concluding reflections, in relation to the bearing of these principles upon the Churches of Christ, as such, their members and their ministers respectively.

In regard (1.) *to the Churches of Christ.* If our views are correct, each one of these bodies is an independent organization, answerable for its whole course directly to the Great Head of the Church, and relying on his promised protection and presence, for all its light, and life, and joy. From Him is derived all that renders a Church honorable to His cause, useful to the world, edifying to its members, happy in itself; just as from the rays of the same sun, wax derives softness and clay hardness, the moon her lustre, the trees their greenness, and all animated creation, its joyousness and life. Should error, or neglect, cause Him to remove the candlestick out of its place, or to withdraw his presence, but for a moment, the Church becomes as dark and gloomy as a world without a sun.

2. To the Churches, as such, Christ has solemnly committed in charge, the ordinances of his house. To neglect them must be displeasing to Him. The power of organized bodies of men, to propagate any truth, or revive an obsolete opinion or practice, is naturally immense. It emboldens the timid, and decides the wavering. It incites *to* action, because it exhibits truth *in* action. Apart from these sources of power, there is in these bodies, another and a greater; the presence and indwelling Spirit of Christ. A Church therefore, is both a human and a divine institution. As in man, one person is formed by the union of soul and body, of powers infinitely greater than many persons would possess with but one of these alone; so is each visible Church of Christ possessed of resources, and strength, and influence, illimitable for good, and far transcending the sum of its individual powers. Its effects on the customs of society, for instance, apart from the saving results that attend its efforts and worship in the hearts of individuals, are incalculable. The morals and manners of a nation, and of an age; its intelligence; even its form of government, will generally have their archetype in the congregations of its saints.*

3. He who has given to these bodies their peculiar strength—He who first applied the power of voluntary social organization to religious purposes in His own Churches, and has, guarded, guided, and actuated that power, so far as religion is concerned, ever since—has

* See Appendix K.

committed two sacramental ordinances specially to their care, Baptism and the Lord's Supper. These, as mere outward signs, might seem of little importance, but that He has connected with them, in a remarkable manner, a whole system of doctrines and practice, of which He has made them the symbols and exponents; to which indeed, He has united them in a unique manner, so that practically, it should no more be thought of severing them, than of disuniting the body and the soul, or Christ and His Churches. He has made it the duty of these organizations, as such, to convert the whole world to the system of Christianity, in all its wholeness, just as he committed it to them: the parts balanced like the various powers of man, and adjusted by His own hand. They have no right to proclaim Baptism, or the Lord's Supper, without the faith they symbolize; nor yet, on the other hand, the faith without the symbols. The body, without the soul, is a mere carcass. But the soul without the body cannot be realized in the present state. Symbol is the appointed dwelling place for piety, as the body clothes the living spirit, with the firm bones, and the soft warm flesh.

4. To the Churches, we say, is this system, Christianity, committed, in all its symmetry. The Bible is indeed its text book, and only unfailing standard. But each Church of Christ is a *living body*, to which He has given in charge, both the lively oracles, and the living ordinances. It is for these Churches to draw from the Scriptures, the system of life, and to propagate it through the whole earth, by their divine powers, energies, example, and organization. " *Ye* are my witnesses, saith the Lord." " *Ye* are the light of the world." The Church and the Bible stand in the same position to the guilty dying world, that the physician

and his books stand to the sick patient. The patient looks upon the physician usually as the living embodiment of his books. So the sinner looks to the Church, as the true exponent of what Christianity, as a system *is*. Right or wrong, each Church of Christ is thus regarded by the great masses of men. Hence they derive more of their religious ideas, than from any other source. These two Ordinances then, should be upheld by the Churches, *in living exhibition*, just in the same position in which they are placed in the New Testament, and they stand very conspicuously in that volume. Much is said of them there. They are held up as the symbols and embodiment of many vital truths. The one is called *"putting on Christ,"* the other, *"the communion of the body and blood of Christ."*

5. These ordinances have been greatly misapprehended and abused. It is therefore the peculiar duty of the Churches as such, above all other bodies, to exert their influence, the power of their public example, and their social organization as the appointed executors of the Will of Christ, to restore them to their original position, to reform current abuses, and to revive their primitive order. All Baptist Churches are agreed as to what those abuses are, and what that order was. The only question, so far as they are concerned, is whether they shall exert their influence to produce a reformation in the most effectual manner? They have immense powers conferred. Are they bound thus to use them? We believe that they are. We have seen that our plan of Communion practically exerts an incalculable influence for the restoration of primitive Baptism. Are we at liberty to use less effectual means, because they may be less painful to our feelings? All must perceive that this would be a solemn breach of

trust. We should not execute faithfully the Will of the Testator; and, by misplaced tenderness, we should defraud the legatees.

6. But a single objection can be urged to this, *i. e.*, that the Ordinances are but *a part* of those duties entrusted to the Churches, and that they may be sacrificed for the good of the whole; as for example, to promote Christian Charity.

The points at issue are in fact these. 1st. Have we, as Churches, a right, practically, to separate and disjoin symbols and things signified; to invert, omit, or alter any of them? And 2nd. If we have the right, is it one that can be safely exercised? Can the constitution of the Churches be *improved?* Will the body and the soul be better sundered? Or can even a member of the body be spared without injury? Are not bone and marrow, joint and sinew, flesh and blood, nerve and tendon, so wondrously and mysteriously bound together, that all are needed, for any to perform their functions perfectly? So are ordinances and doctrines, symbols and things signified, means of grace and the grace of means, things spiritual and things outward, all bound and blended together, and committed to the Churches to keep and maintain, and propagate throughout the whole earth.

7. One word more. In a former part of the work, we have said that we did not unchurch other denominations. Nor do we. We will not deny the claims of any body of evangelical Christians, organized for maintaining social worship, to be considered a Christian Church. Not a *regular* Church indeed. Still we do not doubt that such assemblies realize many Church blessings, particularly this, that when they gather together, though but two or three, in the name of Jesus, He is with them.

But then it cannot be forgotten that privileges and duties go together. They must not be sundered. They are both links of the same chain. To all evangelical Churches therefore, we make this appeal. We feel that a great reormation is needed, one wide-spread throughout Christendom, in regard to Baptism. Great abuses have crept into its administration, defeating its entire object. The system of Pedobaptism, as a system, has been the embodiment, and is now the main support of some of the most cardinal errors that have ever afflicted Christendom; such as Baptismal Regeneration, and an unconverted Church membership and Ministry.* So far as its influence extends, it sweeps the world into the Church, and keeps thousands upon thousands from expecting or praying for any other regeneration than that of baptism. So completely has baptism been perverted from its original intention, which was to draw a line between Christians and the world; so completely has it been changed in the course of centuries, both as to the mode in which it administered, and the subjects who receive it, that it is, as generally given,—*a nullity.*

8. To the Churches of Christ, as such, belongs the solemn task of *restoring* it to its original position. The only object of Baptist Churches, in the ground they take on the subject of Communion, is to keep the ordinances, as they were originally delivered, and to revive their primitive use. If it is not the duty of Churches, as *Churches*, to promote this reform and restoration of primitive Baptism, upon whom does the obligation devolve? Our desire to see this change, is from a love, not of names or sects, or parties, but of a pure Christianity. We are not acting

* See Appendix M.

in antagonism to other Evangelical Christians, of whatever name. The cause in which we are all engaged, is *one*. We are different divisions of the same army. We are all Christian brethren, if we are Christ's. Our position is not taken out of opposition to any who love Christ, but to promote his cause, in what we believe, and feel sure is the best way. We would, in all the warmth and brotherhood of Christian affection, urge a solemn sense of the relation they sustain to this matter, upon all Pedobaptist Churches, and entreat them to examine the whole subject afresh, and defer baptism, as Tertullian insists, until it is *asked for*,* and can be used as a true sign of the admission of a penitent believer, into the Communion of the Church. Let it ever be administered by immersion, so that each of those who receive it will be able to say, as originally, " We are buried with Christ by baptism." We urge this appeal more earnestly, both because this is the only way by which this difficulty with regard to the Lord's Supper can ever be adjusted satisfactorily; and because this reformation, if it were simultaneously adopted by the Churches, would, we are convinced, have the most powerful effect in promoting a general revival of pure religion throughout Christendom.

9. (2.) In regard to the members of such Churches, *as individuals*, we may be permitted to add a few remarks, for to each one, as a part of the whole, is his share of the responsibility and custody of the ordinances committed. Very many of these persons have lost all faith in Infant Baptism. Numbers even do not practise it; or if they do, it is with much hesitation. They are ready to admit, in general terms, that the Baptists are right in everything except their Strict Communion. They are members of

---

* Tertullian de Baptismo, 18.

Pedobaptist Churches, and yet have great misgivings that they themselves are not truly baptized. But they have been taught that Baptism is a subject of no importance, and there they rest. If this work should fall under the eye of any such, the Author trusts, it may at least induce them to regard the correct observance of religious ordinances as a matter of solemn responsibility, and to use their influence and example to promote the restoration of Baptism to its primitive position in the Churches of Christ. How many have been converted by witnessing this ordinance properly administered! Who can say what might be the influence arising from the conscientious action of a single person? Who will dare to keep back that influence, whatever it may be? Surrounded as we all are by a complicated network of associations and influences, perchance a brother or a sister, a husband or a wife, a parent or a child, might be awakened by the baptismal self-consecration of so near a relative. Let no sluggishness hinder; no fear of man; no love, even of Christians, keep us from the supreme love of Christ. Were all who now neglect Infant Baptism, and hold generally to Baptist sentiments, to act up to them consistently and firmly, it is impossible to conjecture the result. In England at this moment, one individual, by a bold avowal of his change of sentiments, by abandoning what he saw to be erroneous, throwing the weight of his influence on the side of truth, and being baptized, has, perhaps, rendered the separation of Church and State inevitable.

10. (3.) And here, it may not be improper to add a word, finally, upon the special obligations resting on *Christian Ministers,* in regard to the entire subject of Ordinances. They are their appointed *administrators.* To those who can conscientiously and firmly say that they

have examined this subject impartially, and have ever had *undoubting conviction* of the Scripturalness of Infant Baptism, we have nothing here to say. But what we fear in regard to this subject, is not investigation, but *indifference*. We are anxious that it should not be laid aside as a matter of no importance. How can a minister dip his finger into the font, and deliberately put the water on the face of an unconscious infant, in the name of the Father, Son, and Holy Ghost, doubting all the time, and perhaps feeling inwardly conscious that this is not a New Testament Baptism; thus helping to carry out a system, which, though now comparatively harmless in some of the more evangelical denominations, is still, not only in the dark corners of Europe, but also in this country, one of the main pillars of Romish superstition, and of all mere traditional religion as opposed to that of the New Testament?

11. Let not any Christian, of whatever name, feel hurt at the plainness of these remarks. They originate not in indifference to the feelings of a brother, much less in that bitterness that could regard any fellow-Christian as a foe. They are not uttered in the bigotry of a partizan, or for sectarian effect. They are made in the frankness of a sincere affection, one that raises all who possess it, above the atmosphere of sect or party. If we are allied to Christ, we must be *allied* and not opposed to each other. We are arrayed in the same army, and marching against the same enemy. The differences that separate us are as nothing to the strong ties that unite us. For we are one in the heart of love to a common Father, in the faith of a common Redeemer, and in spiritual consecration to the interests of his Universal Church.

12. Where those interests are concerned, all true Chris-

tians, of whatever name, have awakened in them a love, infinitely more warm and glowing than their attachment to any peculiar views of ordinances. These respect the means, but that *is* the end. These are the symbols and instruments of Communion, but that is something higher and holier, for it is the Spiritual Communion itself. We love Baptism because it is an instituted symbol of union with Christ and means of grace. We love the Lord's Supper, because it is also an instituted symbol and means of the nearest Communion earth will admit with Him who died for us. But we love the Communion itself better than the symbol, the end better than the means.

And as we have ourselves, so we feel confident all true Christians have love to Christ, and to His cause, so infinitely transcending that of all mere symbols, that we venture to speak of these latter with so much freedom. It is because we believe most fully, that our Pedobaptist brethren love the cause of Christ more than Pedobaptism, that we entreat them to reconsider and abandon the latter, for the sake of the former. What, compared with the growth of that heavenly kingdom founded by the Saviour, what, compared with the salvation of a single soul, are all names, and sects, and parties? They are but as "the small dust of the balance." Time will soon have swept the most of them away.

13. Let any student glance his eye over the list of sects presented in a text book of Church History; how uncandid and irrelevant to the interests of truth do their squabbles for the most part now appear! And what has become of the mass of these? After dancing for a while like a bubble on the wave, they have been dissipated into thin air. So, too, when some future Church Historian writes down the history of our age, what will then be thought

of most of the parties and names and denominations which now so agitate Christendom? Time will have killed them. Meantime, there are in each age, some one or two great principles at work among the masses. These are long treated as insignificant by those of established reputation. They work their way silently and slowly, with a force very inadequately represented, even by the progress of any party. They move along, not like the tornado that sweeps and levels everything at once, but calmly and quietly, unseen, but effectually, like a change in the seasons. As the breaking up of the frosts and snows of winter; as the opening of the buds and blossoms beneath the warm sun, so do these ideas and principles gradually prevail after many apparent reverses, and then, silently and without controversy, carry away sects, and names, and parties, just as the opening up of a river in spring, carries off, without molesting, the chips and straw that lie upon the field of ice that covered it. Thus originally did Christianity arise and sweep clean the Pantheon of its gods. Thus has every great reforming truth arisen since. In morals we have, in our own times, all beheld, in the spread of Temperance, one idea sweep before it the most inveterate prejudices, the oldest habits and customs of hospitality.

14. In religion, one or two great ideas are evidently at work among the masses of thinking men. One is what may be termed *the essential voluntariness of all true Religion, and, therefore, of all true Church Membership.*— That piety is not a thing of mere education, to be learned by rote simply through creed and catechism; not a thing to be professed by proxy, or indeed to be professed at all without the surrender of a man's own heart to God; and that all forms and rites without that are worthless. It

is evident, on a moment's reflection, that either this idea must destroy Pedobaptism, or else Pedobaptism must destroy it. Which does the pious Christian wish to be victorious? Certain as destiny it is that the aggressive principle will here prove triumphant.

15. There is another great truth at work with progressive power, throughout the whole world, both in Church and State. It is *the principle of self-government*, as the most proper of all authorities, because resting with greatest faith and most immediately upon the universal government of God. To that all the revolutions of Europe are tending; to that, the peaceful extension of our own national principles. It were as useless to attempt to silence the thunder by a word, or to roll back the falling waters of Niagara, as to stay the progress of these opinions. The world is full of them, and the Churches are full of them.

16. We believe that whoever examines carefully will perceive that our principles, as Baptists, present the most complete living embodiment of these ideas.* Of the spread and prevalence, therefore, of our denominational views, we feel assured; both because they are true, and because they contain just those truths which the Christian world of the present age needs, those truths for which it hungers and thirsts, which it will, therefore, surely incorporate, and upon which it will grow and thrive.

17. These great changes, as to the ideas which agitate the Christian world, in each successive age, are all *progressive*. They never go backward. As the revolutions and changes which the physical surface of the earth has undergone at different periods, even to every speck of

---

* See Appendix K.

granite and every layer of mica that has crumbled beneath the finger of Time, do all modify the face of the globe, and each modification exhibits progressive order and beauty; so do these alterations and convulsions of opinion, that seem to come blindly, and that overturn and destroy creeds and systems with a ruthless hand, spring not from chance, but from the intervention of a Higher Power. They are parts of a mighty system of beneficence and progress in the Church, and a new illustration of the truth, that "the goodness of God is over all his works." Each of these embodies all that went before, and is necessary to all the future developments of the glory and beauty of Christianity. Nor do we ever labor so successfully, as when in accordance with the movements and tendencies of providence and grace. That Christianity will produce effects, such as we can now hardly anticipate, changes that will alter the whole aspect of society, we may not doubt.

18. The true Christian, however, while he labors on with hope for the good and progress of the cause of Christ on earth, looks for his home and his final reward beyond all Churches of earth, even the most perfect, to the one glorious and Universal Church of God in heaven,—the New Jerusalem. The beauties of that heavenly city will increasingly fix his gaze, and fire his heart;—that city, that has "no need of the sun, neither of the moon to shine in it, for the glory of God lightens it, and the Lamb is the light thereof." There, the spirits of just men made perfect are fast congregating. In that blessed assembly there are no convulsions, no barriers, no changes; but the state of bliss which it exhibits, is the embodiment of all the most glorious results of every conflict of the people of God here below. "These are they," said the angel, describing the saints in glory, "that came out of great tribulation,

and have washed their robes, and made them white in the blood of the Lamb."

19. The glory and honor of the whole Church triumphant will derive no small measure of its lustre from the perfect development of that knowledge, wisdom and love, obtained by Saints in the struggles and experiences of all ages and of all climes. To that season, and to that city, as the result, in part, of all the longings and labors of each individual after the truth, the believer looks forward, with increasing confidence and hope, and learns to bear with patience, and work on with energy, amid the jarrings and disorders of the present state.

It is a comforting and an animating thought, that on this very earth, now so disfigured by the scaffolding and rubbish, so disturbed by the noise of the hammer fashioning out the stones, and the confusion of builders running to and fro; when it has been purified by the final convulsions of the last great day, the heavenly city shall at length appear, in all the magnificence of its goodly proportions. "I saw," says the blessed Apostle, "the holy city, the New Jerusalem, coming down from God, out of heaven. And I heard a great voice, saying, Beholed th tabernacle of God is with men, and he will dwell with them; and he shall wipe away all tears from their eyes; and there shall be no more death, neither sorrow nor crying, neither shall there be any more pain: for the former things are passed away."*

* Rev. 21 : 2, 3, 4.

APPENDIX.

APPENDIX.

A.—Page 23.

"The first instance that I remember of that sort of inward sweet delight in God and divine things, that I have lived in since, was on reading those words, 1 Tim. 1: 17. 'Now, unto the King eternal, immortal, invisible, the only wise God, be honor and glory for ever and ever. Amen.' As I read these words, there came into my soul, and was, as it were, diffused through it, a sense of the glory of the Divine Being, a new sense, quite different from anything I ever experienced before. Never any words of Scripture seemed to me as these words did. I thought within myself how excellent a Being that is, and how happy I should be, if I might enjoy him, and be taken up to him in heaven, and be as it were swallowed up in him forever! I kept saying over these words of Scripture to myself, and went to pray to God that I might enjoy him, and prayed in a manner quite different from what I used to do, with a new sort of affection. . . . . I began to have a new kind of apprehension and idea of Christ, and the work of redemption, and the glorious way of salvation by him. *An inward sweet sense of these things at times came into my heart, and my soul was led away in pleasant views and contemplations of them.* And my mind was greatly engaged to spend my time in reading and meditating on Christ, on the beauty and excellency of his person, and the lovely way of salvation by free grace in him. I found no books so delightful to me, as those that treated of these subjects. . . . . I found from time to time an inward sweetness that would carry me away in my contemplations. This I know not how to express otherwise, than by a calm delightful abstraction of the soul from all the concerns of this world; and sometimes a kind of vision or fixed ideas and imaginations of being alone in the mountains, or some solitary wilderness, far from all mankind, sweetly conversing with Christ, and rapt or swallowed up in God. The sense I had of divine things, would often of a sudden, kindle up an ardor in my soul, that I know not how to express."—(Memoirs of Jonathan Edwards, by Sereno E. Dwight, chap. 1.)

B.—Page 36.

It has been very frequently maintained, or rather taken for granted, that the term Church is sometimes used in the New Testament, in a third sense, *i. e.* for *the Church Universal Visible*, composed of all those, throughout the world, who make a credible profession of true religion. This subject has been ably treated; and the idea of a *Visible Church Universal*, in any literal sense of the term Church, like that maintained by Dr. J. M. Mason, completely refuted by the Rev. Dr. Dagg in a work of Rev. J. L. Reynolds, entitled "The Kingdom of God," (pp. 186–195,) to which the reader is referred. Even should it be granted that the word Church is in one or two places in the New Testament, used by an obvious figure, for the body of *Professors* of religion on earth as such, it would not impair the force of the distinction drawn from the more regular and literal application of the word, between our fellowship with a particular Church, and with all other professed believers.

Of the five or six passages, (*i. e.* Acts 2 : 47, and 8 : 3; 1 Cor. 15 : 9; Rom. 10 : 32,) produced by Dr. Mason, in support of his idea of an organized Universal Church Visible, embracing all who profess true religion; as Dr. Dagg has shown, three refer to the Church at Jerusalem, before the establishment of any church elsewhere, and when, therefore, it was of necessity, for a time, the only visible Christian body. Rom. 16 : 23 : Gaius, " the host of the whole church;" and 1 Cor. 10 : 23 : " Give none offence to the Church of God; "import," as Dr. Dagg says, "hospitality to saints generally, and offence to saints generally," *i. e.* not those of a particular church exclusively. He adds, that it is "not necessary to suppose that they belong to a Visible Church Catholic, in order to be entertained or offended," and appears to suppose that we might rather consider the term as applying to the general assembly and Church of the firstborn, entertained in the persons of those of its members who could thus be ministered to; as the Saviour, in Matt. 25 : 45, represents himself fed, clothed and visited in the persons of his disciples. I am not prepared to express an opinion on this particular point. It is one of great nicety.

To suppose the term Church, however, applied *by a figure* collectively to those who were generally members of the Invisible Church, and also members of some particular Visible Church, and who might temporarily, therefore, without inconvenience, be regarded as members of any body of Christians with whom they sojourned, or were even in the habit of being so regarded; would be far enough from involving the idea of a regularly organized *Church Universal Visible*. Dr. Mason's theory is, therefore, untenable. There may be a figurative use of the word Church in two or three passages of the New Testament, without all their ideas of a regular organization being involved.

In some points of view, unquestionably, those who make a credible profession of the Christian faith must be regarded *as a whole*. They are a body, distinct from the world, but operating upon it with a certain degree of uniformity, and with immense power. This body is distinct from the Invisible Church Universal, in that all who are professors of religion, and some, therefore, who are only professors are mixed up with true Christians in the present world. It is distinct from any particular visible Church, since it embraces members of all truly Christian Churches, throughout the whole world. Such a body as this, however, cannot in any other than *a merely figurative sense* be called a Church, since it never can or does assemble, has no visible earthly representation, government, or organization; all its oneness arises from the general sameness of the aim, and actuating principle of all its members, *i. e.* allegiance to Christ. Who would think of considering all the various tribes and hordes that poured from Northern into Southern Europe for successive centuries, Huns, Goths and Vandals, as *one* literal army! And yet considering the sameness of principle by which they were actuated, the general similarity of course they pursued, and the oneness of result brought about, it would be quite appropriate for the historian to speak of them, *figuratively*, as the successive waves of an overflowing tide, or the several detachments of an immense army. Nor would any one think of inferring from such a figure in Gibbon, that the historian had intended to represent all the bands as organized into a confederate whole, acting in concert, and moving in detachments only by mutual agreement.

There is another form of expression, much more frequently occurring in the New Testament, in such a connection as to seem intended to express the oneness of all who profess the religion of Christ. It is the phrase, "Kingdom of Heaven," or "Kingdom of God," (for they are continually used synonymously.) In nearly all the cases in which these phrases occur in the four Gospels they refer to that kingdom established on earth by Christ, and which perhaps might be fairly expressed in other words by "the Christian dispensation." As Matt. 3 : 2. "The kingdom of heaven is at hand." The figure is obvious and just. This kingdom consists of all those living under the dominion of Heavenly or Spiritual principles, and all acknowledging one Supreme Head, Christ.—Col. 1: 14; Rom. 14: 17.

The only point, however, in which we are here interested, is to ascertain if the phrase βασιλεία τῶν οὐρανῶν is ever used to denote what has been termed *the Visible Church Universal*, *i. e.* the professed followers of Christ on earth as a body. The word rendered kingdom, βασιλεία, as Dr. Campbell has, with great beauty and discrimination shown, has *two senses*, one referring to the *duration*, the other to *the place* over which the authority is extended. The first he translates "*reign*," the second "*kingdom.*" The difference of sense is obvious in such a case as this, "The reign of heaven is approaching." We cannot say that a 'kingdom' is drawing near, but we may say that a '*reign*' is approaching, and thus accordingly in most cases, he translates the word, rendered in our version 'kingdom.' Sometimes, as for instance, when the state of perfect felicity of the righteous is intended, he retains 'kingdom,' as more exactly expressive of the thought of the original. To apply now these principles to such a passage as Matt. 13 : 41, (see also 5 : 24 and 47,) He "shall gather out of *his kingdom* them which do iniquity." This Dr. Campbell translates, and with apparent justice, 'kingdom,' not 'reign.' This clause would seem to mean, not that such characters 'shall be removed from under the kingly dominion of Christ,' but 'removed from the society of those under professed allegiance to Christ.' It will be said, however, that all the parables of this chapter refer to the progress of the dominion of Christ in the earth,—that he claims the world as his of right, that its kingdoms shall all become his kingdom, out of which he at last gathers his enemies; in other words, that the parables of the Tares and of the Net are intended rather to account for the Divine sufferance of sinners in the world, under the Christian dispensation, than the permission of hypocrites in the Church; and this view is probably correct. Robinson, in his Lexicon, however, quotes the above, and several other passages as relating to "the external form of Christ's spiritual kingdom, as embodied in the Visible Church, and the universal reign of the Gospel." Neander, in his Planting and Training, Book 6, chap. 1, on the Pauline doctrine of the Kingdom of God, (Ryland's Translation, p. 279,) says there, perhaps accurately, "the kingdom of Christ coincides with the idea of the Church existing in the hearts of men, the invisible Church, the totality of the operations of Christianity on mankind." The visible body of Christ's followers so nearly corresponded to the invisible, originally, and in the purpose for which each was intended, that it is very difficult to distinguish where the one is meant, and where the other, distinctively in Scripture. Nor am I sure it can be shown that "the kingdom of God," or "of heaven," is anywhere put for the visible company of Christians upon earth, as distinguished from the invisible company of true believers, unless in the Parables. "The totality of the operating power of Christianity on mankind," is the idea which ever accompanies the use of this phrase.

The following remarks, given on the authority of Count Montholon, as uttered by Napoleon, at St. Helena, portray with singular accuracy and graphic force, the true nature and wonderful power of that kingdom.

"Alexander, Cæsar, Charlemagne and myself founded empires, but upon what did we rest the creations of our genius? Upon *force*. Jesus Christ, alone, founded his empire upon *love*, and at this hour, millions of men would die for him.

"It was not a day or a battle which achieved the triumph of the Christian religion in the world. No; it was a long war, a contest for three centuries, begun by the Apostles, then continued by the flood of Christian generations. In this war, all the kings and potentates of earth were on one side; on the other I see no army but a mysterious force, *some men scattered here and there in all parts of the world, and who have no other rallying point than a common faith in the mysteries of the Cross.*

"I die before my time, and my body will be given back to the earth, to become food for worms. Such is the fate which so soon awaits him who has been called the great Napoleon. What an abyss between my deep misery and the eternal kingdom of Christ, which is proclaimed, loved and adored, and which is extending over the whole earth! Call you this dying? Is it not living, rather? The death of Christ is the death of God."

The foregoing remarks on the expressions 'Church,' and 'kingdom of heaven,' will show why the fellowship of

Churches, Denominations, &c., is not more specifically treated of in these pages. Because no collection of these bodies is in the proper sense of the term, *a Church*, and therefore we cannot have a Church fellowship with it as such. If any of the members of one body are brought into company with another Church of the same views, they may either permanently change their relations, or be considered temporarily as having done so, if all parties so desire, and thus enjoy Church privileges. But Churches as such, being responsible to their Great Head, are essentially independent and separate bodies. That they may rightly, and ought to, interchange the most fraternal feelings with other bodies of Christians, as such, cannot be doubted; but then it is not a Church fellowship, but something distinct from it; it is a fellowship, closer and stronger in exact proportion, as we think we see *through the profession* of supreme allegiance to Christ (which all have in common) indications of conformity to the laws and spirit of Christ. It is a fellowship, therefore, of every variety and degree. With those Christians, Churches, or Denominations, most closely agreeing with our views of divine truth, it will be very near and fraternal, while with those in which truth and error, the pious and the irreligious, are all amalgamated, it may hardly exist at all.

By this view we are saved from all trouble of deciding which are, and which are not true Christian Churches, or when a particular body so far apostatizes, as to lose claim to that title altogether. Each Church, *i. e.*, Christian congregation, and each Christian for himself, are left to judge how far to carry their Christian fellowship with other bodies than their own, according as they perceive in them obedience to the will of the Saviour. In proportion as such persons seem to walk according to the spirit and re-

APPENDIX. 289

vealed will of Christ, they will be regarded as forming parts of that kingdom, set up on the earth; and whose sole point of centralization, is Christ. All such will feel united in the kingdom of Christ, while quite distinct in Church relations.

C.—PAGE 42.

I find the following placed as the 24th Maxim of Confucius, in a work labelled, Ancient Fragments from the Chinese, &c.; but called in the Title page "The Phœnix," published by William Gowan, Chatham Street, New York, 1835. The work does not appear to be a very respectable authority; but as it contains some genuine and curious fragments, I insert the quotation, suspecting it will prove to be of much later date than is professed in regard to it.

"Do unto another as thou wouldst be dealt with thyself. Thou only needest this law alone; it is the foundation and principle of all the rest."

D.—PAGE 68.

The following account given by the Hon. and Rev. Baptist W. Noel, at the water's edge, of his reasons for embracing Baptist sentiments, states this part of our views, so briefly and clearly, that I insert them here as given in a recent number of the Christian Watchman and Reflector.

"Mr. Noel then pointed out the reasons why a person who is unbaptized should be baptized, even after he had made a profession of Jesus Christ in other ways, and stated the ground which had led him to obey what he believed to be Christ's command. He said, that after he had fully weighed every considerable argument that had ever been adduced in favour of infant baptism, he had come distinctly to these two conclusions, which appeared, to him at least, to be certain; '*first, that Baptism as ordained by Christ is an immersion in water, a being buried in water; and secondly, that immersion is meant to be a profession of faith in Christ.*' Mr. Noel observed, if those two conclusions were correct—and he believed they would completely prevail with the Christian world eventually—that it followed that a person, who like himself, had only been sprinkled in infancy, is unbaptized; because such a person had neither been immersed, nor had he made a baptismal profession of faith, and these two things constituted Christian baptism. So that if these conclusions were correct, then he and others who had been only sprinkled in infancy, were in neither sense baptized.

"Among the reasons which had led him to embrace believers' baptism, were these;—that there is no instance in the New Testament of any person unbaptized, after the institution of Christian baptism by our Lord, coming to the Lord's Table; and therefore, if we continue to attend the Lord's Table, without being baptized, knowing that Pedobaptism is not the baptism appointed by Christ, we act contrary to all the precedents of the New Testament—that Christ has required a baptismal profession of faith,—and that our blessed Lord has set us an example in this matter."—Watchman and Reflector, Sep. 6, 1849.

E.—PAGE 60.

There are, perhaps, more traces of the idolatry of the outward part of Baptism in the writings of Augustine than in almost any of the Fathers, certainly than in any of equal spirituality. In his account of the baptism of Victorinus, there are expressions that show this very error. And yet who can read the account of it, which he puts into the mouth of Simplicianus, unaffected? I insert it, curtailed of some of those expressions, as an illustration of a reverence for baptism, of which it would not hurt us to have more.

"That aged man, most learned and skilled in the liberal sciences, and who had read and weighed so many works of the philosophers; the instructor of so many noble senators; who also as a monument of his excellent discharge of office, had (which men of this world esteem a high honour) both deserved and obtained a statue in the Roman Forum, he, to that age, was a worshipper of idols, and a partaker of the sacrilegious rites to which almost all the nobility of Rome were given up." . . .

"O Lord, Lord, which hast bowed the heavens and come down, touched the mountains and they did smoke, by what means didst Thou convey Thyself into that breast? He used to read (as Simplicianus said) the Holy Scriptures; most studiously sought, and searched into all the Christian writings, and said to Simplicianus, (not openly, but privately and as a friend,) 'Understand that I am already a Christian.' Simplicianus answered, 'I will not believe it, nor will I rank you among Christians, unless I see you in the Church of Christ.' The other, in banter, replied, 'Do walls, then, make Christians?' And this he often said, that he was already a Christian; and Simplicianus as often made the same answer; and the conceit of the 'walls' was, by the other, as often renewed. For he feared to offend his friends, proud demon-worshippers, from the height of whose Babylonian dignity, as from cedars of Lebanon, which the Lord had not yet broken down, he supposed the weight of enmity would fall upon him. But when, by reading and earnest thought, he had gathered firmness, and feared to be denied by Christ before the holy angels, should he now be afraid to confess Him before men, and appeared to himself guilty of a heavy offence, in being ashamed of the Sacraments, of the humility of thy Word, while he was not ashamed of the sacrilegious rites of those proud demons, whose pride he had imitated, and their rites adopted, he became bold-faced against vanity, and shame-faced towards the truth, and, suddenly and unexpectedly, said to Simplicianus, (as himself told me,) 'Let us go to the Church; I wish to be a Christian.' And not long after, he further gave in his name for baptism—Rome wondering, the Church rejoicing. The proud saw, and were wroth; they gnashed their teeth and melted away. But the Lord God was the hope of Thy servant, and He regarded not vanities, and lying madness.

"In fine, when the hour was come for making profession of his faith, (which at Rome, they . . . . deliver from an elevated place in the sight of all the faithful,) . . . . the presbyters, he said, offered Victorinus (as was done to such as seemed likely through bashfulness to be alarmed,) to make his profession more privately: but he chose rather to profess his salvation in the presence of the holy multitude. 'For it was not salvation that he taught in rhetoric, and yet that he had publicly professed. How much less, then, ought he, when pronouncing Thy word, to dread Thy meek flock, who when delivering his own words, had not feared a mad multitude!' When, then, he went up to make his profession, all, as they knew him, whispered his name one to another, with the voice of congratulation. And who there knew him not? And there ran a low murmur through all the mouths of the rejoicing multitude, Victorinus, Victorinus! Sudden was the burst of rapture, that they saw him; suddenly were they hushed, that they might hear him. He pronounced the true faith, with an excellent boldness, and all wished to draw him into their very hearts: yea, by their love and joy, they drew him hither; such were the hands wherewith they drew him."—(Confessions of Augustine, Book 8, sect. 2.)

F.—PAGE 77.

That the Lord's Supper is here alluded to, and that the subsequent "innocent meal" spoken of was the *agape*, is, it seems to me, unquestionable. "It is plain here," says Bingham, (Antiquities, Book 15, ch. 7, sect. 8,) "the Communion was first, and the *agape* sometime after." A passage from Chrysostom, quoted by him in another section (sect. 6,) is decisive. Speaking of the first Christians having all things common, he says, "From this law and custom there arose then another admirable custom in the Churches. For when all the faithful had met together, and had heard the sermon and prayers, *and had received the Communion*, they did not immediately return home, upon the breaking up of the assembly, but the rich and wealthy brought meat and food from their own houses, and called the poor and made a common table, and a common dinner, a common banquet in the Church.—(Chrys. Hom. 27 in 1 Cor. p. 559.)

G.—Pages 81, 153.

Most commentators, who do not hold to the independence of each Church, quote 1 Cor. 10 : 17, as a proof that the Lord's Supper is a symbol of that Communion which the Christian enjoys with the whole body of believers in Christ, and not as a symbol of Church Communion. How far this opinion is just, we will briefly consider.

The following is Macknight's version of the passage:—
"*Because there is one loaf, we, the many, are one body, for we all participate of the one loaf.*"

Bishop Warburton remarks on the passage in question, "Our being partakers of one bread (or loaf,) in Communion, makes us *many* [which we are by nature] to become by grace *one body* in Christ, the Communion of the body and blood of Christ uniting the receivers into one body by an equal distribution of one common benefit." "The loaves or rather cakes of Judea," adds Dr. Bloomfield, after quoting the above, "were usually, especially at the Paschal feast, of a very large size, so that a considerable number may be supposed to partake in common of *one* of them."

The meaning of this passage must turn upon the sense we ascribe to οἱ πολλοί. Most commentators seem to suppose that it means "the many," and is equivalent to "all Christians;" but on this we remark :—

1. That the article combined with the plural here, by no means necessarily gives it the sense of "*the* many," and might, perhaps, fairly be translated, "many," as in Matt. 24 : 12, "and because the love of *many* (τῶν πολλῶν) shall wax cold;" or as in 2 Cor. 2 : 17, "We are not as *many* (οἱ πολλοί) which corrupt the word of God." So our English translators render it in the passage we are

considering. The sense would then be fairly paraphrased thus, "*Because* every time we celebrate the Lord's Supper, *there is one loaf* used, of which all the communicants participate, *we* who eat of it, and who are naturally *many*, *become* thereby symbolically *one body* with the rest of the communicants, *because we all participate of that one loaf.*"

2. Even if οἱ πολλοί be translated "*the* many," it must still mean that we are proved to be one body, not with "*all Christians*," but with all *with whom we partake* of the symbolic elements. The meaning of παντες, '*all*,' in the next clause, is in terms circumscribed to those who "participate of the same loaf."

That by "*all* who participate" ἐκ τοῦ ἑνὸς ἄρτου is not primarily intended all who partake of one *kind of bread* —(*i. e.*, those through the whole world who are in the habit of eating the Sacramental bread, or *Christians*,) but rather those who partake *together* of the same emblems, is confirmed by New Testament usage, in regard to ἑνὸς ἀρτος, the sense of which clearly is not "*one kind of bread*," as our English translators would leave the impression, but one "*loaf*" of bread.

On this, I subjoin the judicious remarks of Macknight. "The Greek word ἀρτος, especially when joined with words of number, always signifies *a loaf*, and is so translated in our Bibles: Matt. 16 : 9, " Do ye not understand, neither remember the five (ἀρτους) *loaves* of the five thousand ?" Matt. 4 : 3, " Command that these stones be made (ἀρτους) *loaves*." (See Note 1, on 1 Cor. 10 : 17.)

That there may be an indirect inference drawn from the Apostle's remark that all those who, by Divine authority, partake of the same kind of bread and wine in the Communion, must sustain a relation to each other as Christians, we do not deny. They do; and so far the Lord's

Supper may be considered a symbol of the *Christian* oneness or Communion of all who rightly partake, wherever or in what age soever they may be. But this is far enough from showing that this Supper does not indicate a more close, even a *Church* Communion between those who partake together the same loaf. This latter I believe to be the specific meaning of the Apostle, certainly no inference contrary to it can be drawn from this passage. In the Lord's Supper, whenever we sit down to it, we symbolize that we are of one body with those with whom we partake, by eating of the same loaf. The error so wide spread, by which the distinctness of Visible Churches has been confounded through the Universality of the One Invisible Church, has led, I am convinced, to the popular misinterpretation of this passage. That the Lord's Supper is a complex symbol, we have before shown. In such cases, it is only when all the relations symbolized, have a corresponding reality, that the symbol is appropriate.

H.—Page 104.

The Rev. Mr. Wheelock in a letter from England, published in the Christian Watchman, dated December, 1847, is my authority for these last facts. He also says, " While in London, I casually learned that the ordinance of baptism was to be administered in one of the largest and most popular Baptist churches of that city. At the hour appointed, about twilight, on Thursday evening, I went to the chapel to witness the baptism. The church contained rising of eight hundred members. On entering, I perceived the lamps were lit, but few in attendance, and the pastor addressing the people. Eleven were baptized, and after changing their raiment, they returned into the chapel, and received the right hand of fellowship. I asked the administrator why the baptism was on a week day evening, and at an hour when so few could attend. He answered, that about one-half of the church were Pedobaptists; and for the peace of the church, they were careful to select an evening and an hour when there was no other appointment, not even for a committee meeting, or meeting of Sabbath school teachers, or Bible class, or anything else, lest the peace of the church might be disturbed by the Pedobaptist members, thinking they had been entrapped to secure their presence at the baptism. For the same reason, he told me, the right hand of fellowship was given at the Baptism, instead of the Communion, on the following Sabbath, that nothing might be said then that might endanger the harmony of the church. In some mixed churches, the Baptist members have been disciplined and excluded, because they propagated among the people, Baptist sentiments. In Bedford, one of John Bunyan's successors was permitted to retain his pastoral relations, only on condition that 'he should not introduce the controversy' on the subject of Baptism—'into the pulpit, nor into conversation, unless it was first mentioned by others.'"

As a further illustration of what must result from this plan, the following facts are added, also detailed in the same letter. The Rev. Mr. Kinghorn of Norwich, was the well known and able opponent of Mr. Hall on the Communion question. He died, and has been succeeded by Rev. Mr. Brock. "After the Rev. Mr. Brock of Norwich, had revolutionized the Rev. Mr. Kinghorn's church, and received into it Pedobaptists, he began to discipline those members that refused to go to the Lord's Table with the Pedobaptist members. The first one excluded was brother

APPENDIX.

Kelf. The 28th of June last, I perceive this church by a vote of 95 to 22, have for the same reason excluded ten more. The published account of it says, 'it was strongly objected that as these brethren were worthy and tried men, they ought not to be excluded in consequence of their objections to this new practice, as unscriptural. It was said, in reply, that the church did not exclude them, *they excluded themselves!* by absenting themselves from the Lord's Supper.' I have a full account of these melancholy proceedings, but I forbear to give them in detail, as I have already extended this communication much beyond what I at first intended." "In a Summary of principles, for the government of a Mixed Church in St. Andrews, Scotland," the Magazine of 1841 says, "it is held to be 'disorderly' and 'subjecting to discipline,' for the Baptists to use any direct influence, either in public or in private, to inculcate or propagate their peculiar sentiments, by the circulation of tracts or books, by conversation or otherwise among the members of the church," and moreover, " that they should abstain from controverting the sentiments taught from the pulpit on the points of difference." The Magazine adds, "We have heard of another Mixed Church in Scotland under a Baptist pastor, in which the Independent (Pedobaptist) members have made objection to the mention of the subject from the pulpit." A Baptist Church in Dublin, Ireland, after having maintained strict communion, "for about one hundred and fourteen years," had open communion introduced by their pastor, Rev. Mr. Ford. He moved that six persons, holding strict Baptist principles, one of whom had been a member of the Baptist denomination for thirty years, be expelled. That motion was carried, and the brother adds, "Several years have now elapsed since that occurrence, and the members thus expelled have not returned."

J.—Page 200.

In Robert Hall's "Letter to a Clergyman," Works, vol. 4, p. 630, he says, "Our sentiments upon the baptismal rite exempt us from any temptations to lay undue stress upon it; we consider it merely as the symbol of a Christian profession, while you profess to believe it regenerates the partaker, and makes him a child of God."

The disposition to submit to whatever is clearly and deliberately perceived to be the will of God on every subject is an essential part of saving piety, and therefore is, *in every case*, essential to salvation. Hence it is that *unwillingness*, even to submit to baptism, or any other divine appointment, may be at times, where known to be the will of God, fatal to the soul. But no outward *act* of confession (I speak of the outward act, as distinct from the act of the will) can be essential to membership in the invisible Church, while yet some outward act *must be* essential to visible membership.

K.—Page 266.

The following anecdote was communicated to the Christian Watchman, several years ago, by the Rev. Dr. Fishback of Lexington, Kentucky.

"Mr. Editor:—The following circumstance, which occurred in the State of Virginia, relative to Mr. Jefferson, was detailed to me by Elder Andrew Tribble, about six years ago, who since died when ninety-two or three years old. The facts may interest some of your readers. Andrew Tribble was the pastor of a small Baptist Church, which held its monthly meetings at a short distance from Mr.

Jefferson's house, eight or ten years before the American Revolution. Mr. Jefferson attended the meetings of the church several months in succession; and after one of them, he asked Elder Tribble to go home and dine with him, with which he complied.

Mr. Tribble asked Mr. Jefferson how he was pleased with their Church government? Mr. Jefferson replied, that it had struck him with great force, and had interested him much; that he considered it the only form of *pure democracy* that then existed in the world, and had concluded that it would be the *best plan of government for the American colonies.* This was several years before the Declaration of Independence. To what extent this practical exhibition of religious liberty and equality operated on Mr. Jefferson's mind, in forming his views and principles of religious and civil freedom, which were afterwards so ably exhibited, I will not say."

L.—Page 175.

It is a well known fact, that at the time of the commencement of the revival in Boston, under the preaching of Drs. Baldwin and Stillman, half a century since, there was but one Orthodox Congregational Church remaining in the city—the Old South; and that was in so declining a state that it was unable to sustain a weekly prayer meeting. A few of the most spiritual members, by attending the Baptist Churches, were aroused to new sensibility, and gained courage to establish a prayer meeting, and make other efforts to establish Gospel preaching among them once more. From this came the settlement of Mr. Huntington, the publication of the "Panoplist," the erection of Park Street Church, the call of Dr. Griffin, and other events connected with the revival of Orthodox Christianity in Boston. The number of Orthodox Congregational Churches in this city is now fourteen.

In Geneva, the movement in favor of Evangelical Theology dates from the winter of 1818. At that time Robert Haldane, Esq., of Edinburgh, (who had embraced Baptist principles about ten or twelve years before,) passed the winter in Geneva. This excellent man felt his soul stirred within him, at finding the University and all the pulpits of the city closed against the Gospel. He invited several University students to meet at his lodgings, by nights, for the study of the Bible. Some of them were converted as a consequence—and among them, Merle D'Aubigné! What followed is well known.

The present Evangelical movement in Germany, which is restoring Apostolic Churches to the land of Luther, has a similar origin. It dates from the baptism of Mr. Oncken and six others at Hamburg, in 1834. Besides a Church of 500 members in that city, about sixty more, of similar scriptural purity, martyr zeal, and missionary spirit, have already arisen in Central Europe as the result, and are rapidly multiplying amid all the political storms and convulsions of the times.

One more fact may be added. The First Congregational Church in Salem, Mass., from which Roger Williams was driven in 1636, (together with the First in Boston, which did the deed,) is now, and long has been Unitarian; while the First Baptist Church in Providence, R. I., founded by Roger Williams, always has been, and still is, Evangelical; and last year, among other charities, contributed about $5000 to the Foreign Missionary Enterprise.

Such facts have some significance. He is a wise man who learns wisdom even in the school of Experience.

J. N. B.

M.—Page 244.

Dr. Wall, in his History of Infant Baptism, has collected the most melancholy and ample proof of this statement, from the Fathers of the Third and Fourth centuries, though this was far from his design.

How this matter appeared to the Waldenses of the Middle Ages, is most forcibly and concisely expressed in the "TREATISE CONCERNING ANTICHRIST"—a book most carefully cherished among that ancient people, and which bears date, according to Perrin, as early as 1120. The last words we shall quote are omitted by Milner, in his extracts, (Church History, Vol. II. p. 61, Phil. Ed.,) for what reason we know not. They are, however, too memorable to be forgotten. We take them from Jones' History of the Church. (pp. 337–338, Phil. Ed.)

After sketching the origin of ANTICHRIST "in the times of the Apostles," and his comparative weakness "in his infancy," the Treatise proceeds to say, "But growing up in his members, that is, in his blind and dissembling ministers, and in worldly subjects, he at length arrived at full maturity; when men whose hearts were set upon the world, blind in the faith, multiplied in the Church, and *by the union of Church and State, got the power of both into their hands.* Christ never had an enemy like this, so able to pervert the way of truth into falsehood, *insomuch that the true Church with her children is trodden under foot.*"

After specifying the perversions in the objects of worship, particularly in the idolatrous adoration of the Eucharist, the Treatise thus describes that perversion of Baptism of which ANTICHRIST is guilty, and points out its fundamental and all-pervading evils. "*He teaches to baptize children into the faith,* and attributes to this the work of regeneration; thus confounding the work of the Holy Spirit in regeneration with the external rite of baptism; and *on this foundation bestows Orders,* and *indeed grounds all his Christianity.*"

J. N. B.

A
Biographical Sketch
of
Thomas Fenner Curtis
(1816-1872)

By
John Franklin Jones

A BIOGRAPHICAL SKETCH OF THOMAS FENNER CURTIS (1816-1872)

Thomas Fenner Curtis—pastor, denominationalist, professor, author—was born in England in 1815 to Thomas Curtis and Susan Reynoldson. He came with his parents to Augusta, Maine in 1833 (*ESB*).

Curtis pastored churches in Georgia (ca. 1838-43) and moved to pastor the First Baptist Church, Tuscaloosa, Alabama (March 1843-1848) (*ESB*).

He was one of fifteen representing Alabama at the organizational meeting of the Southern Baptist Convention in August, Georgia. He was elected to the first Board of Domestic Missions (Home Mission Board), became professor of theology, Howard College, Marion, Alabama and recording secretary of the missions board and the Alabama Baptist State Convention in 1849. He served the latter for one year (*ESB*).

Curtis was elected corresponding secretary for the board in 1851 and removed therefrom in 1853. He relocated to the University of Lewisburg (later Bucknell), where he taught theology until ca. 1867 (*ESB*).

He authored *Communion:The Distinction Between Christian and Church fellowship and Between Communion and Its Symbols. Embracing a Review of the Arguments of the Rev. Robert Hall and Rev. Baptist W. Noel in Favor of Mixed Communion* (1850); *Progress of Baptist Principles in the Last*

JOHN FRANKLIN JONES

Hundred Years (1856; 1856; 1857; n.d.; 1860; n.d.; rev. ed: 1880) (Starr); *The Human Element in the Inspiration of the Sacred Scriptues* (1867); and numerous articles (*ESB*). Curtis also wrote a few extanct discourses: an ordination sermon on the Christian preacher (1853); and on other unusual religious efforts (1846) (Starr).

He died in Boston, Massachusetts, 1872 (*ESB*).

BIBLIOGRAPHY

Encyclopedia of Southern Baptists, vol. 3 (supplement). S.v. "Curtis, Thomas Fenner" by A. Ronald Tonks.

Starr, Edward C., ed., *A Baptist Bibliography Being a Register of Printed Material By and About Baptists; Including Works Written Against the Baptists*. S.v. "Curtis, Thomas Fenner, 1816-1872."

BY JOHN FRANKLIN JONES
CORDOVA, TENNESSEE
JUNE 2006

THE BAPTIST STANDARD BEARER, INC.

a non-profit, tax-exempt corporation
committed to the Publication & Preservation
of the Baptist Heritage.

CURRENT TITLES AVAILABLE IN
THE BAPTIST *DISTINCTIVES* SERIES

KIFFIN, WILLIAM A Sober Discourse of Right to Church-Communion. Wherein is proved by Scripture, the Example of the Primitive Times, and the Practice of All that have Professed the Christian Religion: That no Unbaptized person may be Regularly admitted to the Lord's Supper. (London: George Larkin, 1681).

KINGHORN, JOSEPH Baptism, A Term of Communion. (Norwich: Bacon, Kinnebrook, and Co., 1816)

KINGHORN, JOSEPH A Defense of "Baptism, A Term of Communion". In Answer To Robert Hall's Reply. (Norwich: Wilkin and Youngman, 1820).

GILL, JOHN Gospel Baptism. A Collection of Sermons, Tracts, etc., on Scriptural Authority, the Nature of the New Testament Church and the Ordinance of Baptism by John Gill. (Paris, AR: The Baptist Standard Bearer, Inc., 2006).

CARSON, ALEXANDER	Ecclesiastical Polity of the New Testament. (Dublin: William Carson, 1856).
BOOTH, ABRAHAM	A Defense of the Baptists. A Declaration and Vindication of Three Historically Distinctive Baptist Principles. Compiled and Set Forth in the Republication of Three Books. Revised edition. (Paris, AR: The Baptist Standard Bearer, Inc., 2006).
BOOTH, ABRAHAM	Paedobaptism Examined on the Principles, Concessions, and Reasonings of the Most Learned Paedobaptists. With Replies to the Arguments and Objections of Dr. Williams and Mr. Peter Edwards. 3 volumes. (London: Ebenezer Palmer, 1829).
CARROLL, B. H.	*Ecclesia* - The Church. With an Appendix. (Louisville: Baptist Book Concern, 1903).
CHRISTIAN, JOHN T.	Immersion, The Act of Christian Baptism. (Louisville: Baptist Book Concern, 1891).
FROST, J. M.	Pedobaptism: Is It From Heaven Or Of Men? (Philadelphia: American Baptist Publication Society, 1875).
FULLER, RICHARD	Baptism, and the Terms of Communion; An Argument. (Charleston, SC: Southern Baptist Publication Society, 1854).
GRAVES, J. R.	Tri-Lemma: or, Death By Three Horns. The Presbyterian General Assembly Not Able To Decide This Question: "Is Baptism In The Romish Church Valid?" 1st Edition.

	(Nashville: Southwestern Publishing House, 1861).
MELL, P.H.	Baptism In Its Mode and Subjects. (Charleston, SC: Southern Baptist Publications Society, 1853).
JETER, JEREMIAH B.	Baptist Principles Reset. Consisting of Articles on Distinctive Baptist Principles by Various Authors. With an Appendix. (Richmond: The Religious Herald Co., 1902).
PENDLETON, J.M.	Distinctive Principles of Baptists. (Philadelphia: American Baptist Publication Society, 1882).
THOMAS, JESSE B.	The Church and the Kingdom. A New Testament Study. (Louisville: Baptist Book Concern, 1914).
WALLER, JOHN L.	Open Communion Shown to be Unscriptural & Deleterious. With an introductory essay by Dr. D. R. Campbell and an Appendix. (Louisville: Baptist Book Concern, 1859).

For a complete list of current authors/titles, visit our internet site at:
www.standardbearer.org
or write us at:

he Baptist Standard Bearer, Inc.

NUMBER ONE IRON OAKS DRIVE • PARIS, ARKANSAS 72855
TEL # 479-963-3831   FAX # 479-963-8083
EMAIL: Baptist@centurytel.net   http://www.standardbearer.org

Thou hast given a standard to them that fear thee; that it may be displayed because of the truth. — Psalm 60:4

www.ingramcontent.com/pod-product-compliance
Lightning Source LLC
Chambersburg PA
CBHW021802220426
43662CB00006B/159